Praise for previous edit[...]

"In this era of globalization, we are in desperate need of accurate information that demonstrates how crucial women are to the whole process... This atlas does just that. Congratulations: Joni Seager has done it again!"
Kum-Kum Bhavnani, Professor of Sociology,
University of California, Santa Barbara

"An imaginative, useful book... unlike anything I've ever seen. Also fun to use."
Alice Walker

"Here is the innovative atlas no thoughtful person, male or female, should be without."
The Washington Post

"A fascinating atlas: a compilation of facts about women's status, work, health, education, and personal freedom across the globe."
The Independent

"A major reference tool. The atlas format and highly original colorful statistical illustrations make this a book as enjoyable as it is important."
Library Journal

"Much of the plethora of information contained within the pages is shocking. A fascinating document, and an extremely valuable one."
Independent Magazine

"An appealing idea, imaginatively executed."
Times Higher Education Supplement

"No-one wishing to keep a grip on the reality of the world should be without these books." *International Herald Tribune*

Available now:

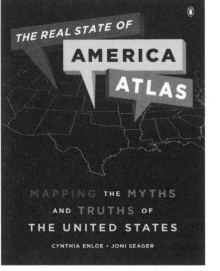

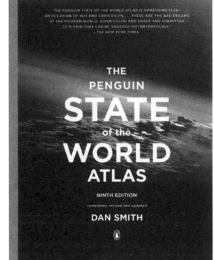

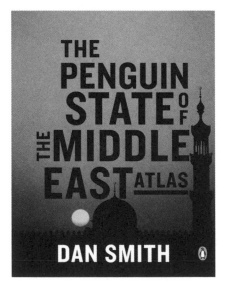

"Invaluable...I would not be without the complete set on my own shelves." *Times Educational Supplement*

"Fascinating and invaluable." *The Independent*

"A new kind of visual journalism." *New Scientist*

THE WOMEN'S ATLAS

JONI SEAGER

A Fully Revised and Updated Edition of
The Penguin Atlas of Women in the World

PENGUIN BOOKS

PENGUIN BOOKS
An imprint of Penguin Random House LLC
penguinrandomhouse.com

This fifth edition first published in Penguin Books 2018

Previous editions published under the title
The Penguin Atlas of Women in the World

Produced for Penguin Books by Myriad Editions,
An imprint of New Internationalist Publications,
The Old Music Hall, 106–108 Cowley Road, Oxford OX4 1JE,
United Kingdom

ISBN 9780143132349 (paperback)

Printed by Jelgavas Tipografija in Latvia

3 5 7 9 10 8 6 4 2

Publishing direction: Candida Lacey
Creative direction: Corinne Pearlman
Edited and co-ordinated by Dawn Sackett
Maps and graphics by Isabelle Lewis
Design consultant: Caroline Beavon

Contents

Introduction

This is not just an atlas about women. It's a feminist remapping of the world through the lens of taking women's experiences seriously.

Feminism, to me, means giving women's lives as much attention, curiosity, and analysis as men's lives routinely receive. The ordinary lives of ordinary men and women often appear to have a great deal in common. And sometimes they do. But in truth, the everyday realities of forming relationships, making livelihoods, and securing autonomy vary significantly between men and women – and, intersectionally, among women.

There can't be any feminist writer who hasn't been on the receiving end of a "why women" challenge. In her trenchant essay, "We Should All Be Feminists", Chimamanda Ngozi Adichie answers for us all:

"Some people ask, 'Why the word *feminist*? Why not just say you are a believer in human rights, or something like that?' Because that would be dishonest. Feminism is, of course, part of *human rights* in general – but to choose the vague expression human rights is to deny the specific and particular problem of gender. It would be a way of pretending that it was not women who have, for centuries, been excluded. It would be a way of denying that the problem of gender targets women. That the problem was not about being human, but specifically about being a female human. For centuries, the world divided human beings into two groups and then proceeded to exclude and oppress one group. It is only fair that the solution to the problem should acknowledge that."

There have been remarkable improvements in the state of women since the first edition of the atlas was published in 1986. Advances in women and girls' literacy and education top the list of global success stories; women have won full voting rights in all but a few places; most of the world's governments have signed international treaties committed to women's rights; acknowledgement of the gender earnings gap has entered the mainstream; the nearly-ubiquitous harassment of and attacks on women by men on streets, in workplaces, and in the home has been pushed into public view by women's organizing.

The importance of such gains should not be underestimated. However, overall the "success story" list is discouragingly short. People who stand outside feminism often imagine that feminists are angry. To which I say, "only part of the day"! In truth, there's a lot to be angry about. In the past decade, many women around the world have experienced an absolute decline in the quality of their life. Improvements in one place are not necessarily transferrable to other places: we remain a world divided. Economic inequality is so extreme that even the IMF recognizes it as a global crisis. At all spatial scales, wealth is concentrated in fewer and fewer hands; mostly, the hands of men. The globalizing world economy is based on exploiting "flexible" markets of underpaid workers; in this context, increases in women's participation in waged work is not an unalloyed sign of progress. Persistent armed conflicts wrack many countries. From Sudan to Afghanistan, millions of people are living under regimes of armed terror under wrenching conditions. Women bear a special burden of masculinized militarization, including mass rapes, erosion of their rights, and trying to meet the unrelenting demands of sustaining families and households in the midst of chaos. Religious fundamentalism and a resurgent conservative intolerance threaten women's rights in a wide range of states across the globe. Millions of women around the world live their daily lives as little more than chattel. Large-scale systems of enslavement and oppression of women, including, prominently, sex trafficking are flourishing.

In the world of women, there are few "developed" nations. Looking at the world through the experiences of women raises questions about the validity of conventional distinctions between "developed" and "underdeveloped" countries: women hold virtually the same proportion of representation in elected governments in Madagascar, Kyrgyzstan, and the USA; the indifference of the state to the murder of indigenous women in Canada, Yazidi women in Iraq, and maquiladora women in Mexico offers a sharp rebuke to the notion of the modern state; married women in South

> ## In the world of women, there are few 'developed' nations.

Korea, the UAE, and Malawi all need their husbands' approval for an abortion.

These may seem to be cheap shots – glib comparisons that don't acknowledge the real advances in women's lives. But for the women living under these realities, it is glib to say that things are getting better for women somewhere else. A rising tide does not necessarily lift all boats. Women do not automatically share in broad social advances – unless there is a commitment to ensure social equity. Feminists have long warned that gains in women's empowerment should not be taken for granted: they are fragile, reversible, and always under pressure. This warning has never seemed so pertinent. At best we can say that from Poland to the USA, from Nigeria to Russia, the halls and hallmarks of power remain remarkably unperturbed by the oppression of women. At worst, evidence suggests that a remarkable number of governments in 2018 seem committed to turning back advances in women's autonomy.

To the extent that real improvements have been made in women's lives, it is mostly due to feminist organizing – which is stronger, more diverse, and more skilled than ever. International feminist networks have broken the isolation of women from one another; feminists everywhere are more informed about issues and perspectives from cultures and places outside their immediate realm. As we define the twenty-first century, we need public and civic leaders who will build on these feminist foundations to make real – not rhetorical – commitments to social justice for women.

As a feminist, I believe that an international and broadly comparative perspective can enrich social analysis and activism. However, working at the global scale inevitably entails a degree of generalization that is troubling – and, indeed, if left unexamined, can undermine feminist analysis. The world of women is defined both by commonality and difference. Women everywhere share primary responsibility for having and rearing children, for forming and maintaining families, for contraception. Rich and poor, they suffer rape, health traumas from illegal abortions, the degradation of pornography. Nonetheless if we have learned anything from modern feminist movements, it is that global generalizations must not be used to mask the real differences that exist among women. These differences travel along fracture lines of race, class, age, sexuality, religion, and place.

It is as a geographer that I have found a way to strike a balance between the demands of acknowledging both commonality and difference. At its best, data visualization – and especially mapping – can simultaneously illuminate both. Mapping is a powerful tool to reveal patterns, continuities, and contrasts. Having presented these patterns, it is my hope that this atlas raises as many questions as it answers.

It "takes a village" to bring a project such as this to fruition. I am fortunate to have several. Strong networks of friends and family provide support, hope, political solidarity, humor, and intellectual spark. You know who you are – thank you!

Without my partner Cynthia Enloe, nothing works. Remarkably, she blends an ingrained impulse towards generosity and kindness with a razor-sharp analytical acuity, the one magnifying the other. She makes me a better thinker and a better person.

This book literally would not be possible without Myriad Editions, a women-run small publisher with an outsize influence and expansive vision. Candida Lacey and Corinne Pearlman, the Publishing and Creative Directors, respectively, perform astonishing feats of imagination, friendship, and persistence. Dawn Sackett and Isabelle Lewis brought both heat and light to this book with their respective editorial and design feats of magic and intelligence. This project tested the patience of us all, but the Myriad equanimity carried the day.

Beyond these particular acknowledgements, I have never lost sight of the broader social and intellectual debt that I owe to the countless feminists – most unnamed and unrecognized – who, for years, and often at great personal cost, have been the only ones insisting that it is important to ask questions about where the women are.

Joni Seager
Cambridge, Massachusetts
2018

Women in the world

The role of the state in shaping women's lives should not be underestimated. Governments and ruling regimes set the context within which families and households are formed and thrive – or not.

State regimes of power draw the boundaries of acceptable behavior, sexual expression, and economic and civic participation. States set the terms of access to health, education, suffrage, reproductive rights, civil protection, and environmental sustainability.

For many millions of people the world over, states and aspirant state actors create chaos and crisis. States set the terms of discrimination that are then enacted in structural, institutional, small and everyday ways.

All states are patriarchal. Even at the individual level, and in countless everyday ways, men benefit from the ubiquity and apparent normalcy of patriarchy in ways that women do not.

> "Patriarchy is everyday sexism, but it is more than everyday sexism. Patriarchy embraces misogyny, but relies on more than misogyny. Patriarchy produces gender inequality, but its consequences run deeper than gender inequality."

Cynthia Enloe, *The Big Push*

Ending discrimination

Signatories to the UN Convention on the Elimination of All Forms of Discrimination Against Women (CEDAW)

March 2018

- signed but not ratified
- neither signed nor ratified
- signed and ratified

USA

USA

President Carter signed CEDAW in 1980, but for it to become law the Senate must ratify it. Conservative politicians and religious groups strenuously oppose CEDAW. At Senate hearings in 2010, Family Watch International claimed that: "ratification of CEDAW would weaken existing protections for women...by seeking to redefine...the indispensible roles women play in our society...as wives and mothers. The objective of CEDAW is to create gender-neutral societies around the world... Many of the groups pressuring the US to ratify CEDAW are doing so in an effort to advance radical women's rights with which most Americans disagree..."

Latecomers

Recent signatories to CEDAW   • 2006: Cook Islands • Brunei • Marshall Islands • Oman

CEDAW is the only comprehensive global treaty on women's rights. Governments that ratify it are committed, at least on paper, to developing policies to eliminate discrimination against women.

Only the USA and Palau have signed without ratifying, which means they are not bound by the treaty. Four countries have neither signed nor ratified.

Iran

In 2001, an Iranian government proposal to accept CEDAW (with limitations) was rejected by the Guardian's Council that said CEDAW contradicted several articles of the Iranian Constitution and the "essential principles of Islam on inheritance, blood-money, divorce, testimony, age of puberty, Hijab, and polygamy." Women's groups in Iran continue to press for its acceptance.

Palau

In 2010, Queen Bilung Gloria Salii of Palau said: "We don't want to enter into some kind of agreement to join other nations and then [find] it will have a conflict with our culture. We will support [CEDAW], but we are not yet ready..."

IRAN

SUDAN

SOMALIA

PALAU

TONGA

Sudan

President Omar al Bashir has long opposed CEDAW on the basis that it contradicts Sudan's values. "We will not sign the CEDAW convention because it is against the morality and principles of the family."

Tonga

In 2015, the Tongan government announced plans to move forward with CEDAW ratification. Groups opposing CEDAW, including the Tonga Catholic Women's League, protested these plans, and petitioned the King to stop the government from ratifying the convention. Opponents argued that CEDAW, among other implications, would force same sex marriage and abortion on the country.

• 2009: Qatar • 2011: Nauru • 2014: Palestine • 2015: South Sudan

Measuring discrimination

There is no easy way to compare the status of women around the world and it is unwise to attempt to use any single lens through which to do so. Nonetheless, there are interesting ways to shed light on questions of overall status and general quality of life.

The Global Gender Gap Index developed by the World Economic Forum measures the size of the gap in each country between women and men in terms of various aspects of health outcomes, educational participation, economic participation and opportunity, and political empowerment. The highest ranked countries have closed more than 80% of their overall gender gap.

The Social Institutions and Gender Index (SIGI) produced by the OECD measures the degree of discrimination against women embedded in the social institutions of countries. The SIGI examines civil society institutions and norms such as family codes and laws, rights of physical autonomy, son bias, access to resources and assets, and civil liberties, to determine the degree to which the civil structure within countries discriminates against women. The regional summaries on page 16 show the proportion of countries in each region that have high to low degrees of embedded institutional discrimination.

GLOBALLY, THE EDUCATION-SPECIFIC GENDER GAP IS LIKELY BE CLOSED BY ABOUT 2030. BUT AT CURRENT PACE THE GENDER GAP IN ECONOMIC PARTICIPATION AND OPPORTUNITY WILL NOT BE CLOSED FOR ANOTHER 217 YEARS.

One of the points illustrated by both indices is that gender equality is, in part, a result of governmental commitments to equality principles and policies. For example, it is no coincidence that the Scandinavian countries rank very high in both indexes – these countries have adopted gender equality and women's empowerment as explicit national policies.

The Global Gender Gap Index

2017

Country rankings:

- 1 – 20 (most parity, smallest gender gap)
- 21 – 55
- 56 – 90
- 91 – 125
- 126 – 144 (least parity, largest gender gap)
- not included in rankings

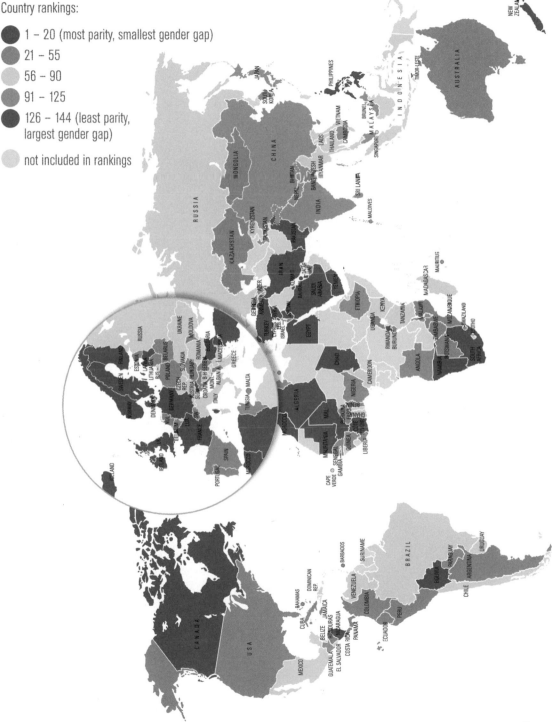

Discrimination against women
Levels of discrimination in society according to the Social Institutions and Gender Index

Proportion of countries in selected regions
2014

- very low discrimination
- low
- medium
- high
- very high discrimination

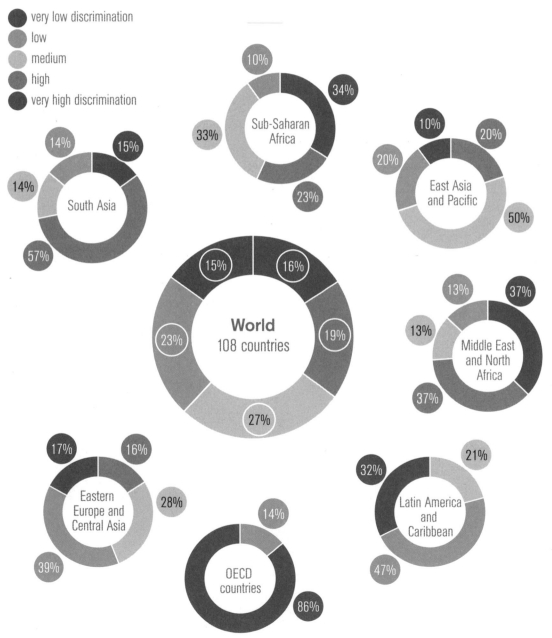

Sub-Saharan Africa
10% · 34% · 23% · 33%

East Asia and Pacific
10% · 20% · 50% · 20% · 20%

South Asia
14% · 15% · 57% · 14%

World
108 countries
15% · 16% · 19% · 27% · 23%

Middle East and North Africa
13% · 37% · 37% · 13%

Eastern Europe and Central Asia
17% · 16% · 28% · 39%

OECD countries
14% · 86%

Latin America and Caribbean
21% · 47% · 32%

Life expectancy

Women's average life expectancy at birth
2015

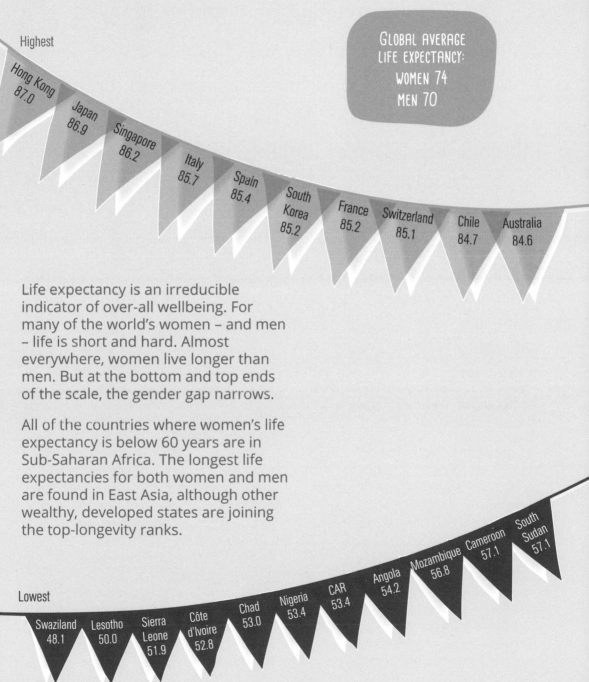

Highest

Hong Kong 87.0
Japan 86.9
Singapore 86.2
Italy 85.7
Spain 85.4
South Korea 85.2
France 85.2
Switzerland 85.1
Chile 84.7
Australia 84.6

GLOBAL AVERAGE LIFE EXPECTANCY:
WOMEN 74
MEN 70

Life expectancy is an irreducible indicator of over-all wellbeing. For many of the world's women – and men – life is short and hard. Almost everywhere, women live longer than men. But at the bottom and top ends of the scale, the gender gap narrows.

All of the countries where women's life expectancy is below 60 years are in Sub-Saharan Africa. The longest life expectancies for both women and men are found in East Asia, although other wealthy, developed states are joining the top-longevity ranks.

Lowest

Swaziland 48.1
Lesotho 50.0
Sierra Leone 51.9
Côte d'Ivoire 52.8
Chad 53.0
Nigeria 53.4
CAR 53.4
Angola 54.2
Mozambique 56.8
Cameroon 57.1
South Sudan 57.1

Lesbian rights

"Lesbian existence comprises both the breaking of a taboo and the rejection of a compulsory way of life. It is also a direct or indirect attack on male right of access to women. But it is more than these, although we may first begin to perceive it as a form of nay-saying to patriarchy, an act of resistance."

Adrienne Rich, *Compulsory Heterosexuality and Lesbian Existence*

When women step outside heterosexual norms, they are being doubly subversive – identifying as members of a sexual minority and also as women who are seen to be rejecting male authority.

Lesbians pay a high price for this nonconformity, subject to "corrective rapes", "honor" killings, social shunning, physical abuse, and material discrimination. In an odd twist, in most of the countries that criminalize homosexuality the specific laws actually only criminalize male same-sex behavior or specific sexual acts identified primarily with gay men. This legal omission doesn't protect women – in all cases, the laws are also applied to lesbians when the state wants them to – but it is an interesting indicator of the capricious disregard of women in general and lesbians in particular.

Even where homosexuality is not criminalized, the rights of LGBTI people are often not protected, nor even recognized. However, lesbian and gay organizing in the past three decades has been impressive, and in many countries lesbian identity is tolerated even if not fully accepted. Within LGBTI communities, the politics of integration into the mainstream is fraught; for lesbians particularly so, as acceptance by and absorption into patriarchal social structures is not necessarily liberating.

Beyond the binary

In most of the world, legal systems of protection have not caught up with gender-identity liberation movements, including transgender, transsexual, and intersex identities.

Gender identity activists are pushing governments to accommodate non-binary sex/gender identities. In most places, this starts with pursuing legal rights for trans and gender-diverse people to change their names and sex/gender identity on official documents.

In many countries, it is not possible to change one's legal gender. Elsewhere, it may be possible to change these markers, but only if certain prohibitive conditions are met such as completing mandated gender reassignment surgery.

Progress is slow, but among other steps forward, Australia, Bangladesh, Germany, India, Nepal, New Zealand, and Pakistan now allow a "third sex" designation on official documents.

Pioneers:

• Canada, 2017: Introduced an "X" gender designation for government-issued documents including passports.

• Bolivia, 2016: A "Gender Identity Law" allows transgender people over age 18 to change their name and sexual identity on official documents upon request.

• Ireland, 2015: The Gender Recognition Act allows for self-declaration of gender identity.

• Bangladesh, 2013: Hijras – biological males who identify as women – are granted official third gender recognition, including for passports and national IDs.

• Germany, 2013: The first European country to recognize "indeterminate" sex on birth certificates. 2017: Federal Constitutional Court rules that all public documents must include an option for a third gender category or dispense with gender designations entirely.

• New Zealand, 2012: Passports can have an "X" sex descriptor, meaning unspecified. In 2015, Statistics New Zealand introduced "gender diverse" as a new identity category.

• Nepal, 2007: A third gender, "other", was added to official documents, and the 2011 census allowed people to register as neither male nor female.

• Australia, 2003: Australians can choose "X" as their gender or sex on birth certificates and passports.

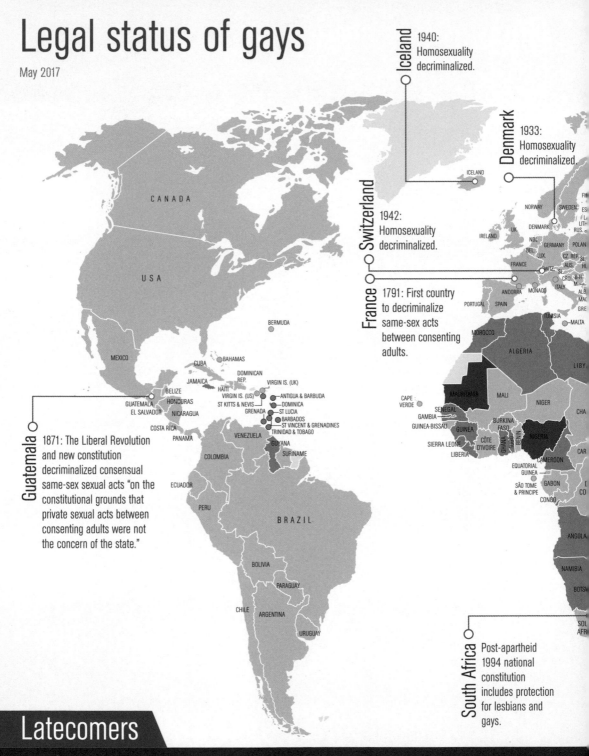

Legal status of gays

May 2017

Iceland — 1940: Homosexuality decriminalized.

Denmark — 1933: Homosexuality decriminalized.

Switzerland — 1942: Homosexuality decriminalized.

France — 1791: First country to decriminalize same-sex acts between consenting adults.

Guatemala — 1871: The Liberal Revolution and new constitution decriminalized consensual same-sex sexual acts "on the constitutional grounds that private sexual acts between consenting adults were not the concern of the state."

South Africa — Post-apartheid 1994 national constitution includes protection for lesbians and gays.

Latecomers

Countries that have recently removed lesbian/gay criminalizing laws (selected examples)

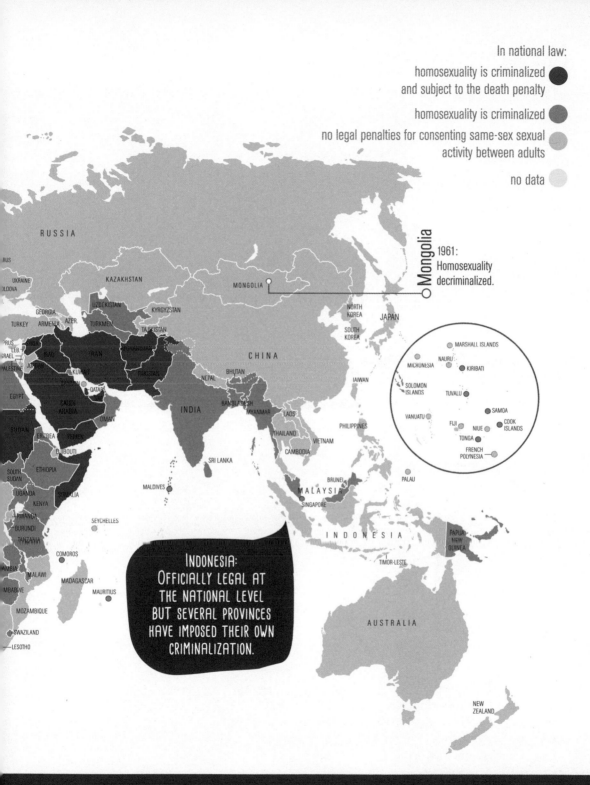

In national law:

homosexuality is criminalized
and subject to the death penalty

homosexuality is criminalized

no legal penalties for consenting same-sex sexual
activity between adults

no data

RUSSIA

RUS

UKRAINE
MOLDOVA

KAZAKHSTAN

GEORGIA
TURKEY ARMENIA AZER.
CRUS LEB. SYRIA
ISRAEL IRAQ
PALESTINE JORDAN KUWAIT
EGYPT PAKISTAN QATAR
SAUDI ARABIA
OMAN
SUDAN ERITREA YEMEN
DJIBOUTI

SOUTH SUDAN ETHIOPIA
UGANDA SOMALIA
RWANDA KENYA
BURUNDI
TANZANIA
ZAMBIA MALAWI
ZIMBABWE
MOZAMBIQUE
SWAZILAND
LESOTHO

COMOROS
MADAGASCAR
MAURITIUS
SEYCHELLES

UZBEKISTAN KYRGYZSTAN
TURKMEN.
TAJIKISTAN
AFGHANISTAN

IRAN

MONGOLIA

NEPAL BHUTAN
INDIA
BANGLADESH
MYANMAR

SRI LANKA

MALDIVES

CHINA

NORTH KOREA JAPAN
SOUTH KOREA

TAIWAN

LAOS
THAILAND
VIETNAM
CAMBODIA

PHILIPPINES

BRUNEI
MALAYSIA
SINGAPORE

INDONESIA

TIMOR-LESTE

PALAU

Mongolia

1961:
Homosexuality
decriminalized.

MARSHALL ISLANDS
NAURU
MICRONESIA KIRIBATI
SOLOMON ISLANDS TUVALU
SAMOA
VANUATU FIJI NIUE COOK ISLANDS
TONGA
FRENCH POLYNESIA

PAPUA NEW GUINEA

AUSTRALIA

NEW ZEALAND

INDONESIA:
OFFICIALLY LEGAL AT
THE NATIONAL LEVEL
BUT SEVERAL PROVINCES
HAVE IMPOSED THEIR OWN
CRIMINALIZATION.

• 2016: Seychelles • Nauru • Belize • 2014: Mozambique • 2010: Fiji • Lesotho • 2008: Nicaragua • 2005: Marshall Is.

Getting married

Average age of women
at first marriage

2015 or most recent data

- 30 and over
- 21 – 29
- 20 and younger
- no data

Or not...

Percentage of women in the USA
aged 45 who have never married

2014

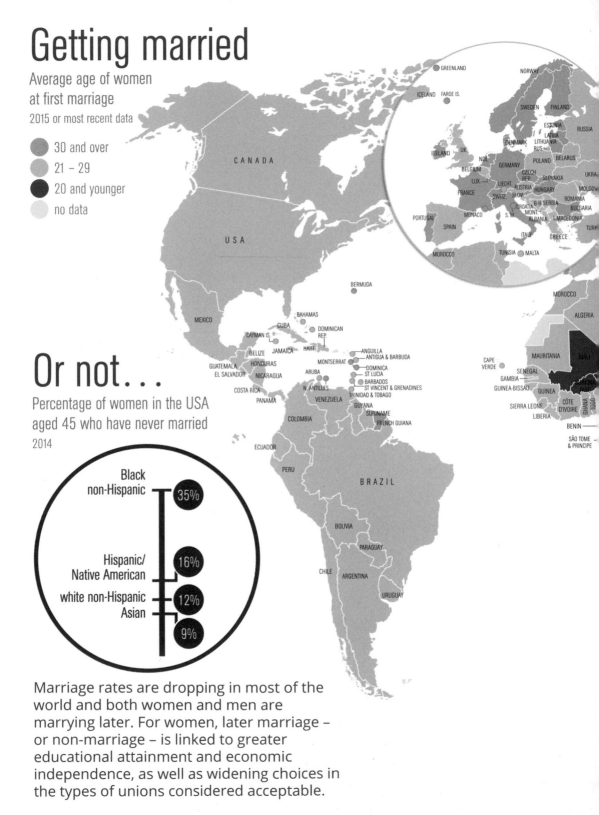

Black
non-Hispanic — 35%

Hispanic/
Native American — 16%

white non-Hispanic — 12%
Asian

9%

Marriage rates are dropping in most of the
world and both women and men are
marrying later. For women, later marriage –
or non-marriage – is linked to greater
educational attainment and economic
independence, as well as widening choices in
the types of unions considered acceptable.

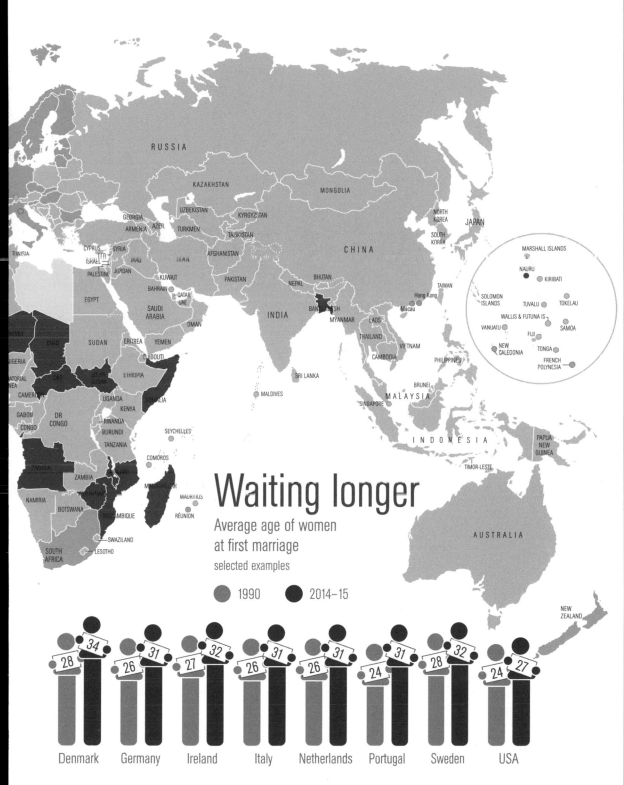

Waiting longer

Average age of women
at first marriage
selected examples

● 1990 ● 2014–15

Denmark	Germany	Ireland	Italy	Netherlands	Portugal	Sweden	USA
28 / 34	26 / 31	27 / 32	26 / 31	26 / 31	24 / 31	28 / 32	24 / 27

Breaking up is hard to do
– but easier now than ever before

Divorces per 100 marriages

selected European examples

 1990   ⬤ 2013–15

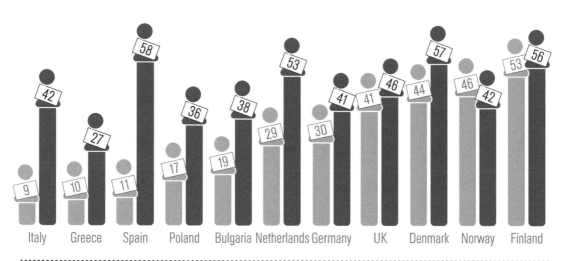

	Italy	Greece	Spain	Poland	Bulgaria	Netherlands	Germany	UK	Denmark	Norway	Finland
1990	9	10	11	17	19	29	30	41	44	46	53
2013–15	42	27	58	36	38	53	41	46	57	42	56

Education and divorce in the USA

Percentage of women's first marriages
ending in divorce by age 46

2013

35%

bachelor's degree
or higher

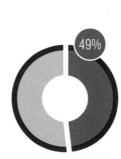

49%

some years of college,
or associate's degree

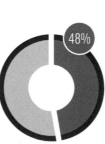

48%

high school graduate

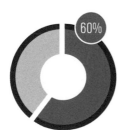

60%

women without a high school
diploma

Same-sex marriage
Recognition in national law
2017

2000	2003	2005	2006	2009	2010
Netherlands	Belgium	Canada Spain	South Africa	Mexico* Norway Sweden *some jurisdictions only	Argentina Iceland Portugal

2012	2013	2014	2015	2016	2017
Denmark	Brazil England/Wales France New Zealand Uruguay	Luxembourg Scotland	Finland Greenland Ireland USA	Colombia	Australia Austria Bermuda Germany Taiwan

Same-sex civil partnerships
Recognition in national law
Typically not on same basis as marriage
December 2017

BUT! BERMUDA'S GOVERNMENT REPEALED ITS SAME-SEX MARRIAGE LAW IN 2018, THE WORLD'S FIRST REVOCATION

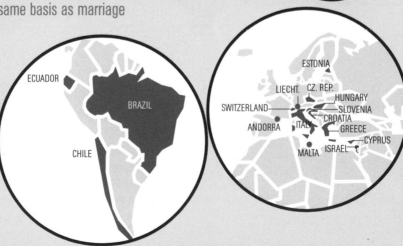

ECUADOR
BRAZIL
CHILE

ESTONIA
LIECHT. CZ. REP.
HUNGARY
SWITZERLAND
SLOVENIA
CROATIA
ANDORRA ITALY
GREECE
CYPRUS
MALTA ISRAEL

Child marriage in the USA

Child marriage rate per 10,000 marriages
2010

- ● 50 or higher
- ● 25 – 49
- ● 10 – 24
- ● lower than 10
- ● no data

Child marriage is legal in most of the USA. More than half the states in the USA do not have a minimum marriage age and every state allows minors (under 18) to get married. Most states allow 16–18-year-olds to marry with parental consent alone and those younger than age 16 to marry with judicial approval, often on the basis of the girl being pregnant.

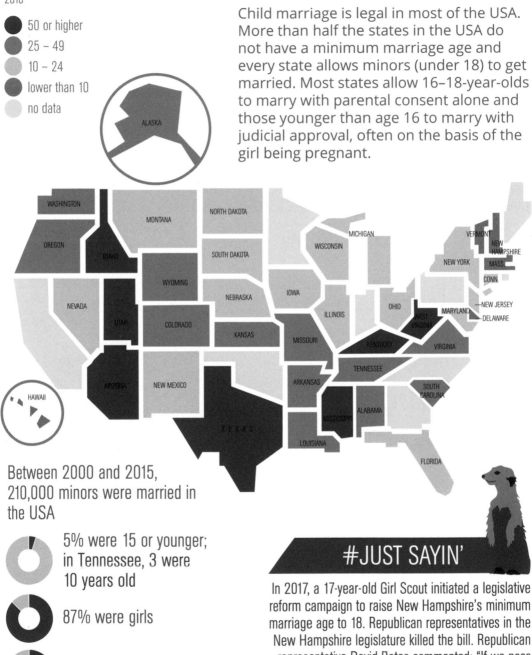

Between 2000 and 2015, 210,000 minors were married in the USA

5% were 15 or younger; in Tennessee, 3 were 10 years old

87% were girls

86% married adults

#JUST SAYIN'

In 2017, a 17-year-old Girl Scout initiated a legislative reform campaign to raise New Hampshire's minimum marriage age to 18. Republican representatives in the New Hampshire legislature killed the bill. Republican representative David Bates commented: "If we pass this, we will ensure forever that every child born to a minor will be born out of wedlock."

Global child marriages

Gender inequality, "traditional practices", patriarchal notions about the necessity of male "protection" to sustain family honor, social and economic insecurity, customary or religious laws that condone the practice, and an inadequate legislative framework fuel child marriage. Girls are often seen as tradeable commodities; girls who are poor and living in rural areas are the most likely to be married young. However, the practice of child marriage is declining; one in four women alive today was married in childhood, compared to one in three in the early 1980s.

Money buys time

CHILD MARRIAGE IS MOST COMMON IN SOUTHERN ASIA AND SUB-SAHARAN AFRICA. 33% OF THE WORLD'S CHILD BRIDES LIVE IN INDIA.

GIRLS IN THE POOREST FIFTH OF THE WORLD'S POPULATION ARE 2.5 TIMES MORE LIKELY TO MARRY — OR TO BE MARRIED OFF BY THEIR PARENTS — THAN THOSE IN THE WEALTHIEST FIFTH.

INDIA: THE AVERAGE AGE OF FIRST MARRIAGE IS 20 YEARS FOR WOMEN IN THE RICHEST QUINTILE; 15 FOR THE POOREST.

DOMINICAN REPUBLIC: HALF OF THE POOREST WOMEN MARRIED AT ABOUT 17; THE RICHEST WOMEN, AT 21.

The youngest brides

Percentage of women now aged 20–24 who were first married before they were 18, highest global rates
most recent year, 2008–14

76% Niger
68% CAR, Chad
55% Mali
52% Bangladesh, Burkina Faso, Guinea, South Sudan
48% Mozambique
47% India
46% Malawi
45% Somalia

Household size

Average number of people per household

most recent data since 2014

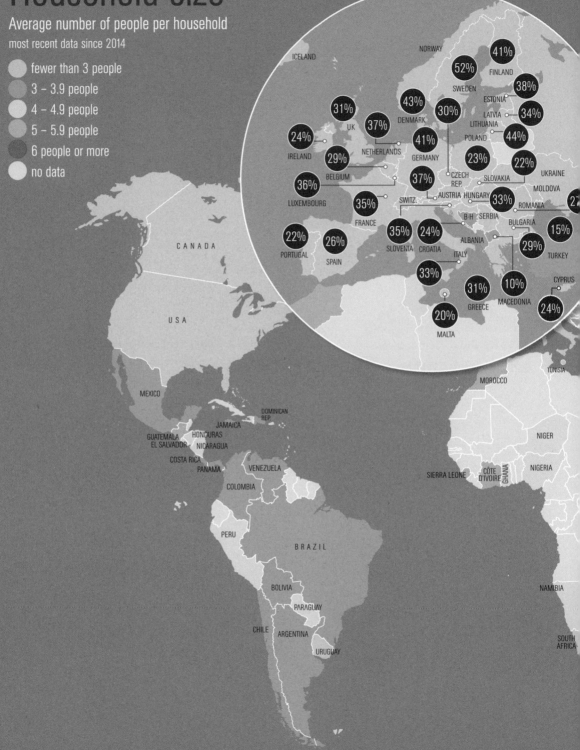

- fewer than 3 people
- 3 – 3.9 people
- 4 – 4.9 people
- 5 – 5.9 people
- 6 people or more
- no data

ICELAND

NORWAY

41% FINLAND

52% SWEDEN

38% ESTONIA

31% UK

37%

43% DENMARK

30%

34% LATVIA

LITHUANIA

24% IRELAND

29% NETHERLANDS

41% GERMANY

POLAND

44%

36% LUXEMBOURG

BELGIUM

37% SWITZ. AUSTRIA

CZECH REP.

23%

SLOVAKIA

22% UKRAINE

MOLDOVA

HUNGARY

33% ROMANIA

2?

35% FRANCE

B-H SERBIA

BULGARIA

15% TURKEY

22% PORTUGAL

26% SPAIN

35% SLOVENIA

24% CROATIA

ALBANIA

ITALY

29%

33%

31% GREECE

10% MACEDONIA

CYPRUS

24%

20% MALTA

CANADA

USA

MEXICO

DOMINICAN REP.

JAMAICA

GUATEMALA HONDURAS

EL SALVADOR NICARAGUA

COSTA RICA

PANAMA

VENEZUELA

COLOMBIA

PERU

BRAZIL

BOLIVIA

PARAGUAY

CHILE ARGENTINA

URUGUAY

MOROCCO

TUNISIA

SIERRA LEONE

CÔTE D'IVOIRE

GHANA

NIGER

NIGERIA

NAMIBIA

SOUTH AFRICA

One-person Europe

The one-person household is the fastest growing household type in the world. On a global scale only about 15% of the world's two billion households are one-person, but in post-industrial wealthier countries, particularly Europe, one-person living arrangements represent the largest block of household types. By 2016, 33% of all households in the EU were one-person. The highest rate in the world is in Sweden, where an astonishing 52% of all households are one-person. Women comprise the majority of one-person households.

Living alone

% one person households as a percentage of all households
most recent data since 2014

Not all households are equal
Poverty, race, and gender in the USA

2016

Percentage of family households living below the poverty rate

US average, all family households
████████ 10%

married couples
████ 5%

male householder, no wife present
██████████ 13%

female householder, no husband present
████████████████ 27%

Percentage of people in female householder families (no husband present) living in poverty

Asian non-Hispanic
████████████████ 19%

white non-Hispanic
███████████████████████ 27%

Black non-Hispanic
██████████████████████████ 34%

Hispanic
███████████████████████████ 35%

Facing hardship in Europe
Percentage of European one-person households facing severe material deprivation
selected examples, 2016

single-female ●
single-male ●

Bulgaria	Romania	Serbia	Italy	Germany	Ireland	France	Netherlands	Iceland	Denmark
55% / 38%	31% / 29%	31% / 28%	14% / 15%	9% / 9%	8% / 11%	7% / 8%	6% / 6%	6% / 2%	3% / 6%

"Material deprivation" expresses the inability to afford some items considered by most people to be desirable or even necessary to lead an adequate life. A combination of nine standard typical items, deemed as representative of a "standard" level of acceptable living conditions, is used for the identification of material deprivation, including the ability to afford: a one-week annual holiday away from home; a meal with meat, chicken, fish, or vegetarian equivalent every second day; adequate heating of the dwelling; durable goods like a washing machine, color television, telephone, or car; ability to pay on time a mortgage, rent, utility bills, or other loan payments; and ability to meet unexpected expenses.

Refugees

16.5 million people are living as refugees outside their countries, and another 32 million are internally displaced. Women make up about 50% of global refugees. For women refugees, whether in camps or in precarious temporary shelter, life is especially fraught; women continue to have primary family and household responsibilities under circumstances where there is little support or protection. Refugee women and girls are subject to rape and sex trafficking, especially in camps, which can be spaces of security but also of exploitation and abuse.

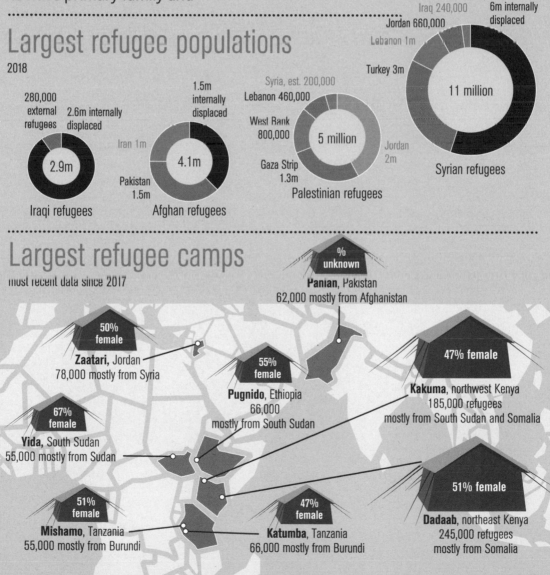

Largest refugee populations

2018

Iraqi refugees
2.9m
280,000 external refugees
2.6m internally displaced

Afghan refugees
4.1m
1.5m internally displaced
Iran 1m
Pakistan 1.5m

Palestinian refugees
5 million
Syria, est. 200,000
Lebanon 460,000
West Bank 800,000
Gaza Strip 1.3m
Jordan 2m

Syrian refugees
11 million
Iraq 240,000
Jordan 660,000
Lebanon 1m
Turkey 3m
6m internally displaced

Largest refugee camps

most recent data since 2017

Panian, Pakistan
62,000 mostly from Afghanistan
% unknown

Zaatari, Jordan
78,000 mostly from Syria
50% female

Pugnido, Ethiopia
66,000 mostly from South Sudan
55% female

Kakuma, northwest Kenya
185,000 refugees
mostly from South Sudan and Somalia
47% female

Yida, South Sudan
55,000 mostly from Sudan
67% female

Mishamo, Tanzania
55,000 mostly from Burundi
51% female

Katumba, Tanzania
66,000 mostly from Burundi
47% female

Dadaab, northeast Kenya
245,000 refugees
mostly from Somalia
51% female

Crisis zones

Prolonged militarized and economic crises

as of 2018

For millions of people in the world, "normal" household and family life has been ripped away. Instead, everyday life is embedded in a state of prolonged and extreme crisis. Women and girls in the midst of conflict and displacement often experience intensified levels of domestic and sexual violence, and trafficking. Families in desperate circumstances often resort to coping mechanisms such as marrying off girl children early, compelling child labor, and using family separation as an economic strategy. Women's work sustaining households and families is the shock absorber of crisis.

Venezuela Political, economic chaos; accelerating political repression; food, and fuel shortages; health system collapse.

Libya Ongoing conflict; fragmented civil society institutions and infrastructure; economic chaos; displacement; hub for international human trafficking.

Lake Chad Basin Environmental collapse of lake system; food insecurity, malnutrition and high risk of famine; terrorist attacks; repeated droughts; decade-long conflict; large-scale displacements.

DR Congo Episodically-intensified armed conflict; political instability; economic decline; epidemic levels of rape, gang rape, sexual slavery.

South Sudan 5-year civil war; war crimes including epidemic levels of rape, gang rape, sexual slavery, torture; economic chaos; destruction of public infrastructure; hunger; displacement.

Palestine Gaza blockade by Israel: food, water, fuel, electricity, and health care shortages; public infrastructure collapse; displacement.

Syria 7-year civil war, also involving external parties; indiscriminate attacks on civilians and civilian infrastructure; destruction of health services, housing, water and food supplies, and livelihoods; large-scale displacements.

Iraq Long-running conflict involving external and internal militaries; fundamentalist terrorism; precarious governance; little civil institution protection for women and girls from rape and violence.

Somalia Consecutive droughts; famine; conflict, terrorist attacks; weak civil society infrastructure and governance.

Yemen War waged by internal and external parties; widespread violence against civilians; destruction of health services, housing, communications, water and food supplies, and livelihoods; famine, cholera crisis.

Afghanistan Re-escalating conflict; sectarian violence; attacks on civilian infrastructure, including hospitals and schools; attacks on girls and women (in 2017, two-thirds of civilian casualties were women and children); displacement; high infant mortality; malnutrition; economic instability and incapacity; endemic polio.

Kashmir Heavily militarized, episodically-intensifying war; rape as tool of civilian repression.

Myanmar Violent repression; forced expulsion of ethnic minority Rohingya; systematic rape and torture of Rohingya women by security forces.

North Korea Epidemic hunger and malnutrition; violent repression of civil and political liberties; economic incapacity; arbitrary executions; forced labor in covert penal systems.

CAR Escalating civil war, sectarian conflict; political instability; attacks on civilians including widespread rapes.

Burundi High food insecurity; cholera outbreaks; political instability; systematic torture and rape by government-allied security forces; economic chaos.

Peacemakers

In many countries, women's movements have made significant and effective interventions to stop or slow armed conflict and to shape the terms of peace.

These countries prominently include: **Argentina, Chile, Colombia, DR Congo, Liberia, Northern Ireland, and Tunisia.**

R1325 After many years of uphill organizing, women persuaded the UN to adopt Resolution 1325 in 2000. **1325** requires governments to include women as authentic and equal partners in peace negotiations and to ensure that women's interests are included in post-conflict reconstruction plans.

Women at the peace table

As a proportion of formal peace negotiators
selected examples

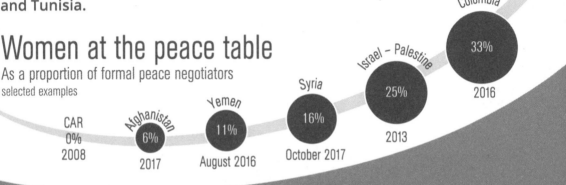

CAR
0%
2008

Afghanistan
6%
2017

Yemen
11%
August 2016

Syria
16%
October 2017

Israel – Palestine
25%
2013

Colombia
33%
2016

Peacekeeping

Women as percentage of military and police forces in UN peacekeeping missions with more than 500 personnel

as of January 2018

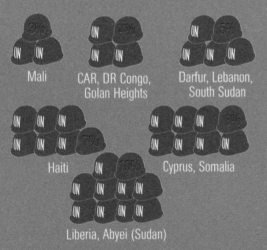

Mali
2%

CAR, DR Congo, Golan Heights
4%

Darfur, Lebanon, South Sudan
5%

Haiti
7%

Cyprus, Somalia
9%

Liberia, Abyei (Sudan)
19%

> "Even the guardians have to be guarded."
>
> Gita Sahgal, Amnesty International

SEXUAL ABUSE AND EXPLOITATION INCLUDING RAPE, SEX TRAFFICKING, AND PROSTITUTION BY MALE UN PEACEKEEPERS HAVE BEEN DOCUMENTED IN PEACEKEEPING MISSIONS SINCE THE 1990s IN BOSNIA AND HERZEGOVINA, CAMBODIA, CENTRAL AFRICAN REPUBLIC, DR CONGO, HAITI, LIBERIA, SIERRA LEONE, SOUTH SUDAN, TIMOR-LESTE.

INDIVIDUAL TROOP-CONTRIBUTING COUNTRIES ARE RESPONSIBLE FOR PROSECUTING MISCONDUCT BY THEIR STAFF, WHICH MAKES ACCOUNTABILITY ESPECIALLY DIFFICULT.

#Hashtagfeminism

Keeping women in their place

As a broad political observation, one might say that women everywhere face de facto restrictions on their public presence and dress, and public and private behavior. But in many countries, "keeping women in their place" is a literal undertaking.

Women are kept in their place in myriad ways – by economic discrimination, by legal structures that treat women as less than full human beings, by denying them reproductive rights. Violence, or the credible threat of it, is by far the most blunt instrument of control. For millions of women, violence starts at home. Far from being a place of safety, the family is often a cradle of violence. Domestic violence is the most ubiquitous constant in women's lives around the world. Statistics on domestic violence are notoriously unreliable. To some extent that's because violence against women is often ignored or even condoned by the state on the grounds that it is a "private" matter.

"Honor" killings and marry-your-rapist laws are among the most blatant expressions of patriarchal commitment to keeping women in the control of men in the confines of marriage and private homes. It is only because of women's extraordinary bravery in organizing against these practices that they are, in some places, crumbling.

"Men are afraid that women will laugh at them. Women are afraid that men will kill them."

Margaret Atwood

Kingdom of boxes

The government most committed to using the power of the state to keep women in their place is **Saudi Arabia**. The legal system in Saudi Arabia is based almost entirely on religious law. Religious fatwas about what women can and can't do are intertwined with government regulations that codify restrictions on women. "Male guardianship" is at the heart of the system of control: every Saudi woman must have a male guardian, normally a father or husband, sometimes a brother or even a son, who has the power to make a range of critical decisions on her behalf.

Control of women:

Women need the permission of a "male guardian" to:

- Travel abroad;
- Obtain a passport;
- Get married;
- Study abroad on a government scholarship.

Restrictions extend to work, health, and social status:

- Private entities/companies are allowed to require male guardianship permission for further activities. The government doesn't require guardian permission for women to work, but doesn't penalize employers who do require it.
- Women may be required to provide guardian consent to work or get health care.
- Recent court cases have supported male guardians prohibiting women from leaving the house on their own.
- In a divorce, male guardianship must be transferred from the husband to another male. But the husband remains in charge throughout divorce proceedings, even if he has been a violent guardian.

> " We all have to live in the borders of the boxes our dads or husbands draw for us. "

Zahra, 25-year-old Saudi woman

Going out in Saudi Arabia

- Women must be dressed "modestly" in public, covered from head to toe. This restriction can be deadly: in 2002, 15 schoolgirls died in a fire in their dormitory after religious police stopped them leaving the building and prevented firefighters from entering, because the girls were not appropriately dressed.

- Women must not spend time with men to whom they're not related. Public buildings, public transportation, parks, banks, and schools are segregated.

- Women are not allowed to use public swimming pools that are available to men.

- Women doctors are not allowed to treat male patients. Male doctors are allowed to treat female patients with a male guardian's permission.

The long road to change

Since the early 2000s, the Saudi government has eased some of the restrictions on work and education for women. The biggest breakthrough may be on the road: until 1990, a "customary ban" prohibited Saudi women from driving. A protest in 1990 by 47 women who drove a convoy of cars through the streets of Riyadh provoked a backlash and the ban then became official government policy. It also provoked more activism from women and a few male supporters: women continued to defy the ban in pop-up protests around the country. Finally, in 2017, the government announced that as of June 2018, Saudi women will be allowed to drive cars, although they may need their guardian's permission to get a driver's license. The government denied that women's activism influenced this decision.

Legally bound

Just some of the countries where married women are required to obey their husband

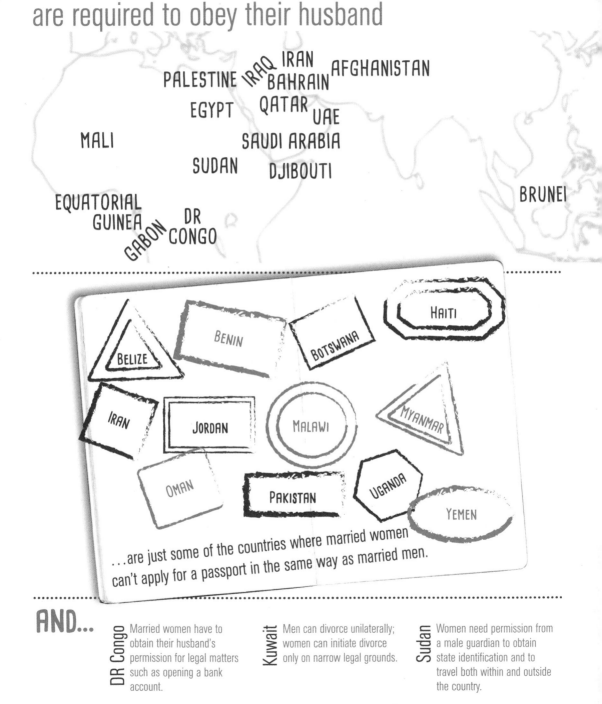

PALESTINE   IRAQ   IRAN   AFGHANISTAN
BAHRAIN
EGYPT   QATAR   UAE
MALI   SAUDI ARABIA
SUDAN   DJIBOUTI
BRUNEI
EQUATORIAL GUINEA   GABON   DR CONGO

HAITI
BENIN   BOTSWANA
BELIZE
IRAN   JORDAN   MALAWI   MYANMAR
OMAN   PAKISTAN   UGANDA   YEMEN

...are just some of the countries where married women can't apply for a passport in the same way as married men.

AND...

DR Congo
Married women have to obtain their husband's permission for legal matters such as opening a bank account.

Kuwait
Men can divorce unilaterally; women can initiate divorce only on narrow legal grounds.

Sudan
Women need permission from a male guardian to obtain state identification and to travel both within and outside the country.

Dress offensive

2013–14

50 countries had at least one law or policy at some level of government (from local to national) regulating the items women wear for religious reasons:

- **38 countries** had regulations prohibiting women wearing religious attire under certain circumstances.

- **11 countries** had regulations requiring women to wear religious attire under certain circumstances.

- **1 country**, Russia, had both: in Chechnya women were required to wear headscarves in public buildings; in Stavropol, hijabs were banned in public schools.

Just some of the things that can get you into trouble

Government-imposed bans on women's dress in the name of upholding moral propriety and social order:

- **Sudan** "indecent clothing" including short skirts and trousers
- **North Korea** trousers
- **Uganda** short skirts, shorts
- **Saudi Arabia** exposed skin or hair
- **France** burqas, niqabs
- **Belgium** burqas
- **Austria** burqas

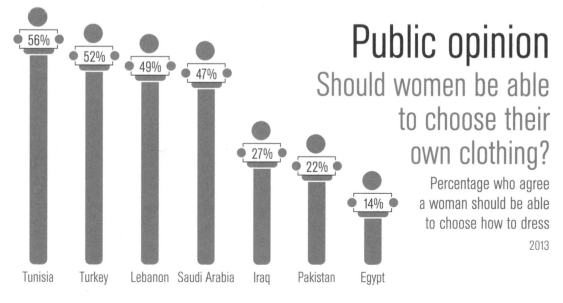

Public opinion
Should women be able to choose their own clothing?

Percentage who agree a woman should be able to choose how to dress

2013

Tunisia	56%
Turkey	52%
Lebanon	49%
Saudi Arabia	47%
Iraq	27%
Pakistan	22%
Egypt	14%

AFGHANISTAN
Under the Afghan penal code, a man convicted of "honor" killing after finding his wife committing adultery cannot be sentenced to more than 2 years' imprisonment.

IRAN
The penal code reduces punitive measures for fathers and other family members who commit "honor" killings.

EGYPT
"Honor" killings occur particularly in rural areas.

MOROCCO

IRAQ
The law permits "honor" considerations to mitigate sentences. For example, a provision limits a sentence for murder to a maximum of 3 years in prison if a man is on trial for killing his wife or a female dependent due to suspicion that the victim was committing adultery.

BANGLADESH

INDIA
Police registered 251 cases in 2015.

PAKISTAN
A 2004 law on "honor" killings and the 2011 Prevention of Anti-Women Practices Act already criminalize acts committed against women in the name of traditional practices. Despite these laws, hundreds of women are estimated to be victims of "honor" killings each year. A 2009 study found that "honor" killing of women constituted at least 21% of all homicides (both male and female victims) in Pakistan. 55% of known "honor" murders were committed using firearms, 11% using axes.

YEMEN
"Honor" killings occur particularly in rural areas.

KUWAIT
The penal code categorizes some "honor" crimes as misdemeanors.

JORDAN

SYRIA
The law permits judges to reduce legal penalties for murder and assault if the defendant asserts an "honor" defense.

CHECHNYA

"Justified" beatings

Percentage of women and men aged 15–49 who say a husband is justified in hitting or beating his wife for one or more of five reasons: burning food, arguing with him, going out without telling him, neglecting the children, refusing sex.

selected examples, most recent since 2011

SURPRISINGLY, IN MOST COUNTRIES WOMEN ARE MORE WILLING THAN MEN TO SAY THAT WIFE-BEATING MAY BE JUSTIFIED.

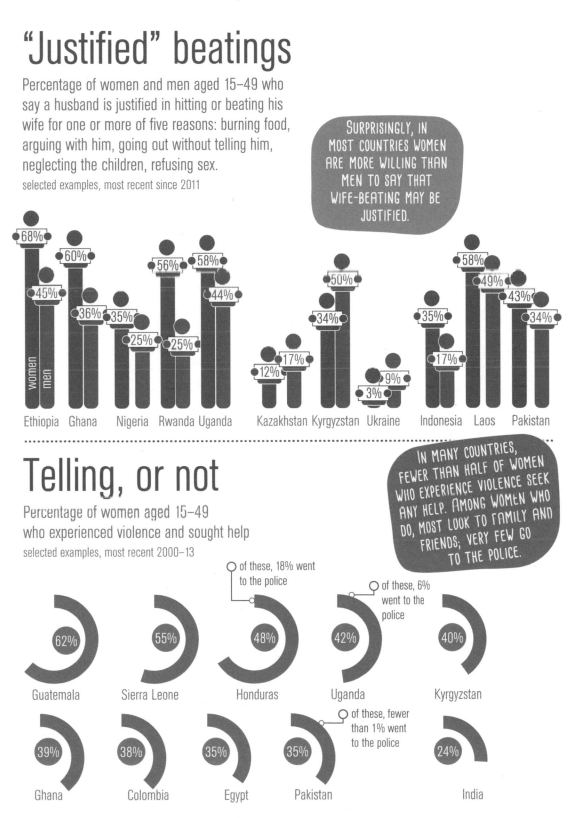

women / men

68% · 60% · 56% · 58% · 45% · 36% · 35% · 44% · 25% · 25% · 50% · 34% · 17% · 12% · 9% · 3% · 58% · 49% · 43% · 35% · 34% · 17%

Ethiopia Ghana Nigeria Rwanda Uganda Kazakhstan Kyrgyzstan Ukraine Indonesia Laos Pakistan

Telling, or not

Percentage of women aged 15–49 who experienced violence and sought help

selected examples, most recent 2000–13

IN MANY COUNTRIES, FEWER THAN HALF OF WOMEN WHO EXPERIENCE VIOLENCE SEEK ANY HELP. AMONG WOMEN WHO DO, MOST LOOK TO FAMILY AND FRIENDS; VERY FEW GO TO THE POLICE.

of these, 18% went to the police

of these, 6% went to the police

62% Guatemala 55% Sierra Leone 48% Honduras 42% Uganda 40% Kyrgyzstan

of these, fewer than 1% went to the police

39% Ghana 38% Colombia 35% Egypt 35% Pakistan 24% India

43

Domestic violence by country

Women who have experienced intimate partner
physical violence at least once in their lifetime
most recent data since 2010

- 20% and fewer
- 21% – 35%
- 36% – 50%
- more than 50%

FIJI 61%

AUSTRALIA 16%

JAPAN 26%

PHILIPPINES 13%

VIETNAM 32%

BANGLADESH 65%

NEPAL 23%

KYRGYZS. 25%

PAKISTAN 27%

TAJIKISTAN 20%

AZERBAIJAN 5%

PALESTINE 31%

CYPRUS 14%

COMOROS 6%

UGANDA 43%

TANZANIA 39%

MALAWI 22%

MOZAMBIQUE 32%

RWANDA 56%

ZIMBABWE 29%

CAMEROON 45%

GABON 46%

NIGERIA 14%

EQUATORIAL GUINEA 54%

MALI 30%

BURKINA FASO 11%

CÔTE D'IVOIRE 25%

SIERRA LEONE 44%

LIBERIA 32%

NIGERIA 12%

HAITI 16%

COLOMBIA 31%

PERU 36%

ECUADOR 35%

TURKEY 36%

ROMANIA 23%

BULGARIA 22%

FINLAND 27%

ESTONIA 19%

LITHUANIA 24%

LATVIA 31%

GREECE 18%

POLAND 12%

SLOVAKIA 22%

HUNGARY 19%

CROATIA 13%

SWEDEN 24%

CZECH REP. 19%

AUSTRIA 12%

SLOVENIA 12%

ROMANIA 12%

DENMARK 29%

GERMANY 20%

ITALY 17%

TUNISIA 20%

NETH. 22%

BELGIUM 22%

LUX. 21%

FRANCE 25%

SPAIN 12%

UK 28%

IRELAND 14%

PORTUGAL 18%

Domestic violence by region

Proportion of ever-partnered women aged 15–69
who have experienced intimate partner violence
most recent data since 2010

"Significant numbers of the world's population are routinely subject to torture, starvation, terrorism, humiliation, mutilation, and even murder simply because they are female. Crimes such as these against any group other than women would be recognized as a civil and political emergency as well as a gross violation of the victims' humanity."

Charlotte Bunch

North America
21%

Caribbean
27%

Central Latin America
30%

Andean Latin America
41%

Southern Latin America
24%

World average
30%

Western Europe
19%

North Africa/ Middle East
35%

Central Europe
28%

Eastern Europe
26%

West Sub-Saharan Africa
42%

East Sub Saharan Africa
39%

Central Asia
23%

Central Sub-Saharan Africa
66%

Southern Sub-Saharan Africa
30%

South Asia
42%

East Asia
16%

Southeast Asia
28%

Oceania
35%

Focus on intimate partner abuse

USA Intimate partner physical abuse has declined **67%** since the passage of the Violence Against Women Act in 1994.

BUT! *IT IS STILL WIDELY PREVALENT*

USA: Physical violence by race and ethnicity

Women who have experienced physical violence by an intimate partner during their lifetimes
2011

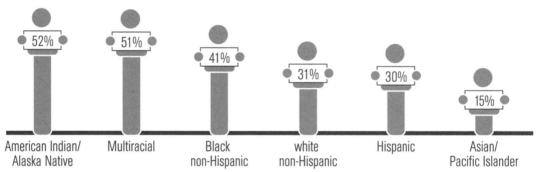

American Indian/ Alaska Native	Multiracial	Black non-Hispanic	white non-Hispanic	Hispanic	Asian/ Pacific Islander
52%	51%	41%	31%	30%	15%

England & Wales

Domestic violence accounts for one-third of all reported violent crimes in England and Wales.

In one year alone, from March 2015 – March 2016, 1.2 million women and 651,000 men were victims of domestic abuse.

In the decade up to 2016, 9% of all women aged 16–59 in England and Wales experienced domestic violence; for young women aged 16–19 this was 13%.

India

From 2001–2012, 45% – 50% of all crimes categorized as being specifically "against women" (versus general crimes such as robbery), were "cruelty by husband or his relatives."

China

The government agency in charge of promoting women's rights estimates that 1 in 4 married women is beaten.

China's first law against domestic violence, the Family Violence Law, came into effect in 2016.

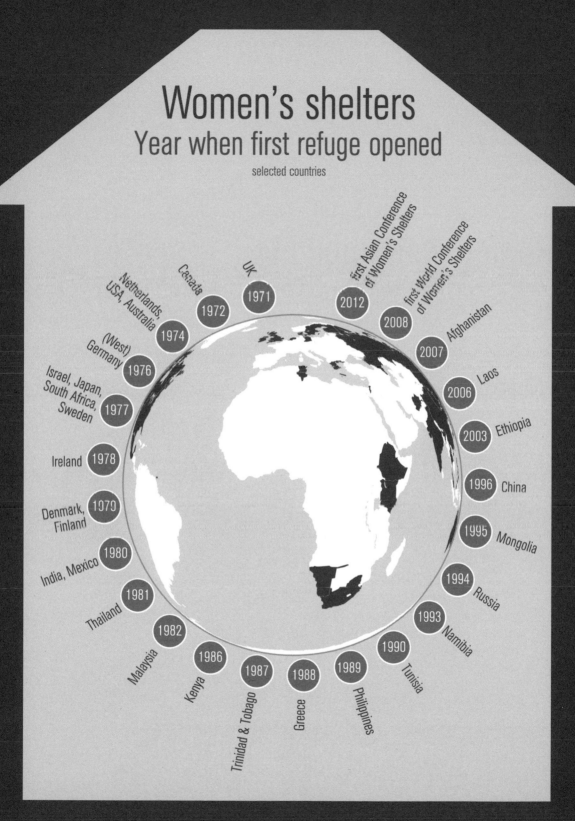

Women's shelters
Year when first refuge opened
selected countries

Canada — 1972
UK — 1971
Netherlands, USA, Australia — 1974
(West) Germany — 1976
Israel, Japan, South Africa, Sweden — 1977
Ireland — 1978
Denmark, Finland — 1979
India, Mexico — 1980
Thailand — 1981
Malaysia — 1982
Kenya — 1986
Trinidad & Tobago — 1987
Greece — 1988
Philippines — 1989
Tunisia — 1990
Namibia — 1993
Russia — 1994
Mongolia — 1995
China — 1996
Ethiopia — 2003
Laos — 2006
Afghanistan — 2007
first World Conference of Women's Shelters — 2008
First Asian Conference of Women's Shelters — 2012

Marry-your-rapist laws

Legal codes in many countries allow a rapist to avoid punishment if he marries his victim – in most cases, whether she agrees to the marriage or not. In the name of preserving family "honor", it is often family members who coerce women victims into these marriages. Feminist and human rights organizations are raising fierce opposition to these laws, with accelerating success.

Raping with impunity

Rape-marriage exemption laws and loopholes remain in effect in:

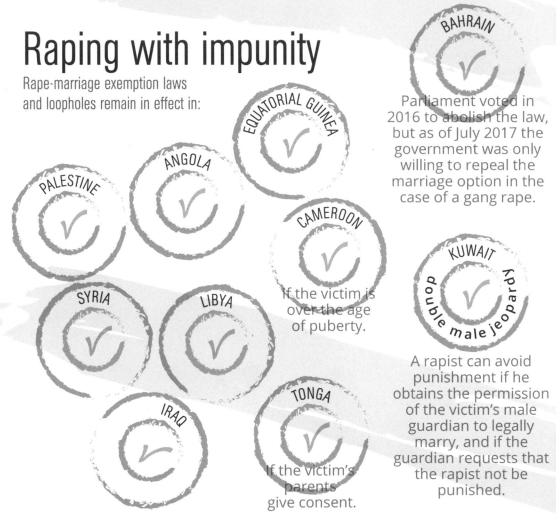

BAHRAIN ✓

Parliament voted in 2016 to abolish the law, but as of July 2017 the government was only willing to repeal the marriage option in the case of a gang rape.

EQUATORIAL GUINEA ✓

ANGOLA ✓

PALESTINE ✓

CAMEROON ✓

If the victim is over the age of puberty.

KUWAIT ✓
double male jeopardy

A rapist can avoid punishment if he obtains the permission of the victim's male guardian to legally marry, and if the guardian requests that the rapist not be punished.

SYRIA ✓

LIBYA ✓

IRAQ ✓

TONGA ✓

If the victim's parents give consent.

Repealed! Thank a feminist!

أبعاد
abaad

A WHITE DRESS DOESN'T COVER THE RAPE

#Undress522

ARTICLE 522 OF THE LEBANESE PENAL CODE EXONERATES A RAPIST IF HE MARRIES HIS VICTIM.

What does the Lebanese Penal Code provide in its article 522?

"In the event a legal marriage is concluded between the person who committed any of the crimes mentioned in this chapter [including rape, kidnapping and statutory rape], and the victim, prosecution shall be stopped and in case a decision is rendered, the execution of such decision shall be suspended against the person who was subject to it. Prosecution or the execution of the penalty shall be resumed before the lapse of three years in cases of misdemeanors and five years in cases of felonies, in the event such marriage ends by the divorce of the woman without a legitimate reason or by a divorce which is decided by court in favor of the woman."

Article 522 includes the crimes already mentioned in the chapter "offenses against honor" that deals with rape, kidnapping, seduction, indecency, and the violation of women's private spaces.

Why is ABAAD working on abolishing article 522? And how?

Article 522 of the Lebanese Penal Code is considered as a blatant discrimination against girls and women and their human rights and applies all over Lebanese territory. Our campaign Abolish 522 aims to:
- Push for the abolition of article 522.
- Stress on the right of women survivors of rape to refuse to marry their rapist, and put an end to their stigmatization and shaming
- Encourage people to join our cause, through the clear differentiation between the act of rape as a crime, and what society considers as the women's honor.
- Emphasize that forcing women to marry their rapist is a repressive act that legitimizes rape against women on a daily basis. Parents should therefore be convinced that the marriage of the victim to her rapist is not the solution and does not protect women.
- Rape is a crime, and the rapist should be punished.

ABAAD, a women's group in Lebanon, has been advocating for gender and sexual rights since 2011. In 2017, they launched an ambitious media campaign against the rapist-marriage law, including #Undress522, across social media. Later that year, the rapist-marriage law was repealed. Other discriminatory laws remain.

Rape

Proportion of women who have experienced sexual violence
at least once in their life

most recent data since 2011

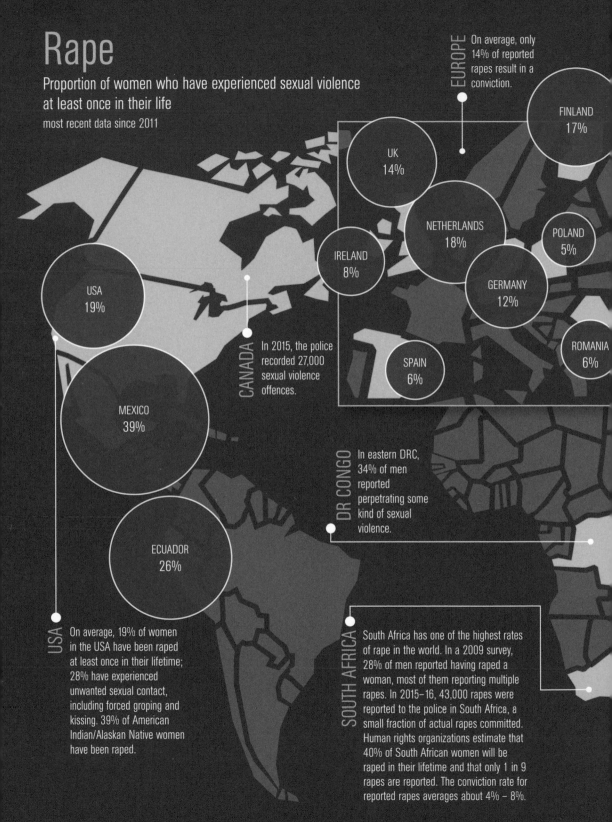

EUROPE On average, only 14% of reported rapes result in a conviction.

FINLAND
17%

UK
14%

NETHERLANDS
18%

POLAND
5%

IRELAND
8%

GERMANY
12%

ROMANIA
6%

USA
19%

SPAIN
6%

CANADA In 2015, the police recorded 27,000 sexual violence offences.

MEXICO
39%

DR CONGO In eastern DRC, 34% of men reported perpetrating some kind of sexual violence.

ECUADOR
26%

USA On average, 19% of women in the USA have been raped at least once in their lifetime; 28% have experienced unwanted sexual contact, including forced groping and kissing. 39% of American Indian/Alaskan Native women have been raped.

SOUTH AFRICA South Africa has one of the highest rates of rape in the world. In a 2009 survey, 28% of men reported having raped a woman, most of them reporting multiple rapes. In 2015–16, 43,000 rapes were reported to the police in South Africa, a small fraction of actual rapes committed. Human rights organizations estimate that 40% of South African women will be raped in their lifetime and that only 1 in 9 rapes are reported. The conviction rate for reported rapes averages about 4% – 8%.

In 2014, the police recorded almost 9,000 sexual violence offences.

SOUTH KOREA
20%

FIJI
36%

In 2013, the police recorded 117,000 rapes. An estimated 1% of victims report the crime to police. Adolescent girls account for 24% of rape cases, although they represent only 9% of the total female population.

Out of 100 sexual assaults, an estimated 9 are reported to the police; of those, 3 cases are prosecuted, and 1 will result in a conviction.

AUSTRALIA
19%

It is not unusual for women to be punished for adultery – often with floggings and prison sentences – if they report being raped.

Rape in war zones

Systematic or widespread rape of women by soldiers / paramilitaries as part of armed conflict

1990s–2018, where known

THE 1998 ROME TREATY DEFINED RAPE, SEXUAL SLAVERY, ENFORCED PROSTITUTION, FORCED PREGNANCY, AND ENFORCED STERILIZATION AS CRIMES AGAINST HUMANITY AS WELL AS WAR CRIMES. IN 2008, THE UN SECURITY COUNCIL DEMANDED AN END TO THE USE OF SEXUAL VIOLENCE AS A TOOL OF WAR.

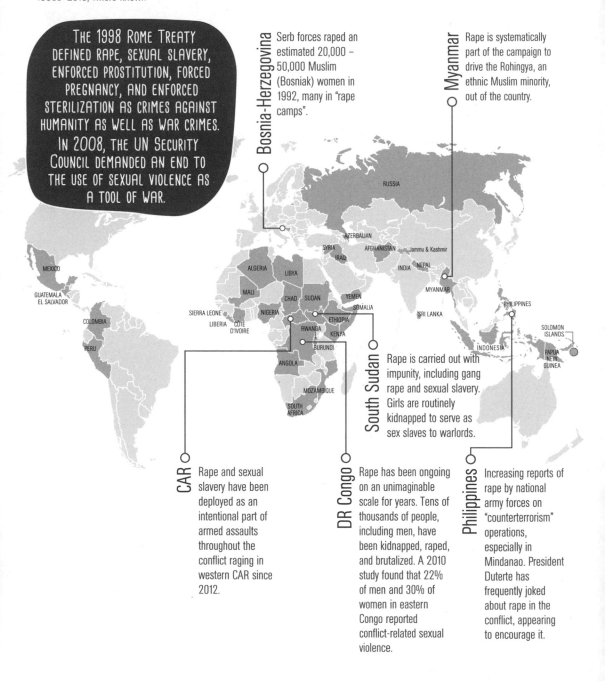

Bosnia-Herzegovina
Serb forces raped an estimated 20,000 – 50,000 Muslim (Bosniak) women in 1992, many in "rape camps".

Myanmar
Rape is systematically part of the campaign to drive the Rohingya, an ethnic Muslim minority, out of the country.

South Sudan
Rape is carried out with impunity, including gang rape and sexual slavery. Girls are routinely kidnapped to serve as sex slaves to warlords.

CAR
Rape and sexual slavery have been deployed as an intentional part of armed assaults throughout the conflict raging in western CAR since 2012.

DR Congo
Rape has been ongoing on an unimaginable scale for years. Tens of thousands of people, including men, have been kidnapped, raped, and brutalized. A 2010 study found that 22% of men and 30% of women in eastern Congo reported conflict-related sexual violence.

Philippines
Increasing reports of rape by national army forces on "counterterrorism" operations, especially in Mindanao. President Duterte has frequently joked about rape in the conflict, appearing to encourage it.

The rapist at home

Proportion of women who have experienced sexual violence by an intimate partner at least once in their life

selected examples, most recent data since 2011

Country	%
Spain	4%
Australia, Nigeria	5%
Mexico	6%
Peru	8%
USA, France, Jordan	9%
UK, Sweden	10%
Haiti, Netherlands	11%
Turkey	12%
Mali, Japan	14%
Palestine	15%
Cameroon	20%
Zimbabwe	26%
Bangladesh	37%

WOMEN IN VIOLENT RELATIONSHIPS HAVE 4 TIMES THE RISK OF CONTRACTING SEXUALLY TRANSMITTED INFECTIONS, INCLUDING HIV, THAN WOMEN IN NON-VIOLENT RELATIONSHIPS.

Marital rape

In many countries, marital rape is not explicitly defined as a crime. In others, including the countries below, rape in marriage is permissible.

IRAN

Article 1108 of Iran's Civil Code obliges women to fulfill the sexual needs of their husbands at all times. A woman's refusal to engage in sexual activity with her husband constitutes noshuz [disobedience] and can disqualify her for maintenance rights.

INDIA

In August 2017, the Indian government filed a formal judicial brief opposing the possible criminalization of marital rape. The government expressed concern that criminalizing marital rape might "destabilize the institution of marriage [and become] an easy tool for harassing husbands".

BAHAMAS

In 2009, an MP introduced a legislative bill that would have criminalized marital rape. In the face of considerable opposition, the legislation was abandoned.

NIGERIA

JORDAN

OMAN

SRI LANKA

SINGAPORE

INDONESIA

TANZANIA

GHANA

LESOTHO

Murder of women

In 2015, more than 1,800 women and girls were murdered (in single-victim/single-offender crimes). More than 90% of them were killed by men. 10,018 women were murdered between 2004–14. Very few women are murdered by strangers: intimate partners account for well over 50% of women's murders. Only about 5% of men are murdered by intimate partners.

A woman is 70 times more likely to be murdered in the few weeks after leaving her abusive partner than at any other time in the relationship.

Indigenous women are 3 times more likely than non-indigenous women to experience violent abuse and are 4 times more likely to be victims of homicide. A 2014 report concluded that 1,017 indigenous women had been killed between 1980 and 2012 and that another 164 were missing. This is widely assumed to be an underestimate.

Internationally, women who work as prostitutes are up to 100 times more likely to be murdered than non-prostitute women, and their murders are less likely to be solved. In Canada, for example, between 1991–2014, the overall unsolved rate for murders was 20%; for sex-workers the unsolved murder rate was 34%.

Ethnicity, race, and murder in the USA

	Proportion of murders related to intimate-partner violence	Proportion of murders committed with firearms	Murder rate per 100,000
Black non-Hispanic	51%	58%	4.4
American Indian/ Alaska Native	55%	39%	4.3
Hispanic	61%	49%	1.8
white non-Hispanic	57%	53%	1.5
Asian/ Pacific Islander	58%	40%	1.2

Hundreds, perhaps thousands, of women and girls have been abducted and murdered in northern Mexico in the past two decades. This "femicide cluster" seems to be at the center of colliding forces of organized criminal activity, drug trafficking, and sexual assaults turning deadly – aided and abetted, until recently, by considerable indifference from the authorities. In 2011 alone, 300 women were murdered in one city at the center of this epidemic, Ciudad Juárez.

Every 3 days a woman is killed by her current or former intimate partner.

4,762 women were murdered in 2013.

Every 30 hours, a woman is killed in what Argentinian feminists call "femicide" – a murder usually committed by a husband, boyfriend, family member, or acquaintance of the victim.

Internationally

The 5 countries with the highest murder rates of women and girls are:
El Salvador
Jamaica
Guatemala
South Africa
Russia

Internationally

Men and boys represent the largest share of people who die violently. But, the rate of murder for women matches or exceeds that of men in many countries including several high-income countries such as:
Austria
Germany
Hong Kong
Japan
Luxembourg
New Zealand
Slovenia
Switzerland

England & Wales

Domestic abuse leads to the murder of about 100 women and 30 men a year. On average, a victim of domestic violence endures 35 assaults before she calls the police.

Netherlands

More than half of the women murdered in 2011–15 died at the hands of their current or former partner; in the same period, only about one-third of murdered men were killed by an acquaintance.

Russia

An estimated 14,000 women a year are killed by intimate male partners.

Germany

127,457 persons in relationships were targets of murder, bodily harm, rape, sexual assault, threats, and stalking in 2015. Approximately 82% of these were women.

Belarus

In the first 10 months of 2015, police identified almost 2,000 victims of domestic violence, 76% of whom were women. 96 victims of domestic violence died, and 169 suffered severe bodily injuries.

Japan

On average, a woman is killed by her intimate partner or ex-partner every 3 days.

Turkey

At the end of 2015, the Stop Women Murders Now group reported that 328 women had been murdered during the year.

Australia

In 2015, 80 women were violently killed, 80% as a result of domestic violence.

South Africa

Every 6 hours, a woman is killed by her current or former intimate partner.

Dowry deaths

Traditionally, a bride's family provided the groom and his parents with money or gifts, some extravagant, to ensure that the woman was taken care of in her new home. **The practice of dowry is now illegal in India**, but it continues apace. In thousands of cases each year, the groom's family demands more dowry after marriage, culminating in ever-harsher extortion and harassment that can lead to suicide or murder of the bride. **Dowry murders**, many by burnings that are made to look like kitchen accidents, occur sporadically around the world, but the incidence is particularly **high in Bangladesh, India, and Pakistan.**

Pakistan

- Although the highest absolute number of dowry deaths is found in India, Pakistan has the highest *rate* proportional to the population.
- An average of 2,000 women are known to be killed each year in dowry extortion; the actual number of deaths is likely to be considerably higher.

India

- The Ministry of Women and Child Development estimates that between 2012 and 2014 almost 25,000 women either committed suicide or were killed due to dowry harassment.
- In 2015, an estimated 7,634 women died due to dowry harassment.
- In 2016, 21 dowry deaths a day were reported. Many more go unreported.
- The conviction rate for dowry deaths is less than 35%.

Bangladesh

- Between 2014 and 2016, 350 dowry-related deaths were recorded.
- A Bangladesh human rights organization estimates that in 2016, 108 women were physically tortured in dowry violence, 126 were killed after torture, and another 4 committed suicide after torture.

Fundamentalist wars on women

Women's rights are under increasing pressure from religious fundamentalism in many countries: Buddhist in Myanmar, Catholic in Poland, Christian in the USA, Hindu fundamentalism in India, Islamic in Algeria, among dozens of other examples.

Restrictions on women in the name of religious tradition are in most cases symptomatic of wider human rights abuses and political repression. They are cultivated in a climate of widespread oppression that affects women and men in countless ways.

But in the past two decades, ferociously militarized fundamentalist movements have emerged with theologies that embed extreme oppression of women at their core: Al Qaeda, Boko Haram, Al-Shabab, the Taliban, and ISIL (Daesh/ISIS) have escalated organized misogyny to new extremes. At the same time, manifesting the reality that people can be agents of their own oppression, some women have joined these groups and argue the rightness of their social codes.

The rising tide of fundamentalism is everywhere contested. Feminists have been especially active in challenging the legitimacy of fundamentalist proscriptions, and in offering alternative interpretations of religious texts. Women have also formed armed resistance groups against the fundamentalist forces, notably in Kurdistan and Nigeria.

Boko Haram
Boko Haram misogynist hallmark:
Abducting schoolgirls, raping and forcing them into "marriages"

- 2,000+ women and girls kidnapped in past decade.
- Abducted girls endure systematic physical and sexual violence, are usually gang-raped and typically awarded to fighters as "wives".
- Significantly more men than women have been killed in fighting, but women are an overwhelming majority among the estimated 1.8 million internally displaced persons in Nigeria's northeast.
- Believing that girls will draw less official attention, in 2011 Boko Haram started to systematically use captured girls as suicide bombers. Of the 338 suicide attacks by Boko Haram between 2011 and 2017 in which the bomber's gender could be identified, 244 were women or girls.
- 300 schoolgirls seized near Chibok, Nigeria in 2014, another 110 in Dapchi in February 2018, are just two among several and continuing mass abductions.

ISIS / ISIL / Daesh
ISIS misogynist hallmark:
Creating formal theological justification for raping and enslaving girls and women

- Starting in 2014, ISIS fighters captured and enslaved more than 6,000 Yasidi women in northern Iraq, trading them as sex slaves throughout their territory.
- ISIS religious leaders claim that all females within ISIS-held territory – slaves and non-slaves alike as young as 9 years old – can be enslaved by or married to ISIS militants as rewards of plunder.
- ISIS requires that women should be "hidden and veiled": women in ISIS territory must be accompanied by a male guardian to go out in public, and wear double-layered veils, loose abayas, and gloves.
- ISIS creates women's brigades to enforce other women's compliance with social codes.
- Sexual minorities are tortured and killed, especially gay men, but lesbians are fiercely persecuted.
- Despite losing most of its territory in 2017, individual ISIS fighters and cells are maintaining and expanding the sex markets and trafficking networks they established at their peak.

Birthrights

Many millions of women are engaged in childbearing for most of their lives, sometimes starting when they are still children themselves. Decisions about whether or not to have children, how many to have and when, how to get and control contraceptives, and how to manage reproductive choices are central to most women's lives. In too many instances, the capacity to act on these decisions is denied women. Legal structures and cultural norms that restrict access to contraception and abortion, that protect rape within marriage, and that give men control over women's reproductive choices are widespread. In many instances, economic inequality directly shapes decision-making capacity:

about 12% of the world's married or in-union women want to delay or stop childbearing, for example, but do not have access to contraceptives – too often because they cannot afford them.

The extent to which women control their reproductive choices affects their freedom in all other spheres: their participation in the economy, education, the household, and in political and civic arenas, as well as their capacity to be economically and socially autonomous from men.

The struggle over abortion rights – fiercely contested in many countries – is, at its heart, a struggle about women's autonomy.

" If men could get pregnant, abortion would be a sacrament. "

Florynce R. Kennedy

Births

Average number of births per woman

2015

GREENLAND

ICELAND

FAROE IS.

NORWAY

SWEDEN FINLAND

ESTONIA

RUSSIA

LATVIA

UK

DENMARK LITHUANIA

RUS.

BELARUS

IRELAND

POLAND

NDL

BELGIUM GERMANY

CZECH
REP. SLOVAKIA

UKRAINE

LUX.

LIECH.

MOLDOVA

FRANCE SWITZ. AUSTRIA HUNGARY

SLOV.

ROMANIA

CROATIA B-H SERBIA

BULGARIA

MONT.

KOSOVO

PORTUGAL

ALBANIA MACEDONIA

SPAIN

ITALY GREECE

MALTA

CANADA

USA

MEXICO

BERMUDA

BAHAMAS

CUBA

DOMINICAN
REP. PUERTO RICO

HAITI

ST. MARTIN (FR)

BELIZE JAMAICA

VIRGIN IS. (US)

ANTIGUA & BARBUDA

GUATEMALA
EL SALVADOR

HONDURAS

ARUBA GRENADA

ST LUCIA

NICARAGUA

BARBADOS

COSTA RICA

N. ANTILLES

ST VINCENT & GRENADINES

PANAMA

VENEZUELA

TRINIDAD & TOBAGO

COLOMBIA

GUYANA

SURINAME

ECUADOR

PERU

BRAZIL

BOLIVIA

PARAGUAY

CHILE

ARGENTINA

URUGUAY

MOROCCO

TUNISIA

ALGERIA

LIBYA

MAURITANIA

MALI

NIGER

CHAD

CAPE
VERDE

SENEGAL

GAMBIA

BURKINA
FASO

GUINEA-BISSAU

GUINEA

NIGERIA

CÔTE
D'IVOIRE

GHANA

TOGO

BENIN

CAR

SIERRA LEONE

LIBERIA

CAMEROON

EQUATORIAL
GUINEA

CONGO

GABON

DR
CON

SÃO TOME
& PRINCIPE

ANGOLA

NAMIBIA

SOUTH
AFRIC

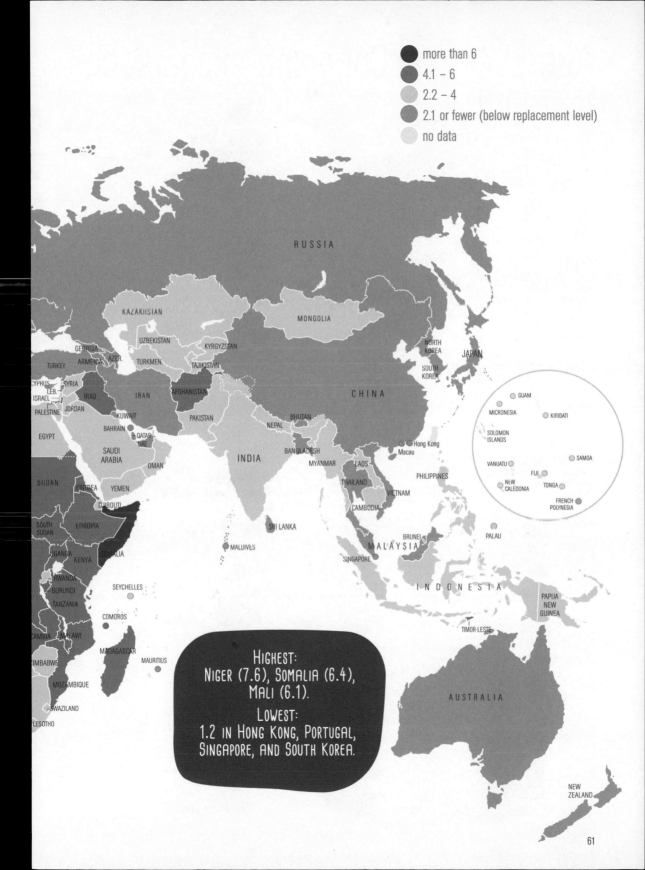

more than 6
4.1 – 6
2.2 – 4
2.1 or fewer (below replacement level)
no data

RUSSIA

KAZAKHSTAN

MONGOLIA

UZBEKISTAN   KYRGYZSTAN

GEORGIA   NORTH
ARMENIA AZER. TURKMEN. TAJIKISTAN   KOREA   JAPAN
TURKEY   SOUTH
CYPRUS   AFGHANISTAN   KOREA
LEB.   SYRIA
ISRAEL IRAQ   IRAN   CHINA
PALESTINE JORDAN
       KUWAIT   PAKISTAN   BHUTAN
BAHRAIN   NEPAL
EGYPT   QATAR   Hong Kong
         UAE   Macau
SAUDI   BANGLADESH
ARABIA OMAN   INDIA   MYANMAR   LAOS
                                            PHILIPPINES
SUDAN   ERITREA YEMEN   THAILAND
DJIBOUTI   VIETNAM
SOUTH   CAMBODIA
SUDAN ETHIOPIA   SRI LANKA   BRUNEI
UGANDA KENYA SOMALIA   MALDIVES   MALAYSIA
RWANDA   SINGAPORE
BURUNDI SEYCHELLES   INDONESIA
TANZANIA
ZAMBIA MALAWI COMOROS   PAPUA
MADAGASCAR   NEW
ZIMBABWE MAURITIUS   GUINEA
MOZAMBIQUE   TIMOR-LESTE
SWAZILAND   AUSTRALIA
LESOTHO

GUAM
MICRONESIA   KIRIBATI
SOLOMON
ISLANDS
VANUATU   SAMOA
NEW   FIJI
CALEDONIA TONGA
           FRENCH
           POLYNESIA
PALAU

HIGHEST:
NIGER (7.6), SOMALIA (6.4),
MALI (6.1).
LOWEST:
1.2 IN HONG KONG, PORTUGAL,
SINGAPORE, AND SOUTH KOREA.

NEW
ZEALAND

61

Age at first birth

Women's average age
selected examples

most recent year since 2010

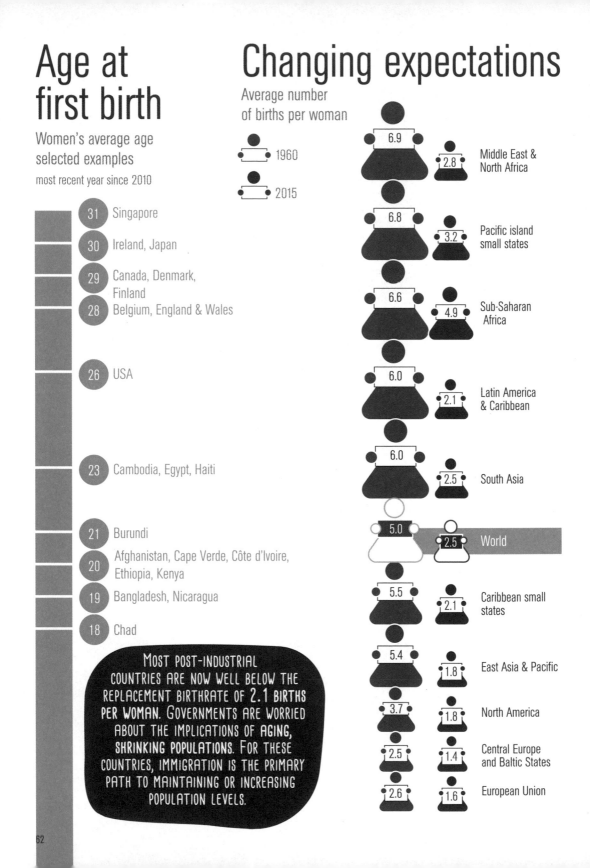

31	Singapore
30	Ireland, Japan
29	Canada, Denmark, Finland
28	Belgium, England & Wales
26	USA
23	Cambodia, Egypt, Haiti
21	Burundi
20	Afghanistan, Cape Verde, Côte d'Ivoire, Ethiopia, Kenya
19	Bangladesh, Nicaragua
18	Chad

MOST POST-INDUSTRIAL COUNTRIES ARE NOW WELL BELOW THE REPLACEMENT BIRTHRATE OF 2.1 BIRTHS PER WOMAN. GOVERNMENTS ARE WORRIED ABOUT THE IMPLICATIONS OF AGING, SHRINKING POPULATIONS. FOR THESE COUNTRIES, IMMIGRATION IS THE PRIMARY PATH TO MAINTAINING OR INCREASING POPULATION LEVELS.

Changing expectations

Average number
of births per woman

● 1960

● 2015

1960	2015	Region
6.9	2.8	Middle East & North Africa
6.8	3.2	Pacific island small states
6.6	4.9	Sub-Saharan Africa
6.0	2.1	Latin America & Caribbean
6.0	2.5	South Asia
5.0	2.5	World
5.5	2.1	Caribbean small states
5.4	1.8	East Asia & Pacific
3.7	1.8	North America
2.5	1.4	Central Europe and Baltic States
2.6	1.6	European Union

Contraception is still women's responsibility

Female sterilization is, worldwide, the most common method of contraception. Male sterilization is more effective, less expensive to perform and has fewer complications than female sterilization but is seldom performed.

Overall, contraceptive methods that require men's direct participation – male sterilization (vasectomy), the male condom and withdrawal – account for only a small proportion of contraceptive practices.

"Modern" methods include: sterilization, IUD, implants, injectables, oral contraceptives, condoms, emergency contraception.

"Traditional" methods include: rhythm, herbal remedies, withdrawal, planned abstinence.

Types of contraception

Worldwide, 64% of women in heterosexual relationships use some kind of contraceptive method or device. This is what they're using:

Global averages, 2015

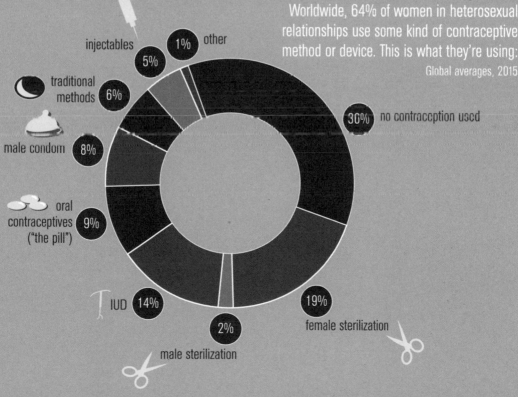

injectables 5%

other 1%

traditional methods 6%

30% no contraception used

male condom 8%

oral contraceptives ("the pill") 9%

IUD 14%

male sterilization 2%

19% female sterilization

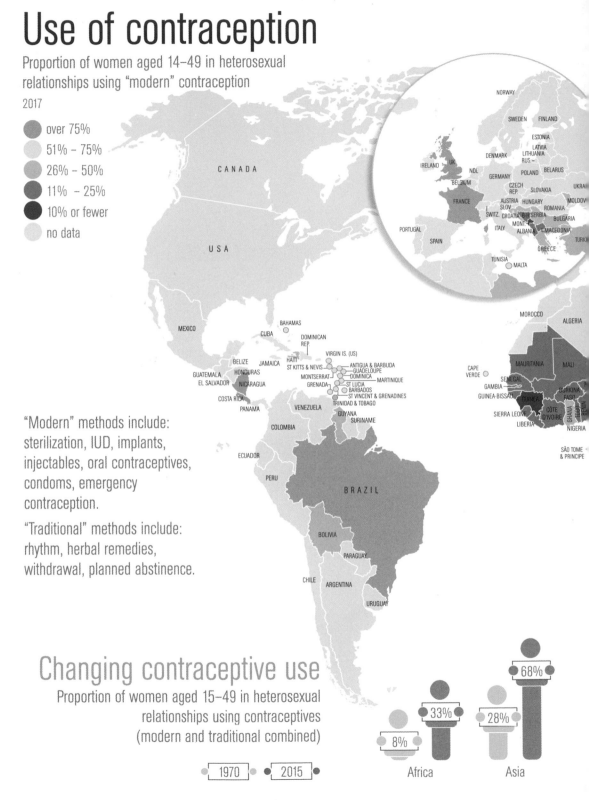

Use of contraception

Proportion of women aged 14–49 in heterosexual relationships using "modern" contraception

2017

- over 75%
- 51% – 75%
- 26% – 50%
- 11% – 25%
- 10% or fewer
- no data

"Modern" methods include: sterilization, IUD, implants, injectables, oral contraceptives, condoms, emergency contraception.

"Traditional" methods include: rhythm, herbal remedies, withdrawal, planned abstinence.

Changing contraceptive use

Proportion of women aged 15–49 in heterosexual relationships using contraceptives (modern and traditional combined)

1970   2015

Africa

- 8%
- 33%

Asia

- 28%
- 68%

Map labels:

NORWAY, SWEDEN, FINLAND, ESTONIA, LATVIA, LITHUANIA, RUS.–, DENMARK, IRELAND, UK, NDL, GERMANY, POLAND, BELARUS, BELGIUM, CZECH REP, SLOVAKIA, UKRAINE, FRANCE, AUSTRIA, SLOV, HUNGARY, MOLDOV, SWITZ., CROATIA, B-H SERBIA, ROMANIA, PORTUGAL, MONT., BULGARIA, ITALY, ALBANIA, L. MACEDONIA, SPAIN, GREECE, TURKEY, TUNISIA, MALTA

CANADA, USA, MEXICO, BAHAMAS, CUBA, DOMINICAN REP, HAITI, JAMAICA, BELIZE, GUATEMALA, HONDURAS, EL SALVADOR, NICARAGUA, COSTA RICA, PANAMA, VIRGIN IS. (US), ST KITTS & NEVIS, ANTIGUA & BARBUDA, GUADELOUPE, DOMINICA, MONTSERRAT, MARTINIQUE, GRENADA, ST LUCIA, BARBADOS, ST VINCENT & GRENADINES, TRINIDAD & TOBAGO, VENEZUELA, GUYANA, SURINAME, COLOMBIA, ECUADOR, PERU, BRAZIL, BOLIVIA, PARAGUAY, CHILE, ARGENTINA, URUGUAY

MOROCCO, ALGERIA, CAPE VERDE, MAURITANIA, MALI, SENEGAL, GAMBIA, GUINEA-BISSAU, GUINEA, BURKINA FASO, SIERRA LEONE, CÔTE D'IVOIRE, GHANA, TOGO, BENIN, NIGERIA, LIBERIA, SÃO TOME & PRINCIPE

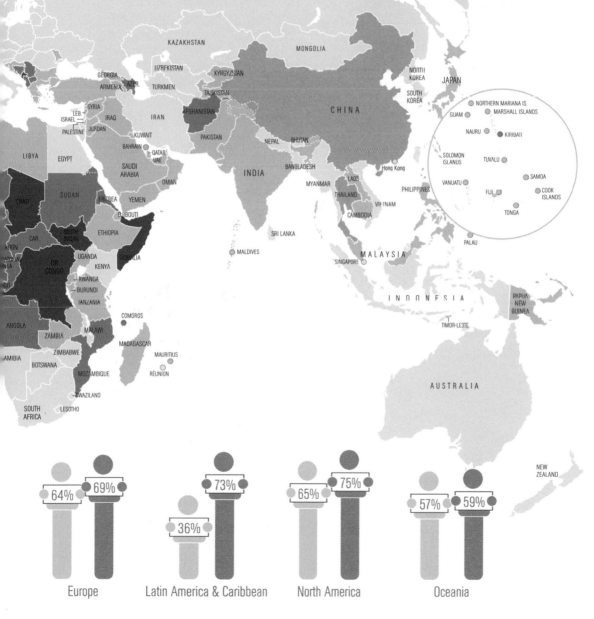

GLOBALLY IN 2015,
57% OF WOMEN OF REPRODUCTIVE AGE USED A MODERN METHOD OF CONTRACEPTION. IN 54 COUNTRIES (34 OF THEM IN AFRICA), LESS THAN HALF THE DEMAND FOR CONTRACEPTION WAS BEING MET WITH MODERN METHODS.

Europe 64% 69%

Latin America & Caribbean 36% 73%

North America 65% 75%

Oceania 57% 59%

Family Planning 2020 Initiative

In poor countries, and for poor women in all countries, buying contraceptives may be beyond reach. A global effort is underway to provide contraception to all women who want it in **69 high-priority countries by 2020**. The coalition of aid groups and governments behind the Family Planning 2020 Initiative (FP2020) is now a major supplier of contraceptives to developing countries.

In 2015 they spent **$269 million** on procuring contraceptives. **The preference for providing long-acting and pharmaceutical-based contraceptives is strongly evident.**

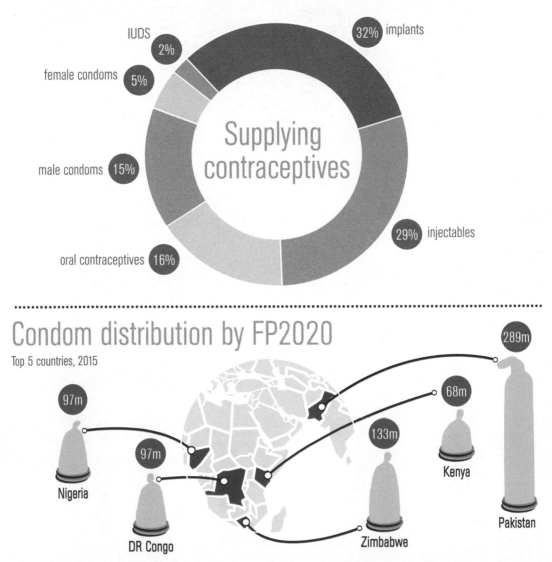

IUDS
2%

female condoms
5%

32% implants

male condoms
15%

Supplying
contraceptives

29% injectables

oral contraceptives
16%

Condom distribution by FP2020

Top 5 countries, 2015

97m
Nigeria

97m
DR Congo

133m
Zimbabwe

68m
Kenya

289m
Pakistan

Unmet need

 20% or more women
have an unmet need for contraception
2017

214 million women of reproductive age in developing regions want to avoid pregnancy but are not using a modern contraceptive method. This includes **155 million who use no contraception** and 59 million who rely on traditional methods.

About 12% of the world's married or in-union women want to delay or stop childbearing, but do not have access to, or are not using, contraceptives.

The costs of unmet contraceptive needs are high in terms of maternal and infant health, unintended pregnancies, and limits on women's social and economic autonomy.

Dying to give birth

Almost everywhere in the world, maternal mortality rates are dropping.

BUT!

NOT IN THE USA, WHERE RATES HAVE MORE THAN DOUBLED SINCE THE LATE 1980s. THE USA NOW HAS THE HIGHEST MATERNAL DEATH RATE IN THE DEVELOPED WORLD AND IT'S GETTING WORSE, ESPECIALLY FOR BLACK WOMEN. THE CAUSES OF THIS INCREASE ARE UNCLEAR, BUT IT IS A GLOBAL ABERRATION.

CANADA

USA

MEXICO

BAHAMAS

CUBA

JAMAICA   HAITI

DOMINICAN REP.   PUERTO RICO

BELIZE

GUATEMALA   HONDURAS

EL SALVADOR   NICARAGUA

COSTA RICA

PANAMA

GRENADA   ST LUCIA

BARBADOS

ST VINCENT & GRENADINES

TRINIDAD & TOBAGO

VENEZUELA

GUYANA

SURINAME

COLOMBIA

ECUADOR

PERU

BRAZIL

BOLIVIA

PARAGUAY

CHILE   ARGENTINA

URUGUAY

ICELAND

NORWAY

FIN

SWEDEN

EST

LA

DENMARK   RUSSIA

IRELAND   UK

NDL   GERMANY   POLAND

BEL

LUX   CZ REP.

AUS.   HUM

FRANCE   SW   SL

CRO   B-H   SH

MONT.

ITALY   ALB

MAC

PORTUGAL   SPAIN   GREE

TUNISIA   MALTA

MOROCCO

ALGERIA

LIBYA

CAPE VERDE

MAURITANIA

MALI

NIGER

SENEGAL

GAMBIA

BURKINA FASO

CHAD

GUINEA-BISSAU

CÔTE D'IVOIRE

GHANA

BENIN

NIGERIA

CAMEROON

GUINEA

LIBERIA

TOGO

EQUATORIAL GUINEA

SÃO TOME & PRINCIPE

GABON

CON

DR CONG

Sierra Leone   Highest: 1,360 deaths per 100,000 live births

ANGOLA

NAMIBIA

BOTSW

SOU AFRI

Danger zones

ⓧ fewer than half of all births are assisted by a skilled health attendant, most recent data since 2010

700 or more
400 – 699
100 – 399
10 – 99
fewer than 10
no data

RUSSIA

RUS

UKRAINE

LDOVA

ANIA

ARIA

GEORGIA

TURKEY

ARMENIA   AZER.

YPRUS

SYRIA

LEB.

RAEL

ALESTINE   JORDAN

EGYPT

SUDAN

KAZAKHSTAN

UZBEKISTAN

TURKMENISTAN

TAJIKISTAN

IRAN

IRAQ

KUWAIT

BAHRAIN

QATAR

UAE

SAUDI
ARABIA

OMAN

KYRGYZSTAN

AFGHANISTAN

PAKISTAN

ⓧ ERITREA

ⓧ YEMEN

DJIBOUTI

ⓧ SOUTH SUDAN

ⓧ ETHIOPIA

SOMALIA

UGANDA

KENYA

RWANDA

BURUNDI

ⓧ TANZANIA

COMOROS

MBIA   MALAWI

MBABWE

ⓧ MADAGASCAR

MAURITIUS

MOZAMBIQUE

SWAZILAND

SOTHO

MONGOLIA

CHINA

NORTH
KOREA

SOUTH
KOREA

JAPAN

NEPAL

BHUTAN

ⓧ BANGLADESH

INDIA

MYANMAR

ⓧ LAOS

THAILAND

VIETNAM

CAMBODIA

SRI LANKA

MALDIVES

BRUNEI

MALAYSIA

SINGAPORE

PHILIPPINES

INDONESIA

ⓧ → TIMOR-LESTE

MICRONESIA

KIRIBATI

SOLOMON
ISLANDS

VANUATU

FIJI

SAMOA

TONGA

PAPUA
NEW
GUINEA

AUSTRALIA

NEW
ZEALAND

GOOD NEWS

Globally, the proportion of births assisted by a trained health attendant, such as a midwife, nurse, or doctor, has increased.

61% 2000

78% 2016

Race, place, ethnicity, and death

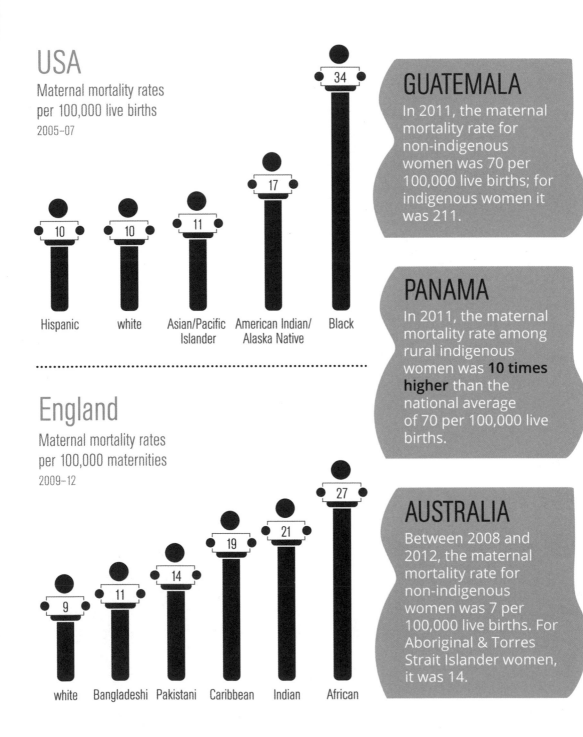

USA

Maternal mortality rates
per 100,000 live births
2005–07

Hispanic	white	Asian/Pacific Islander	American Indian/ Alaska Native	Black
10	10	11	17	34

England

Maternal mortality rates
per 100,000 maternities
2009–12

white	Bangladeshi	Pakistani	Caribbean	Indian	African
9	11	14	19	21	27

GUATEMALA

In 2011, the maternal mortality rate for non-indigenous women was 70 per 100,000 live births; for indigenous women it was 211.

PANAMA

In 2011, the maternal mortality rate among rural indigenous women was **10 times higher** than the national average of 70 per 100,000 live births.

AUSTRALIA

Between 2008 and 2012, the maternal mortality rate for non-indigenous women was 7 per 100,000 live births. For Aboriginal & Torres Strait Islander women, it was 14.

66 How can such a heavy burden of death, disease, and disability have continued for so long with so little outcry?... As one midwife has put it: 'If hundreds of thousands of men were suffering and dying every year, alone and in fear and in agony, or if millions upon millions of men were being injured and disabled and humiliated, sustaining massive and untreated injuries and wounds to their genitalia, leaving them in constant pain, infertile, and incontinent and in dread of having sex, then we would all have heard about this issue long ago and something would have been done'. **99**

UNICEF

Abortion laws

Abortion may be more freely available or more restricted than the national law allows

July 2017

- illegal or severely restricted, only to save a woman's life
- illegal except on narrow grounds: to save a woman's life, preserve her health, and/or if the fetus is impaired
- legal for social and economic reasons
- legal on request, but usually with gestational limits
- no data

ICELAND
NORWAY
CANADA
Northern Island
UK
SWED
IRELAND
NDL
BELGIUM
CZ.
LUX.
LIECH
FRANCE
SWITZ
USA
ANDORRA
MONACO
S.
PORTUGAL
SPAIN
TUNISIA
MOROCCO
ALGERIA
BAHAMAS
MEXICO
CUBA
DOMINICAN REP.
CAPE VERDE
MAURITANIA
MALI
NIGER
JAMAICA
PUERTO RICO
VIRGIN IS. (UK)
GUATEMALA
BELIZE
HAITI
VIRGIN IS. (US)
ANTIGUA & BARBUDA
HONDURAS
ST KITTS & NEVIS
DOMINICA
SENEGAL
BURKINA FASO
EL SALVADOR
ST VINCENT & GRENADINES
ST LUCIA
GAMBIA
NICARAGUA
GRENADA
BARBADOS
GUINEA-BISSAU
GUINEA
COSTA RICA
TRINIDAD & TOBAGO
SIERRA LEONE
COTE D'IVOIRE
GHANA
TOGO
BENIN
NIGERIA
PANAMA
VENEZUELA
GUYANA
SURINAME
LIBERIA
CAMEROON
COLOMBIA
FRENCH GUIANA
EQUATORIAL GUINEA
ECUADOR
SAO TOME & PRINCIPE
GABON
CONGO
PERU
BRAZIL
AN
BOLIVIA
NA
CHILE
PARAGUAY
URUGUAY
ARGENTINA

Male approval, again

Some of the many places where a husband's consent is needed for an abortion

2016

- ✓ Bahrain
- ✓ Indonesia
- ✓ Kuwait
- ✓ Malawi
- ✓ Morocco
- ✓ Qatar
- ✓ Saudi Arabia
- ✓ Solomon Islands
- ✓ South Korea
- ✓ Syria
- ✓ Taiwan
- ✓ Timor-Leste
- ✓ Turkey
- ✓ UAE
- ✓ Yemen

Restrictive laws don't stop women from having abortions. They only make abortions clandestine and unsafe.

Internationally, there are nearly **56 million** abortions every year; there are fewer in places where abortion is safest and where contraception is readily available. Married women account for 73% of abortions.

From 2010 to 2014, average abortion rates for women aged 15–44 were:

37 per 1,000 in countries where abortion is prohibited altogether or permitted only to save a woman's life.

34 per 1,000 in countries where abortion is available on request.

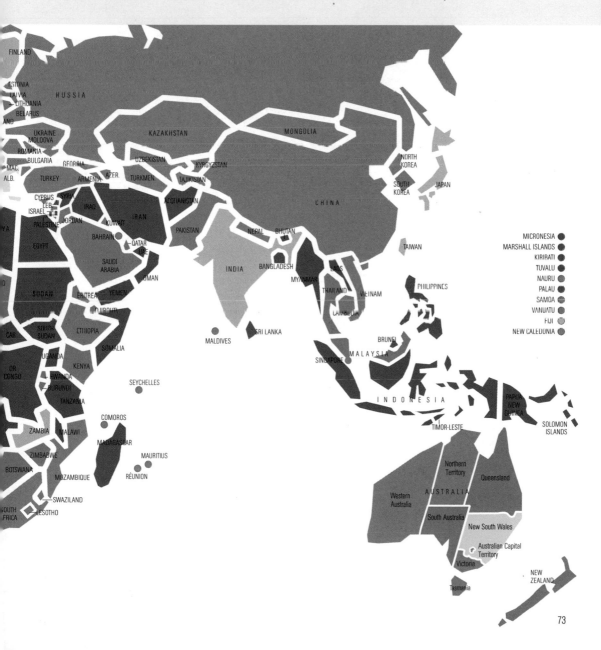

Who's having abortions?

Regional abortion rate

Per 1,000 women
2010–14

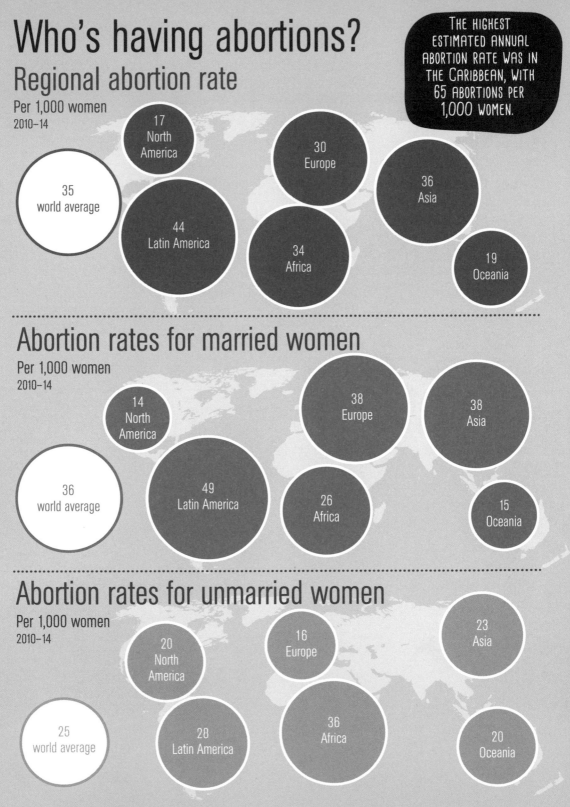

35
world average

17
North America

30
Europe

36
Asia

44
Latin America

34
Africa

19
Oceania

Abortion rates for married women

Per 1,000 women
2010–14

14
North America

38
Europe

38
Asia

36
world average

49
Latin America

26
Africa

15
Oceania

Abortion rates for unmarried women

Per 1,000 women
2010–14

20
North America

16
Europe

23
Asia

25
world average

28
Latin America

36
Africa

20
Oceania

Safety and availability

Almost half of the abortions in the world are performed under unsafe conditions. In countries where abortion is banned or highly restricted, **only 1 in 4 abortions is safe**; in countries where abortion is legal on broader grounds, nearly 9 in 10 are done safely. Restricting access to abortions does not reduce the number of abortions: it reduces the number of safe abortions.

25 million women have unsafe abortions each year. Women in Africa and Latin America suffer the highest rates; a woman's risk of dying from an unsafe abortion is highest in Africa. These inequalities reflect legal, financial, and logistical constraints that render safe abortion – and, often, contraceptives as well – out of reach of many of the world's women.

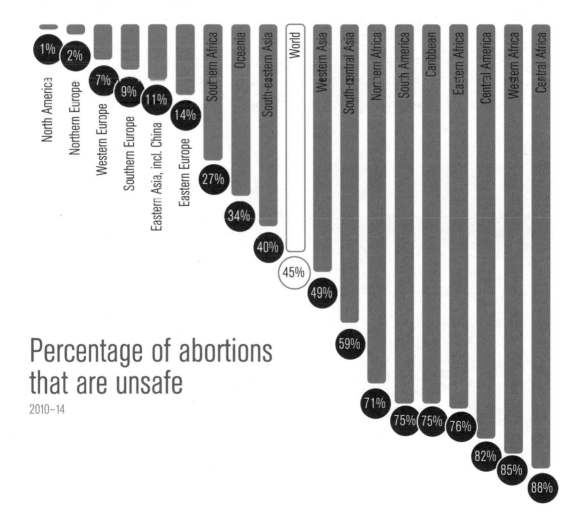

North America 1%
Northern Europe 2%
Western Europe 7%
Southern Europe 9%
Eastern Asia, incl. China 11%
Eastern Europe 14%
Southern Africa 27%
Oceania 34%
South-eastern Asia 40%
World 45%
Western Asia 49%
South-central Asia 59%
Northern Africa 71%
South America 75%
Caribbean 75%
Eastern Africa 76%
Central America 82%
Western Africa 85%
Central Africa 88%

Percentage of abortions that are unsafe

2010–14

Bringing back the coathanger

Despite the USA being a constitutionally secular state, conservative religious beliefs are increasingly being given precedence in public policy on abortion, often explicitly so. Combined with many male legislators' insouciance about their efforts to control women's bodies, the result is an overwhelming assault on reproductive rights in America. Because abortion is still legal at the federal level, the battle has moved to the individual states – where abortion cannot be banned outright, but a concerted effort is underway to undermine women's access to it. Now, access to contraceptives is also under attack.

In the first 6 months of 2017, a total of 431 provisions restricting abortion access were introduced at the state level. Of these, 41 had become law by June.

A Trump directive in October 2017 allows employers to drop contraception coverage from their health insurance plans. Prior to this, it was required as a basic preventive service.

In 2014, 90% of US counties had no clinics providing abortions. 7 states have only one abortion clinic *for the whole state.*

21 states restrict abortion coverage in insurance plans for public employees.

In 32 states, women who rely on public funding for their health care (Medicaid) can have an abortion covered only when the woman's life is in danger or if the pregnancy is the result of rape or incest. South Dakota doesn't allow Medicaid coverage even in cases of rape or incest.

11 states, among them Arizona, Indiana, Kentucky, and Nebraska, have laws that restrict coverage of abortion in *private* insurance plans issued in the state.

Reflecting a religious view that human life begins at conception, many states, including Arkansas, Iowa, Texas, and North Carolina, require a funeral for fetal tissue remains.

Son preference

A cultural preference for sons over daughters is almost universal. In an increasing number of countries, this general preference is acted out in ways that produce demographic distortion. Around 117–126 million women are believed to be "missing" in Asia and Eastern Europe – the result of son preference and gender-biased sex selection. The trend has shifted geographically over time, noted first in Bangladesh, China, India, Pakistan, and South Korea in the 1980s, followed by some countries of the Caucasus (Armenia, Azerbaijan, and Georgia) in the 1990s, and more recently identified in Albania, Montenegro, and in Vietnam. In 1995, only six countries had a marked imbalance of boys to girls. Today, more than 20 countries have skewed sex ratios favoring boys. South Korea is the only country to have effectively reversed its distorted sex ratio in the past three decades.

Son preference takes several forms, often starting in the womb. Birth ratios provide the surest evidence of this form of extreme son preference. The primary tool of prenatal discrimination is the ultrasound – easily-available scans are used to detect female fetuses, which are then aborted. Postnatal discrimination is also widespread, producing skewed sex ratios through active female infanticide or intentional neglect – such as feeding girls less or withholding medical attention.

In several countries the sex ratio is so severely skewed, with as few as 80 girls per 100 boys, that it is now causing widespread social disruption as entire societies are masculinized. Among other consequences, a shortage of women seems to be contributing to local and regional increases in trafficking and kidnapping of women (see pages 98–99). Son preference reflects the combined forces of economics, culture, and religion. As smaller families become the norm, the pressure to have sons accelerates. Girls are widely considered to have a lower economic value than boys – a view often strengthened by marriage, dowry, and inheritance practices. Son preference used to be thought of as a practice of the poor, but evidence suggests the opposite – increasing affluence magnifies perceptions of the greater worth of boys.

Sex preference in the USA

If you could only have one child, would you prefer a girl or a boy?
2011

- boy
- girl
- doesn't matter

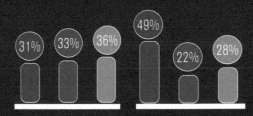

women — 31% | 33% | 36%

men — 49% | 22% | 28%

India: Fewer girls than boys

Child sex ratio: number of 0- to 6-year-old girls
per 100 boys in India
2011

1991: 94.5 girls per 100 boys
2001: 92.7 girls per 100 boys
2011: 91.8 girls per 100 boys

83 girls per 100 boys
84 – 89
90 – 93
94 – 97 girls
per 100 boys

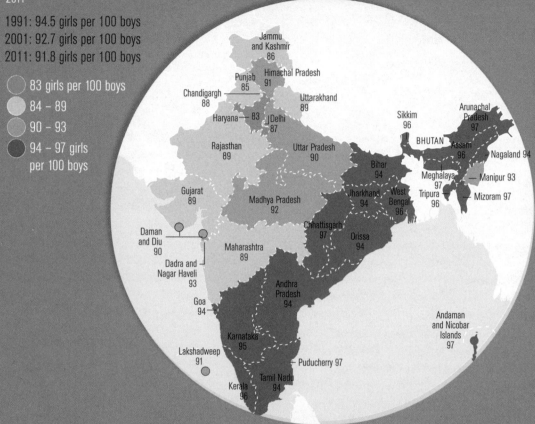

Jammu
and Kashmir
86

Punjab
85

Himachal Pradesh
91

Chandigargh
88

Uttarakhand
89

Sikkim
96

Arunachal
Pradesh
97

Haryana — 83   Delhi
87

BHUTAN   Assam
96   — Nagaland 94

Rajasthan
89

Uttar Pradesh
90

Bihar
94

Meghalaya
97   — Manipur 93

Gujarat
89

Madhya Pradesh
92

Jharkhand
94

West
Bengal
96

Tripura
96   — Mizoram 97

Daman
and Diu
90

Maharashtra
89

Chhattisgarh
97

Orissa
94

Dadra and
Nagar Haveli
93

Goa
94

Andhra
Pradesh
94

Andaman
and Nicobar
Islands
97

Karnataka
95

Lakshadweep
91

— Puducherry 97

Tamil Nadu
94

Kerala
96

Missing women

2010–15 estimates

The discrepancy between the number of girls and
women in the population and the number that would
be expected if there were no son preference.

Nigeria
2m

Pakistan
4m

India
45m

Bangladesh
2m

China: More boys born than girls

Sex ratio at birth: number of boys born per 100 girls

Natural sex ratio at birth: 105 boys per 100 girls

2014

In China, the sex ratio at birth has become increasingly skewed, growing from 109 boys per 100 girls in 1982, to 117–118 boys per 100 girls in recent years.

- 125.00 – 128.6
- 120.00   124.00
- 115.00 – 119.99
- 110.00 – 114.99
- 106.00 – 109.99

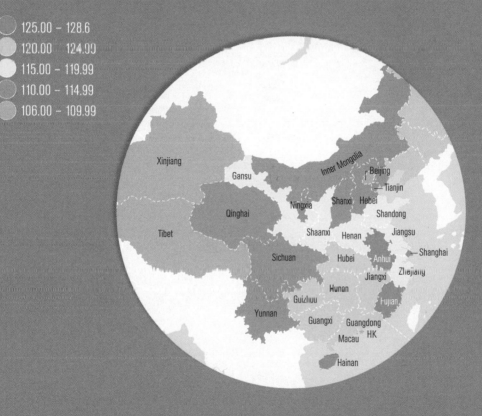

Xinjiang

Gansu

Inner Mongolia

Beijing

Tianjin

Ningxia

Shanxi Hebei

Qinghai

Shandong

Shaanxi Henan

Jiangsu

Tibet

Hubei

Shanghai

Sichuan

Anhui

Hunan

Jiangxi Zhejiang

Guizhou

Fujian

Yunnan

Guangxi

Guangdong

Macau HK

Hainan

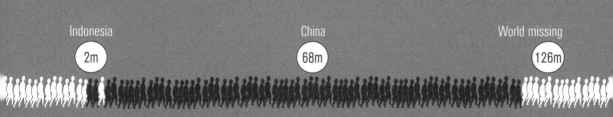

Indonesia	China	World missing
2m	68m	126m

Unnatural selection

strong demographic evidence of son preference
most recent data since 2012

Prenatal sex selection

natural rate = 105 boys per 100 girls
selected countries, most recent since 2012

number of boys born for every 100 girls

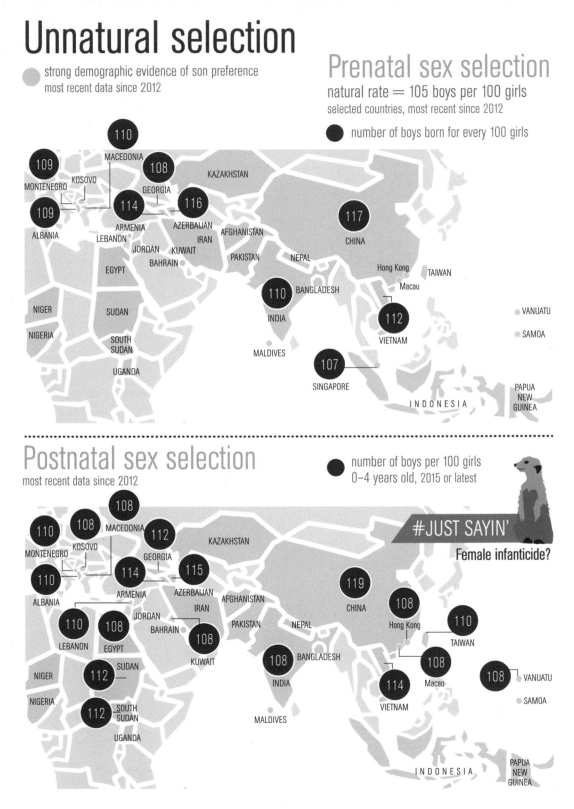

110 MACEDONIA

109 MONTENEGRO KOSOVO

108 GEORGIA

KAZAKHSTAN

109 ALBANIA

114 ARMENIA LEBANON JORDAN KUWAIT BAHRAIN

116 AZERBAIJAN AFGHANISTAN IRAN PAKISTAN

117 CHINA

NEPAL

Hong Kong TAIWAN Macau

EGYPT

110 BANGLADESH INDIA

VANUATU

SAMOA

NIGER SUDAN

NIGERIA SOUTH SUDAN

UGANDA

MALDIVES

112 VIETNAM

107 SINGAPORE

INDONESIA

PAPUA NEW GUINEA

Postnatal sex selection

most recent data since 2012

number of boys per 100 girls
0–4 years old, 2015 or latest

#JUST SAYIN'

Female infanticide?

108 MACEDONIA

110 MONTENEGRO 108 KOSOVO 112 GEORGIA

KAZAKHSTAN

110 ALBANIA 114 ARMENIA 115 AZERBAIJAN AFGHANISTAN IRAN

JORDAN BAHRAIN

110 LEBANON 108 EGYPT 108 KUWAIT

PAKISTAN NEPAL

119 CHINA

108 Hong Kong 110 TAIWAN Macau

NIGER 112 SUDAN

108 BANGLADESH INDIA

108 Macau 108 VANUATU

NIGERIA 112 SOUTH SUDAN

UGANDA

MALDIVES

114 VIETNAM

SAMOA

INDONESIA

PAPUA NEW GUINEA

Body politics

"It was in the air, or so it seemed to Kiki, this hatred of women and their bodies – it seeped in with every draught in the house; people brought it home on their shoes, they breathed it in off their newspapers. There was no way to control it."

Zadie Smith, *On Beauty*

"I love my body, and I would never change anything about it. I'm not asking you to like my body. I'm just asking you to let me be me. Because I'm going to influence a girl who does look like me, and I want her to feel good about herself."

Serena Williams

Women in the Olympics

When women's participation in sports at the Olympics was introduced

Notions of appropriate femininity and masculinity are embedded in and structured by sports. Men who don't like sports are often considered to be suspiciously unmanly; for women, developing strength, muscles, and sports-skills challenges conventional notions of femininity. The participation of women in the Olympics mirrors the larger struggle of women in sports. Gender breakthroughs in the Olympics often improve the funding and legitimacy of women's sports overall.

1900 Tennis, Golf

1904 Archery

1908 Figure skating

1912 Swimming

1924 Fencing

1928 Athletics, Gymnastics

1936 Alpine Skiing

1948 Canoeing

1952 Equestrian sports

1960 Speed skating

1964 Volleyball, Luge

1976 Rowing, Basketball, Handball

1980 Field Hockey

1984 Shooting, Cycling, Marathon

1988 Tennis, Table Tennis, Sailing

Winter Olympics
Percentage of women participants

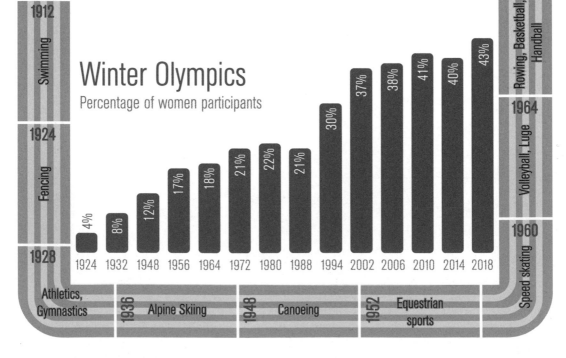

1924	1932	1948	1956	1964	1972	1980	1988	1994	2002	2006	2010	2014	2018
4%	8%	12%	17%	18%	21%	22%	21%	30%	37%	38%	41%	40%	43%

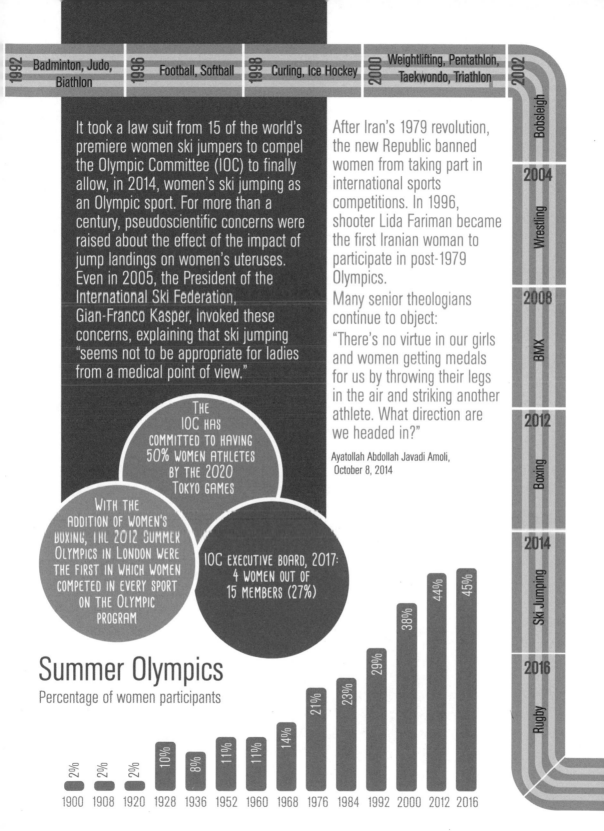

1992 Badminton, Judo, Biathlon

1996 Football, Softball

1998 Curling, Ice Hockey

2000 Weightlifting, Pentathlon, Taekwondo, Triathlon

2002 Bobsleigh

2004 Wrestling

2008 BMX

2012 Boxing

2014 Ski Jumping

2016 Rugby

It took a law suit from 15 of the world's premiere women ski jumpers to compel the Olympic Committee (IOC) to finally allow, in 2014, women's ski jumping as an Olympic sport. For more than a century, pseudoscientific concerns were raised about the effect of the impact of jump landings on women's uteruses. Even in 2005, the President of the International Ski Federation, Gian-Franco Kasper, invoked these concerns, explaining that ski jumping "seems not to be appropriate for ladies from a medical point of view."

After Iran's 1979 revolution, the new Republic banned women from taking part in international sports competitions. In 1996, shooter Lida Fariman became the first Iranian woman to participate in post-1979 Olympics.

Many senior theologians continue to object:

"There's no virtue in our girls and women getting medals for us by throwing their legs in the air and striking another athlete. What direction are we headed in?"

Ayatollah Abdollah Javadi Amoli, October 8, 2014

THE IOC HAS COMMITTED TO HAVING 50% WOMEN ATHLETES BY THE 2020 TOKYO GAMES

WITH THE ADDITION OF WOMEN'S BOXING, THE 2012 SUMMER OLYMPICS IN LONDON WERE THE FIRST IN WHICH WOMEN COMPETED IN EVERY SPORT ON THE OLYMPIC PROGRAM

IOC EXECUTIVE BOARD, 2017: 4 WOMEN OUT OF 15 MEMBERS (27%)

Summer Olympics

Percentage of women participants

Year	Percentage
1900	2%
1908	2%
1920	2%
1928	10%
1936	8%
1952	11%
1960	11%
1968	14%
1976	21%
1984	23%
1992	29%
2000	38%
2012	44%
2016	45%

One step forward...

1972: Title IX in the USA, signed into law, prohibiting sex-based discrimination in education programs, **including athletic programs**, at universities and colleges that receive federal funding (most do). Title IX opened the floodgates for women athletes. **In 1970, there were 16,000 inter-collegiate women athletes; by 2014, more than 200,000.**

Soccer showed especially explosive growth. In 1977 there were women's soccer teams at fewer than three out of a hundred schools. By 2014, 9 out of 10 schools had women's soccer teams.

In 1972, when Title IX was signed into law, 90% of women's college teams were coached by women.

BUT!

> WITH MORE MONEY, ATTENTION, JOBS, AND PRESTIGE COMING INTO WOMEN'S SPORTS, THE MEN CAME TOO: BY 2017 THE NUMBER OF WOMEN COACHES HAD FALLEN TO ABOUT 40%.

2016: Afghan women's cycling team nominated for Nobel Peace Prize for their bravery and persistence in challenging gender norms.

January 2018, Saudi Arabia: Women and girls allowed to enter professional sports stadiums as spectators to watch professional games (from special women's or family sections) for the first time in the country's history.

Tennis

8 of the **10** highest-paid female athletes in the world are tennis players.

A few Grand Slam tournaments pay men and women equally: in 2007, Wimbledon became the last of the four major tournaments to award equal prize money to men and women players, following the US Open in 1973, the Australian Open in 2001, and the French Open in 2006.

BUT!

> John McEnroe on Serena Williams in 2017, the top ranked women's tennis player in the world: "if she played the men's circuit she'd be [ranked] like 700 in the world."

> TOP TENNIS EARNERS AS OF 2017, OVER FULL CAREER: SERENA WILLIAMS: $82 MILLION IN PRIZE MONEY, 39 GRAND SLAM TITLES. NOVAK DJOKOVIC: $108.8 MILLION IN PRIZE MONEY, 12 GRAND SLAM TITLES.

> ANNUAL PRIZE MONEY PAID TO THE TOP 100 EARNERS ON THE WOMEN'S AND MEN'S TENNIS TOURS = 80 CENTS FOR WOMEN FOR EACH DOLLAR MEN EARN.

Golf

2012: Augusta National Golf Club, opened in 1932, home of the Masters Golf Tournament in the USA, invited women to join after a decade-long feminist campaign against the men-only policy.

2016: Muirfield Golf Club in the UK, founded in 1744 and long-time home of the Open Championships, voted to remain men-only.

Peter Alliss, a prominent golf commentator remarked that:

"The women who are there as wives of husbands, they get all the facilities. If somebody wants to join, well you'd better get married to somebody who's a member."

Following the men-only vote, the Open withdrew Muirfield's right to host the prestigious golf tournament.

2017: Muirfield voted again, this time to admit women.

Football (soccer) on the world stage

1930: First men's FIFA World Cup Tournament.

1991: First women's FIFA World Cup Tournament.

WORLD CUP team bonuses from FIFA: The 2015 World Cup-winning women's team (USA) was awarded a $2 million bonus from FIFA. In the men's World Cup, held the year before, the winning team (Germany) collected a $35 million bonus from FIFA. Prior to 2007 the women's teams received no prize money at all from FIFA.

In fact, the 16 men's teams **that were eliminated** in the first round of the 2014 men's World Cup each got $8 million, or four times as much as the championship women. The US men's team, which finished 11th, won $9 million.

2015 OFFICIAL TWEET FROM THE ENGLISH FOOTBALL ASSOCIATION, WELCOMING HOME THE WOMEN'S TEAM FROM THE WORLD CUP TOUR: "OUR #LIONESSES GO BACK TO BEING MOTHERS, PARTNERS AND DAUGHTERS TODAY, BUT THEY HAVE TAKEN ON ANOTHER TITLE – HEROES".

OCTOBER 2017: NORWAY BECAME THE FIRST NATIONAL FA TO AGREE AN EQUAL PAY DEAL FOR THE MEN'S AND WOMEN'S TEAMS. PRIOR TO THE NEW FINANCIAL AGREEMENT, THE WOMEN COLLECTIVELY EARNED 50% LESS THAN THEIR MALE COUNTERPARTS – DESPITE CONSISTENTLY ACHIEVING BETTER RESULTS ON THE INTERNATIONAL STAGE.

The global beauty beat
Countries sending contestants to Miss World or Miss Universe
2017

Miss World is owned by a private family company, Miss World Organization; Miss Universe was sold by Donald Trump in 2015 to the William Morris/IMG talent agency.

THE MOST MISS WORLDS:
VENEZUELA (6), INDIA (5), UK (5).
THE MOST MISS UNIVERSES:
USA (8), VENEZUELA (7), PUERTO RICO (5).

THE PERFECT MISS UNIVERSE:
CONTESTANTS MUST BE BETWEEN THE AGES OF 18 AND 28. CONTESTANTS MAY NOT BE MARRIED OR PREGNANT. THEY MUST NOT HAVE EVER BEEN MARRIED, NOR HAD A MARRIAGE ANNULLED, NOR GIVEN BIRTH TO, OR PARENTED A CHILD. THE TITLEHOLDERS ARE ALSO REQUIRED TO REMAIN UNMARRIED THROUGHOUT THEIR REIGN.

SIERRA LEONE ENTERED THE MISS UNIVERSE CONTEST FOR THE FIRST TIME IN 2017, BUT THE CONTESTANT HAD TO WITHDRAW BECAUSE SHE WAS UNABLE TO GET A VISA FOR TRAVEL TO THE PAGEANT IN THE USA.

ICELAND
NORWAY
FINLAND
N. Ireland
Scotland
England
SWEDEN
DENMARK
IRELAND
Wales
NDL
POLAND
BELARUS
GERMANY
BELGIUM
CZ. REP.
SLOVAKIA
AUSTRIA
HUNGARY
MO
FRANCE
SLOVENIA
ROMANIA
CROATIA
B-H
SERB.
BULGA
M.
ALB.
PORTUGAL
SPAIN
ITALY
GREECE
TUNISIA
MALTA
GIBRALTAR

CANADA

USA

MEXICO
BAHAMAS
CAYMAN IS.
DOMINICAN REP.
L.
BELIZE
JAMAICA
HAITI
PUERTO RICO
GUATEMALA
HONDURAS
GUADELOUPE
EL SALVADOR
ARUBA
ST LUCIA
MARTINIQUE
NICARAGUA
BARBADOS
COSTA RICA
CURAÇAO
TRINIDAD & TOBAGO
PANAMA
VENEZUELA
GUYANA
COLOMBIA

ECUADOR

PERU
BRAZIL

BOLIVIA

PARAGUAY
CHILE

ARGENTINA
URUGUAY

CAPE VERDE
SENEGAL
GUINEA-BISSAU
GUINEA
SIERRA LEONE
CÔTE D'IVOIRE
LIBERIA
GHANA

Global beauty contests promote a narrow, primarily Western view of beauty. Globalization is accelerating the adoption of these standards around the world. Newly sponsoring participants for global beauty contests is one way that governments signal their intention to become global economic players.

NEW COUNTRIES JOINING THE BEAUTY BEAT: MISS WORLD, 2016–17 DEBUTS: ARMENIA, LAOS, RWANDA, SENEGAL. MISS UNIVERSE, 2016–17 DEBUTS: CAMBODIA, LAOS, NEPAL; IRAQ RETURNED IN 2017, HAVING PREVIOUSLY LAST COMPETED IN 1972.

RUSSIA

KAZAKHSTAN

MONGOLIA

GEORGIA

KYRGYZSTAN

TURKEY

ARMENIA

JAPAN

CYPRUS

IRAN

SOUTH KOREA

ISRAEL

LEBANON

CHINA

EGYPT

NEPAL

INDIA

BANGLADESH

Hong Kong

MYANMAR

LAOS

THAILAND

VIETNAM

PHILIPPINES

CAMBODIA

GERIA

SRI LANKA

GUAM

SOUTH SUDAN

ETHIOPIA

FIJI

CAMEROON

COOK ISLANDS

EQUATORIAL GUINEA

KENYA

MALAYSIA

RWANDA

SINGAPORE

SEYCHELLES

TANZANIA

INDONESIA

2017 WINNERS: MISS WORLD, INDIA; MISS UNIVERSE, SOUTH AFRICA.

ANGOLA

ZAMBIA

ZIMBABWE

MADAGASCAR

NAMIBIA

BOTSWANA

MAURITIUS

AUSTRALIA

SOUTH AFRICA

LESOTHO

MISS WORLD CONTESTANTS CHOOSE A CIVIC PROJECT TO HIGHLIGHT AS PART OF THEIR COMMITMENT TO "BEAUTY WITH A PURPOSE". THE 2017 WINNER, MISS INDIA, LAUNCHED A FEMININE HYGIENE AWARENESS CAMPAIGN.

NEW ZEALAND

The big business of beauty

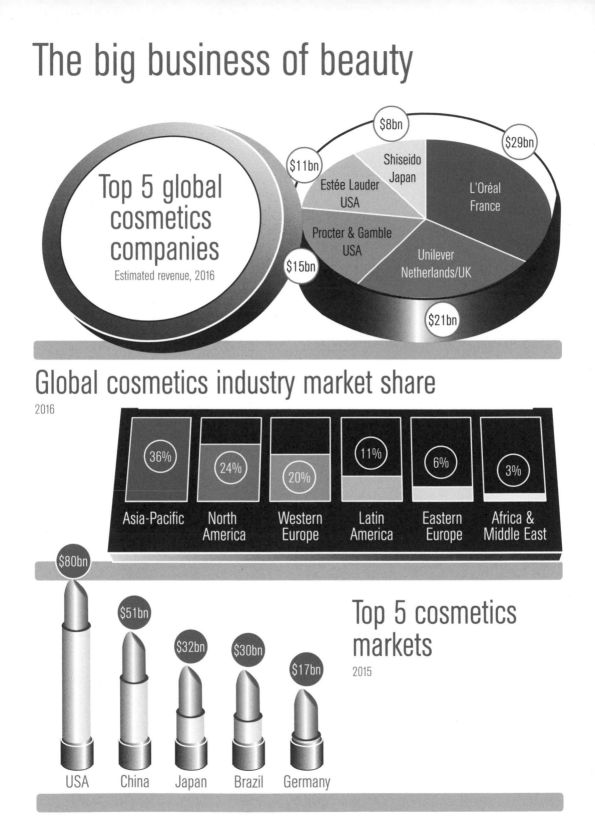

Top 5 global cosmetics companies
Estimated revenue, 2016

$29bn — L'Oréal France
$21bn — Unilever Netherlands/UK
$15bn — Procter & Gamble USA
$11bn — Estée Lauder USA
$8bn — Shiseido Japan

Global cosmetics industry market share

2016

36%	24%	20%	11%	6%	3%
Asia-Pacific	North America	Western Europe	Latin America	Eastern Europe	Africa & Middle East

Top 5 cosmetics markets

2015

- $80bn — USA
- $51bn — China
- $32bn — Japan
- $30bn — Brazil
- $17bn — Germany

Not so pretty

Personal care products routinely include **toxic substances** including lead and other heavy metals, parabens, phthalates, carcinogens, neurotoxins, endocrine disruptors, and formaldehyde. In the USA, women apply an average of **168 chemicals** to their faces and bodies every day through their cosmetics, perfumes, personal care products, and feminine hygiene products. Chemicals in cosmetics in the USA are largely unregulated.

Skin whitening products, heavily marketed in **Africa** and **Asia**, typically contain **mercury** and **steroids**. In Nigeria, **77%** of women use skin-lightening agents; **59%** in Togo; and **27%** in Senegal. In India, the market for whitening cream is expanding at a rate of nearly **18%** a year.

Fat profits

THE SIZE OF THE GLOBAL WEIGHT LOSS AND DIET INDUSTRY IS IMPOSSIBLE TO MEASURE, BUT REVENUES CERTAINLY REACH INTO THE MULTI-BILLIONS.

In the UK, almost two-thirds of people are on a diet "most of the time"; in 2016, **57%** of British women said they were trying to lose weight.

In the USA, 57% of women and **46%** of men say they want to lose weight; about 45 million Americans diet each year and spend **$33 billion** on weight-loss products.

Shaping the elusive body beautiful

Women undergo a staggering amount of suffering in the pursuit of beauty. Everywhere in the world, but especially in the rich countries, tens of thousands of women each year have their bodies cut, shaped, stapled, and manipulated to conform to prevailing – and increasingly globalized – standards of beauty. Globally, the world's most popular elective cosmetic surgery is breast augmentation. But the cosmetic surgery with the fastest rate of growth is labiaplasty – a surgery that removes "excess tissue" from the labia. When combined with vaginoplasty (a procedure to tighten the vagina), this is called "vaginal rejuvenation".

Global league

Top 10 countries by total number of elective cosmetic procedures

(%) percentage share of global cosmetic surgeries

GLOBALLY, 86% OF ALL COSMETIC PROCEDURES ARE PERFORMED ON WOMEN.

THE MOST COMMON NON-SURGICAL PROCEDURE IS BOTOX INJECTION.

IN 2016, 17.1 MILLION COSMETIC PROCEDURES WERE PERFORMED, 92% ON WOMEN; 85% OF BOARD-CERTIFIED PLASTIC SURGEONS ARE MEN.

ON A PER CAPITA BASIS, SOUTH KOREA HAS THE HIGHEST RATE OF COSMETIC PROCEDURES.

Turkey nose reshaping; breast augmentation; liposuction; eyelid surgery; facial fat-grafting

liposuction; facial fat-grafting; tummy tuck
Germany eyelid surgery; breast augmentation;

France breast augmentation; liposuction; eyelid surgery; tummy tuck; breast reduction

USA breast augmentation; liposuction; nose reshaping; eyelid surgery; tummy tuck

India liposuction; nose reshaping; hair transplantation; breast augmentation; tummy tuck

Russia eyelid surgery; breast augmentation; nose reshaping; liposuction; facial fat-grafting

Mexico liposuction; breast augmentation; eyelid surgery; nose reshaping; tummy tuck

Italy breast augmentation; liposuction; eyelid surgery; nose reshaping; facial fat-grafting

Japan eyelid surgery; nose reshaping; breast augmentation; liposuction; facelift

Brazil breast augmentation; liposuction; eyelid surgery; tummy tuck; breast lift

2% 3% 3% 4% 4% 4% 4% 5% 11% 18%

2016

FGM/C

More than 200 million girls and women alive today have undergone female genital mutilation/cutting (FGM/C) and an estimated 3 million more girls are at risk of undergoing it every year. FGM/C encompasses a range of procedures from partially to totally removing external female genitalia, cutting the clitoris, or in the most severe cases, sewing closed the girl's vagina. The practice is mostly carried out by traditional circumcisers using razor blades and scrapers, performed in informal settings without anesthesia.

FGM/C is mostly performed on young girls. Its over-riding purpose is to ensure the desirability and suitability of women for marriage, in large part by controlling their sexual behavior. FGM/C typically reduces women's sexual desire. In some cultures female genitalia are considered unclean, and the ritual of circumcision is thought to smooth and purify girls' bodies.

Traditionally, it is women who perform the actual cutting, and many women are strong proponents of the practice.

Legal status
Banned by national legislation

Guinea	1965
CAR (revised 1996)	1966
Ghana	1994
Djibouti	1995
Burkina Faso	1996
Côte d'Ivoire, Tanzania, Togo	1998
Senegal	1999
Kenya, Yemen	2001
Benin, Chad, Niger	2003
Ethiopia	2004
Mauritania, South Africa	2005
DR Congo	2006
Eritrea	2007
Egypt	2008
Uganda	2010
Guinea Bissau, Kurdistan region of Iraq	2011
Gambia	2015
Liberia	2018

Somaliland: the Somaliland government issued an official fatwa banning FGM/C

Countries where FGM/C is known to occur widely, but with no national legislation banning it

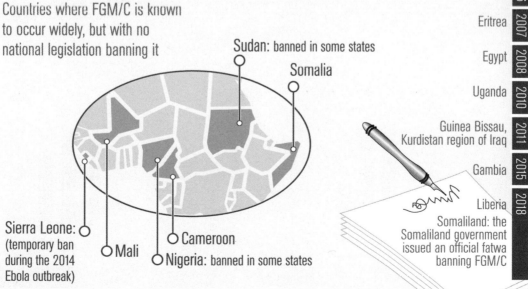

Sudan: banned in some states

Somalia

Sierra Leone: (temporary ban during the 2014 Ebola outbreak)

Mali

Cameroon

Nigeria: banned in some states

Under the knife
Prevalence of female genital mutilation/cutting (FGM/C)

Percentage of girls and women aged 15–49 years who have undergone FGM/C

most recent data since 2011

- more than 90%
- 60% – 90%
- 30% – 59%
- 5% – 29%
- fewer than 5%
- some incidence reported, documentation unclear; often restricted to small communities or groups

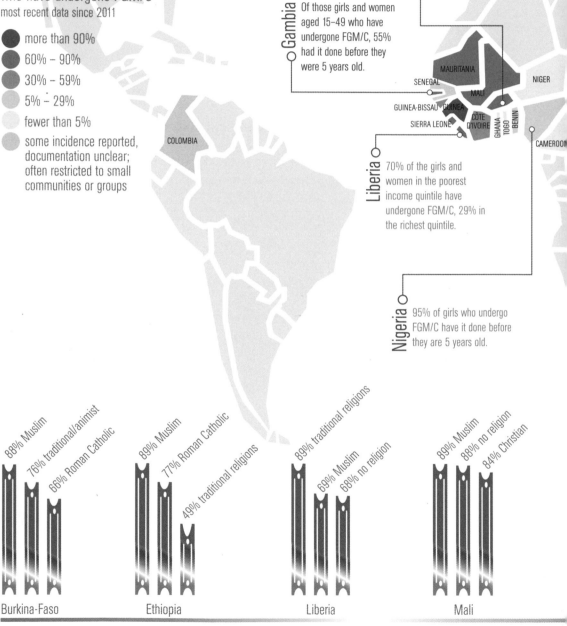

Burkina Faso By 2016, 219 communities had made public commitments to abandon the practice of FGM/C.

Gambia Of those girls and women aged 15–49 who have undergone FGM/C, 55% had it done before they were 5 years old.

Liberia 70% of the girls and women in the poorest income quintile have undergone FGM/C, 29% in the richest quintile.

Nigeria 95% of girls who undergo FGM/C have it done before they are 5 years old.

MAURITANIA
SENEGAL
MALI
NIGER
GUINEA-BISSAU   GUINEA
SIERRA LEONE
CÔTE D'IVOIRE
GHANA
TOGO
BENIN
CAMEROON

COLOMBIA

Burkina-Faso
88% Muslim
76% traditional/animist
66% Roman Catholic

Ethiopia
89% Muslim
77% Roman Catholic
49% traditional religions

Liberia
89% traditional religions
69% Muslim
68% no religion

Mali
89% Muslim
88% no religion
84% Christian

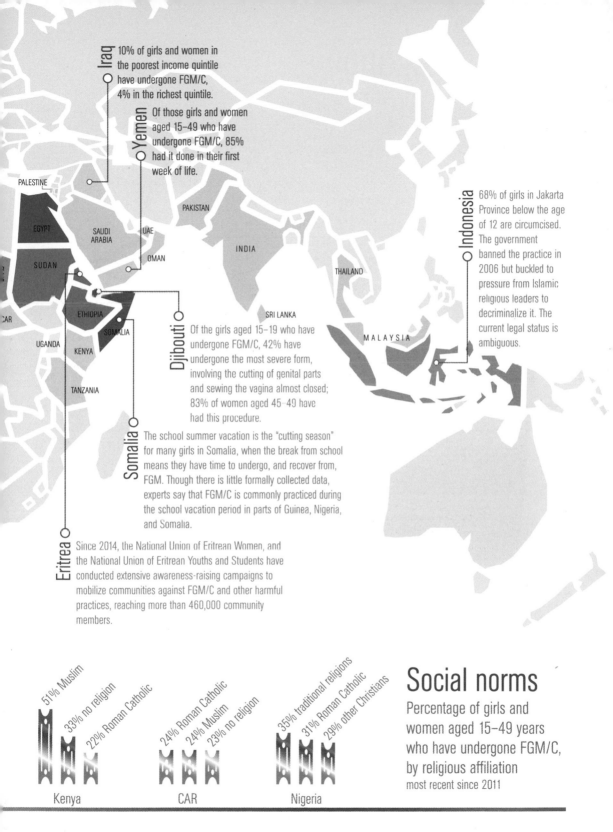

Iraq 10% of girls and women in the poorest income quintile have undergone FGM/C, 4% in the richest quintile.

Yemen Of those girls and women aged 15–49 who have undergone FGM/C, 85% had it done in their first week of life.

PALESTINE

EGYPT

SUDAN

SAUDI ARABIA

UAE

OMAN

PAKISTAN

INDIA

THAILAND

CAR

ETHIOPIA

SOMALIA

UGANDA

KENYA

TANZANIA

SRI LANKA

MALAYSIA

Indonesia 68% of girls in Jakarta Province below the age of 12 are circumcised. The government banned the practice in 2006 but buckled to pressure from Islamic religious leaders to decriminalize it. The current legal status is ambiguous.

Djibouti Of the girls aged 15–19 who have undergone FGM/C, 42% have undergone the most severe form, involving the cutting of genital parts and sewing the vagina almost closed; 83% of women aged 45–49 have had this procedure.

Somalia The school summer vacation is the "cutting season" for many girls in Somalia, when the break from school means they have time to undergo, and recover from, FGM. Though there is little formally collected data, experts say that FGM/C is commonly practiced during the school vacation period in parts of Guinea, Nigeria, and Somalia.

Eritrea Since 2014, the National Union of Eritrean Women, and the National Union of Eritrean Youths and Students have conducted extensive awareness-raising campaigns to mobilize communities against FGM/C and other harmful practices, reaching more than 460,000 community members.

51% Muslim
33% no religion
22% Roman Catholic

Kenya

24% Roman Catholic
24% Muslim
23% no religion

CAR

35% traditional religions
31% Roman Catholic
29% other Christians

Nigeria

Social norms

Percentage of girls and women aged 15–49 years who have undergone FGM/C, by religious affiliation
most recent since 2011

Winds of change

It is women who have taken the lead in organizing against FGM/C. Feminist groups, often led by young women, have taken up the cause of ending the practice. One encouraging trend is that women aged 15–19 years are less likely to have been submitted to FGM/C than are women in older age groups and support for ending the practice is particularly high among younger women.

Campaign against FGM/C, road sign in Kapchorwa, Uganda, 2004

It should stop

Percentage of girls/women, boys/men, aged 15–49, who have heard about FGM/C and think it should stop

most recent data since 2011

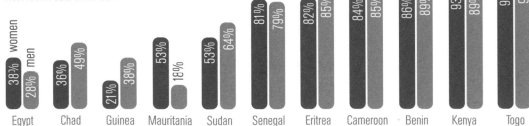

	women	men
Egypt	38%	28%
Chad	36%	49%
Guinea	21%	38%
Mauritania	53%	18%
Sudan	53%	64%
Senegal	81%	79%
Eritrea	82%	85%
Cameroon	84%	85%
Benin	86%	89%
Kenya	93%	89%
Togo	95%	96%

Police-recorded sexual offences against children

Rate per 100,000 population

in one year, 2013–14

Reported sexual offence crimes against children include child pornography offences, procuring a child for prostitution, statutory rape of a person below the age of consent, and other offences related to the sexual exploitation of children. The recording of offences varies considerably.

ENGLAND & WALES 272
JAMAICA 218
NEW ZEALAND 190
CHILE 174
BELGIUM 158
GERMANY 145
FRANCE 128
NORWAY 115
CANADA 64
UGANDA 58
RUSSIA 37
JAPAN 21
KENYA 17
ITALY 10

Forced sex

Percentage of women whose first sexual intercourse was forced

most recent data since 2010

UNICEF ESTIMATES THAT 120 MILLION GIRLS AND WOMEN UNDER THE AGE OF 20 HAVE BEEN SUBJECTED TO FORCED SEXUAL INTERCOURSE OR OTHER FORCED SEXUAL ACTS AT SOME POINT IN THEIR LIVES.

30%
Bangladesh (rural)

29%
Nepal

24%
Peru (rural)

22%
Zimbabwe

20%
Cameroon

17%
Tanzania (rural)

15%
Malawi

5%
Fiji

Sex tourism

Sex tourism is fueled by a toxic mix of masculinized power and privilege combined with a sense of impunity and anonymity. The "allure" of sex tourism, whether undertaken by individual men or as part of organized group tours, is the opportunity to buy sex that would not be available at home. Often, that is sex with a child.

Where sex tourists come from

CANADA, USA

WESTERN EUROPE: AUSTRIA, BELGIUM, CROATIA, DENMARK, FINLAND, FRANCE, GREECE, IRELAND, ITALY, LIECHTENSTEIN, LUXEMBOURG, NETHERLANDS, PORTUGAL, SPAIN, SWITZERLAND, UK

RUSSIA, TURKEY

SAUDI ARABIA

CHINA, JAPAN, KOREA, MALAYSIA, SINGAPORE, SOUTH KOREA, TAIWAN

AUSTRALIA

Where sex tourists go

Hubs are typically located in regular tourist zones such as beach resort towns, or in major urban centers where prostitution hubs already exist

BULGARIA, ESTONIA, GERMANY, MOLDOVA, NETHERLANDS, UKRAINE

MOROCCO, SPAIN

CUBA, DOMINICAN REP, JAMAICA

BELIZE, COSTA RICA, GUATEMALA, MEXICO

INDIA, NEPAL, SRI LANKA

ALGERIA, CAMEROON, GAMBIA, GHANA, SENEGAL

CAMBODIA, INDONESIA, MYANMAR, PHILIPPINES, THAILAND, VIETNAM

BRAZIL, COLOMBIA

DJIBOUTI, KENYA, MALAWI

SOUTH AFRICA

Prostitution

There is considerable disagreement over whether legalization or criminalization is the best way to protect and support women who are in prostitution – and also to delink consensual sex exchange from coerced sex trafficking. The "Swedish model", gaining acceptance in Europe, criminalizes the buyers of sex, not the sellers.

Prostitution in Europe

IN 1999 SWEDEN BECAME THE FIRST COUNTRY TO INTRODUCE A SEX BUYER LAW, MAKING IT ILLEGAL TO PAY FOR SEX, BUT NOT TO BE A PROSTITUTE — THE CLIENT COMMITS THE CRIME, NOT THE PROSTITUTE.

ICELAND

FINLAND

NORWAY

SWEDEN   ESTONIA
          LATVIA   RUSSIA
Northern UK   DENMARK   LITHUANIA
Ireland
IRELAND   NETHERLANDS   POLAND   BELARUS
          GERMANY
          BELGIUM
LUXEMBOURG   LIECHT. CZ. REP. SLOVAKIA   UKRAINE
FRANCE   AUSTRIA
       SWITZERLAND SLOVENIA HUN.   MOLDOVA
          ITALY CROATIA B-H SERBIA
                 MONTENEGRO   KOSOVO BULGARIA
PORTUGAL   ANDORRA   ALBANIA
   SPAIN   MACEDONIA   TURKEY
                        GREECE
                              CYPRUS

● legal, with varying degrees of regulation*
● illegal for buyer
● illegal for seller
● illegal for buyer and seller

* some activities such as soliciting, pimping, or owning a brothel may be illegal

#JUST SAYIN'

Climate change and prostitution: In many parts of the world, natural disasters and escalating environmental degradation are destroying livelihoods and resources – compelling women to turn to temporary sex barter or transactional sex arrangements to support themselves and their families.

Sex trafficking

Major global flows of trafficking

most recent since 2014

← main trafficking flows

 governments that have not ratified the UN "Protocol to Prevent, Suppress and Punish Trafficking in Persons, Especially Women and Children"

as of September 2017

Germany Two-thirds of Germany's estimated 400,000 sex workers come from overseas.

from EAST ASIA & PACIFIC

NORTH AMERICA

WESTERN & SOUTHERN EUROPE

CENTRAL AMERICA & CARIBBEAN

Central America Children represent more than 60% of trafficking victims found in Central America.

SOUTH AMERICA

Internationally In 2016, globally, there were only 14,894 prosecutions and 9,071 convictions for trafficking.

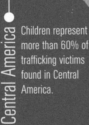

The global trafficked

2014 or most recent

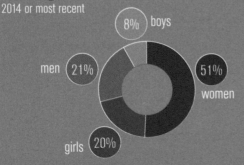

8% boys

men 21%

51% women

girls 20%

There at least **21 million adults and children in the world who have been trafficked** across international borders into commercial sexual servitude, forced labor, or bonded labor. The largest share of them is trafficked for sexual exploitation.

Of those trafficked for sex, 96% are women and girls; of those trafficked for forced labor, 63% are men. Sex trafficking accelerates in regions facing natural disasters and militarized conflicts.

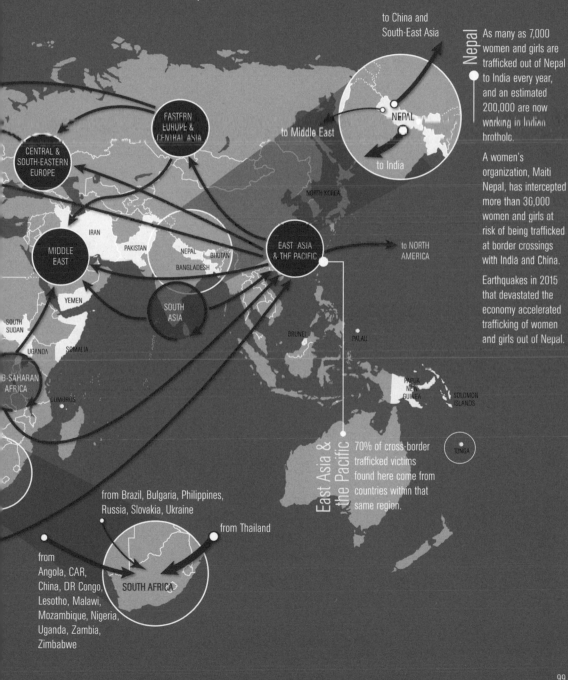

Nepal

As many as 7,000 women and girls are trafficked out of Nepal to India every year, and an estimated 200,000 are now working in Indian brothels.

A women's organization, Maiti Nepal, has intercepted more than 30,000 women and girls at risk of being trafficked at border crossings with India and China.

Earthquakes in 2015 that devastated the economy accelerated trafficking of women and girls out of Nepal.

to China and South-East Asia

to Middle East

to India

NEPAL

EASTERN EUROPE & CENTRAL ASIA

CENTRAL & SOUTH-EASTERN EUROPE

NORTH KOREA

MIDDLE EAST

IRAN

PAKISTAN

NEPAL

BHUTAN

BANGLADESH

EAST ASIA & THE PACIFIC

to NORTH AMERICA

YEMEN

SOUTH ASIA

BRUNEI

PALAU

SOUTH SUDAN

UGANDA

SOMALIA

B-SAHARAN AFRICA

COMOROS

PAPUA NEW GUINEA

SOLOMON ISLANDS

East Asia & the Pacific

70% of cross-border trafficked victims found here come from countries within that same region.

TONGA

from Brazil, Bulgaria, Philippines, Russia, Slovakia, Ukraine

from Thailand

from Angola, CAR, China, DR Congo, Lesotho, Malawi, Mozambique, Nigeria, Uganda, Zambia, Zimbabwe

SOUTH AFRICA

Pornography

Commodification of sex is big business, now most of it online. Pornography is one of the most complicated and divisive issues for feminists. Many believe that porn is part of the systematic oppression and degradation of women, an apparatus of the patriarchy that objectifies women and reduces them to sex objects. Others argue that anti-porn arguments themselves reduce women's agency, and are embedded in the assumption that pornography participants don't have control over their bodies. Context could be everything.

GLOBAL SNAPSHOT:
★ AN ESTIMATED 12% OF ALL WEBSITES ON THE INTERNET ARE PORNOGRAPHY SITES.
★ AN ESTIMATED 13% OF ALL WEB SEARCHES ARE FOR EROTIC SEXUAL CONTENT.

The "world's biggest porn site" reports on itself

2017 year-in-review on PornHub.com

28.5 billion visitors
81 million a day
74% are men

67% of PornHub visitors accessed the website by smartphone
24% by desktop computer

Proportion of women visitors to PornHub:

global average 26%

from the Philippines 36%

from USA and Canada 25%

from Japan 19%

Top 5 categories of sexual activity viewed by men:
- Japanese
- Ebony
- milf
- mature
- anal

Most searched-for terms by men:
- milf
- stepmom
- Japanese
- hentai
- mom

Top 5 categories of sexual activity viewed by women:
- women on women ("lesbian")
- threesome
- big dick
- "popular with women"
- Ebony

Most searched-for terms by women:
- women on women ("lesbian")
- "lesbians" scissoring
- threesome
- hentai
- Japanese

#JUST SAYIN'

Attitudes to pornography score the largest gender gap in Gallup's annual "social values" poll: in 2015, 43% of American men said pornography is "morally acceptable"; 25% of women said the same.

Health

HIV is one of the world's biggest killers of women.

Globally, 51% of people with HIV are women. One of the main contributing factors is the power difference between men and women in negotiating sexual arrangements.

Young women are at a particular disadvantage in negotiating safe sex practices with older male partners.

One in eight women in industrialized countries will develop breast cancer over an 85-year lifespan.

In the 1970s, this number was 1 in 20. In most of Western Europe and North America, the proportion of women who die from breast cancer is dropping, but the benefits of advanced medical care are not evenly distributed. In the USA, for example, the diagnosed incidence is higher among white women, but Black women are more likely to die from it.

Breast cancer incidence is rising around the world, possibly due to the export of "Western" diets and lifestyles.

Environmental disruptions present significant health problems in themselves, and also exacerbate other health problems.

The geographic range of malaria is spreading as climate change expands the habitats of malaria-carrying mosquitos.

Access to basic sanitation and clean water is improving in the poorest parts of the world, but chemical pollution of drinking supplies is a rapidly escalating problem in rich and poor countries alike. Houses are often the most dangerous sites of concentrated pollution, both chemical pollution and, in poorer households, particulate pollution from open fires.

Breast cancer

Incidence per 100,000 women
2012

- 80 and over
- 50 – 79
- 25 – 49
- under 25
- no data

Weekly death toll

Number of women dying
of breast cancer
selected examples, 2012

- numbers given

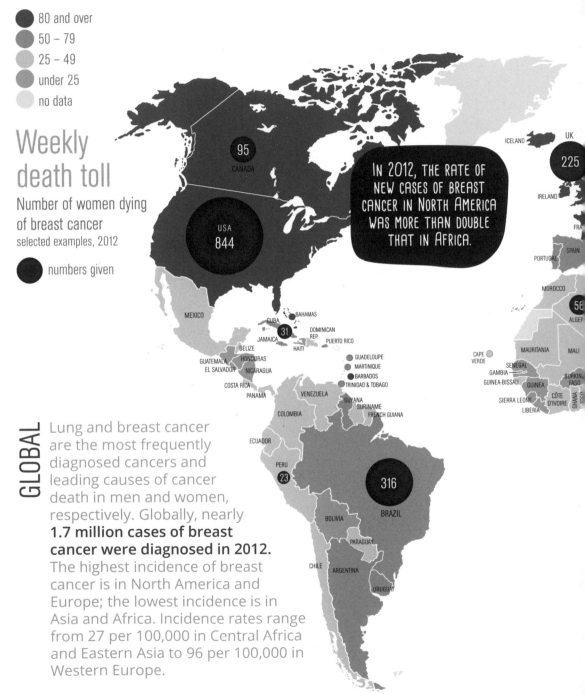

IN 2012, THE RATE OF
NEW CASES OF BREAST
CANCER IN NORTH AMERICA
WAS MORE THAN DOUBLE
THAT IN AFRICA.

CANADA 95

USA 844

MEXICO

BAHAMAS
CUBA
JAMAICA
HAITI
DOMINICAN REP.
PUERTO RICO
31

BELIZE
GUATEMALA
EL SALVADOR
HONDURAS
NICARAGUA
COSTA RICA
PANAMA

GUADELOUPE
MARTINIQUE
BARBADOS
TRINIDAD & TOBAGO

VENEZUELA
COLOMBIA
GUYANA
SURINAME
FRENCH GUIANA

ECUADOR
PERU 23

BRAZIL 316

BOLIVIA
PARAGUAY
CHILE
ARGENTINA
URUGUAY

ICELAND
UK 225
IRELAND
FRA
SPAIN
PORTUGAL
MOROCCO
56 ALGER
MAURITANIA
MALI
CAPE VERDE
SENEGAL
GAMBIA
GUINEA-BISSAU
GUINEA
SIERRA LEONE
LIBERIA
CÔTE D'IVOIRE
GHANA
BURKINA FASO

GLOBAL

Lung and breast cancer
are the most frequently
diagnosed cancers and
leading causes of cancer
death in men and women,
respectively. Globally, nearly
**1.7 million cases of breast
cancer were diagnosed in 2012.**
The highest incidence of breast
cancer is in North America and
Europe; the lowest incidence is in
Asia and Africa. Incidence rates range
from 27 per 100,000 in Central Africa
and Eastern Asia to 96 per 100,000 in
Western Europe.

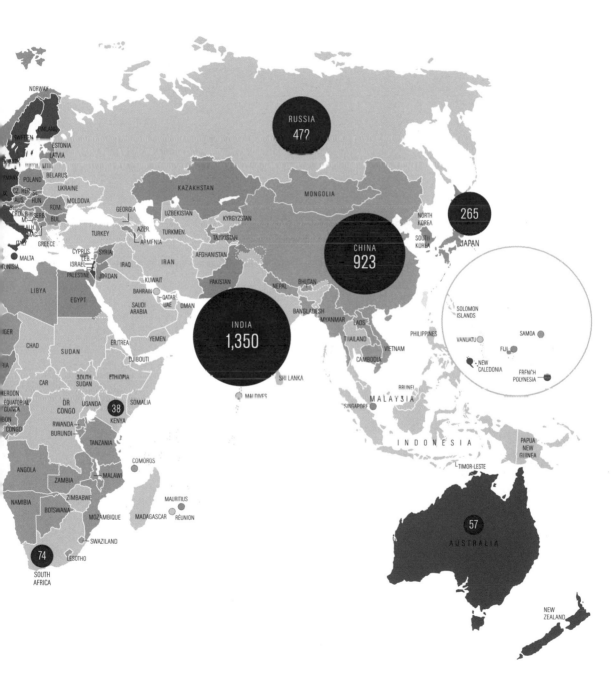

Breast cancer: The regional lottery

Top 5 regions in incidence and death rates per 100,000 women
2012

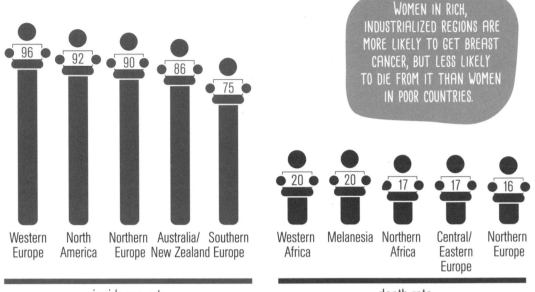

WOMEN IN RICH,
INDUSTRIALIZED REGIONS ARE
MORE LIKELY TO GET BREAST
CANCER, BUT LESS LIKELY
TO DIE FROM IT THAN WOMEN
IN POOR COUNTRIES.

| 96 | 92 | 90 | 86 | 75 | | 20 | 20 | 17 | 17 | 16 |
| Western Europe | North America | Northern Europe | Australia/ New Zealand | Southern Europe | | Western Africa | Melanesia | Northern Africa | Central/ Eastern Europe | Northern Europe |

incidence rate   death rate

Race, ethnicity, and breast cancer

Incidence and death rates in the USA
per 100,000 women
2014

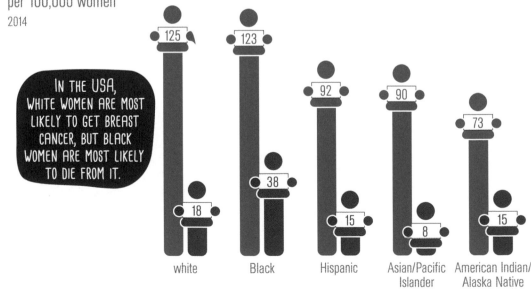

IN THE USA,
WHITE WOMEN ARE MOST
LIKELY TO GET BREAST
CANCER, BUT BLACK
WOMEN ARE MOST LIKELY
TO DIE FROM IT.

125	123	92	90	73
18	38	15	8	15
white	Black	Hispanic	Asian/Pacific Islander	American Indian/ Alaska Native

HIV in East and Southern Africa

Percentage of females aged 15–49 with HIV

2015

- 20% – 34%
- 5% – 19%
- fewer than 5%

EAST AND SOUTHERN AFRICA IS THE REGION HARDEST HIT BY HIV. IT IS HOME TO ONLY 6% OF THE GLOBAL POPULATION BUT OVER 50% OF THE TOTAL NUMBER OF PEOPLE LIVING WITH HIV IN THE WORLD.

ERITREA

SOUTH SUDAN

UGANDA

KENYA

RWANDA

BURUNDI

TANZANIA

ANGOLA

MALAWI

ZAMBIA

MADAGASCAR

ZIMBABWE

NAMIBIA

BOTSWANA

MAURITIUS

MOZAMBIQUE

SWAZILAND

SOUTH AFRICA

LESOTHO

Living with HIV

2015

- all adults with HIV
- adult women with HIV

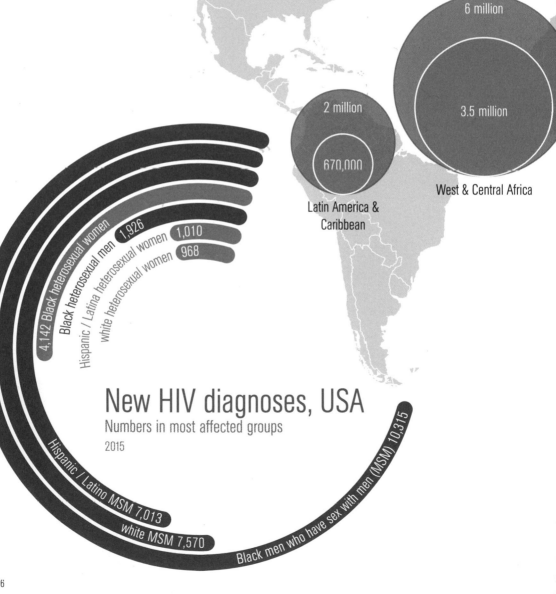

2.4 million

550,000

Western & Central
Europe & North America

6 million

3.5 million

West & Central Africa

2 million

670,000

Latin America &
Caribbean

4,142 Black heterosexual women

Black heterosexual men 1,926

Hispanic / Latina heterosexual women 1,010

white heterosexual women 968

New HIV diagnoses, USA
Numbers in most affected groups
2015

Hispanic / Latino MSM 7,013

white MSM 7,570

Black men who have sex with men (MSM) 10,315

Weekly toll

Number of
AIDS related deaths,
averaged per week
selected examples
2015

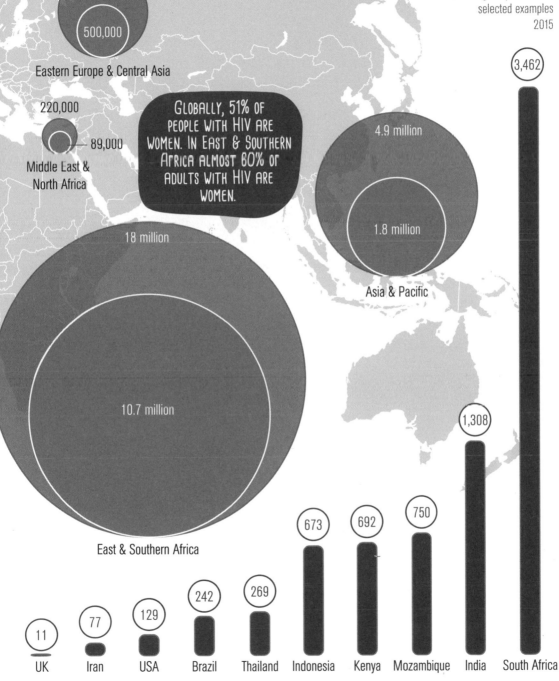

1.5 million

500,000

Eastern Europe & Central Asia

220,000

89,000

Middle East &
North Africa

GLOBALLY, 51% OF
PEOPLE WITH HIV ARE
WOMEN. IN EAST & SOUTHERN
AFRICA ALMOST 60% OF
ADULTS WITH HIV ARE
WOMEN.

4.9 million

1.8 million

Asia & Pacific

18 million

10.7 million

East & Southern Africa

3,462

1,308

11
UK

77
Iran

129
USA

242
Brazil

269
Thailand

673
Indonesia

692
Kenya

750
Mozambique

India

South Africa

Treatment for HIV

Percentage of HIV+ population in East and Southern Africa
receiving anti-retroviral drug therapy
2015

- 50% – 79%
- 20% – 49%
- fewer than 20%

54% OF HIV+ PEOPLE
IN EAST AND SOUTHERN
AFRICA RECEIVE ARV
TREATMENT.

ERITREA

SOUTH
SUDAN

UGANDA

KENYA

RWANDA

BURUNDI

TANZANIA

ANGOLA

MALAWI

ZAMBIA

ZIMBABWE

NAMIBIA

BOTSWANA

MADAGASCAR

MAURITIUS

MOZAMBIQUE

SWAZILAND

SOUTH
AFRICA

LESOTHO

New HIV infections and young women

Harmful gender norms and inequalities, insufficient access to education and sexual and reproductive health services, poverty, food insecurity, widespread violence against women, and sexual coercion of young girls are at the root of their increased HIV risk. In high HIV prevalence areas, men often seek out young girls for sex, presuming them less likely to be infected. Young women may find it difficult to negotiate safe sex practices with older male partners.

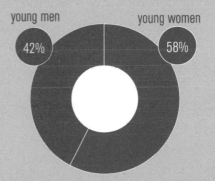

IN 2015, THERE WERE 2.1 MILLION NEW HIV INFECTIONS WORLDWIDE. YOUNG WOMEN MAKE UP A DISPROPORTIONATE SHARE OF NEW INFECTIONS.

New HIV infections
In young adults aged 15–24
worldwide, 2015

young men **42%**

young women **58%**

Age and gender inequalities in new HIV infections

2015

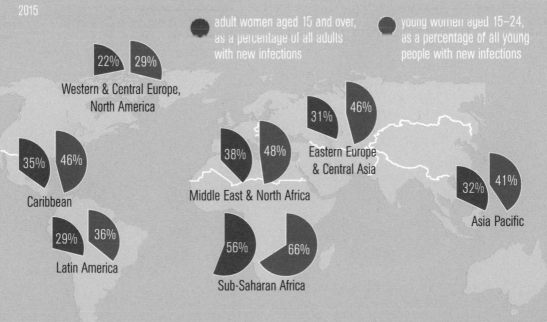

● adult women aged 15 and over, as a percentage of all adults with new infections

● young women aged 15–24, as a percentage of all young people with new infections

22% **29%**
Western & Central Europe, North America

35% **46%**
Caribbean

29% **36%**
Latin America

38% **48%**
Middle East & North Africa

56% **66%**
Sub-Saharan Africa

31% **46%**
Eastern Europe & Central Asia

32% **41%**
Asia Pacific

Tuberculosis
Global incidence

2016

Tuberculosis (TB) is one of the world's deadliest diseases. An estimated one third of the world's population is infected with TB, many without knowing until it is too late. In 2016, 10.4 million people around the world became ill with TB, and 1.7 million died from it. It is a leading killer of HIV-positive people: in 2016, 40% of HIV deaths were due to TB.

20 COUNTRIES ACCOUNT FOR 84% OF THE GLOBAL INCIDENCE OF TB

Bangladesh • Myanmar • Russia • North Korea • China • Thailand • Indonesia • Philippines • Vietnam

Brazil • South Africa • Mozambique • Angola • DR Congo • Tanzania • Kenya • Nigeria • Ethiopia • Pakistan • India

GENITAL TUBERCULOSIS IS A RELATIVELY RARE CONDITION IN MEN. HOWEVER, ONE IN EIGHT WOMEN WHO HAVE PULMONARY TUBERCULOSIS MAY ALSO HAVE GENITAL TUBERCULOSIS — A SIGNIFICANT CAUSE OF INFERTILITY IN WOMEN IN HIGH-TB COUNTRIES.

Global deaths from TB

2016

boys under age 15 **8.5%**
girls under age 15 **7.5%**
women, age 15 and older **29%**
Total: 1.3 million
men, age 15 and older **55%**

HIV-negative people

boys under age 15 **7.5%**
girls under age 15 **6.5%**
women, age 15 and older **31%**
Total: 374,000
men, age 15 and older **55%**

HIV-positive people

Malaria

Malaria deaths worldwide are on the decline, but this disease is still one of the world's major scourges, killing a half-million people a year and debilitating millions more. **In 2016, there were about 216 million new malaria cases worldwide, almost 90% of which were in Africa.**

Malaria kills more children than adults; **16% – 24% of all child deaths in Africa are due to malaria.** The death toll from malaria, globally, is slightly higher for women than men. Women's household responsibilities, such as cooking the evening meal outdoors or waking up before sunrise to fetch water, may put them at particular risk of malaria infection.

Pregnant women are especially susceptible: their rate of infection is higher because of their decreased immunity, and infection during pregnancy carries substantial risks for the mother, the fetus and the newborn child. An estimated 60% of pregnant women in Africa do not have access to preventative treatment. Health care is often too distant, too expensive, and in many places women often have to ask for their husband's permission to access treatment for themselves and their children.

10,000 WOMEN DIE ANNUALLY IN AFRICA AS A RESULT OF MALARIA INFECTION DURING PREGNANCY.

Annual malaria mortality

most recent since 2013

♀ higher mortality rates for women

0 — deaths per 100,000 people — 238

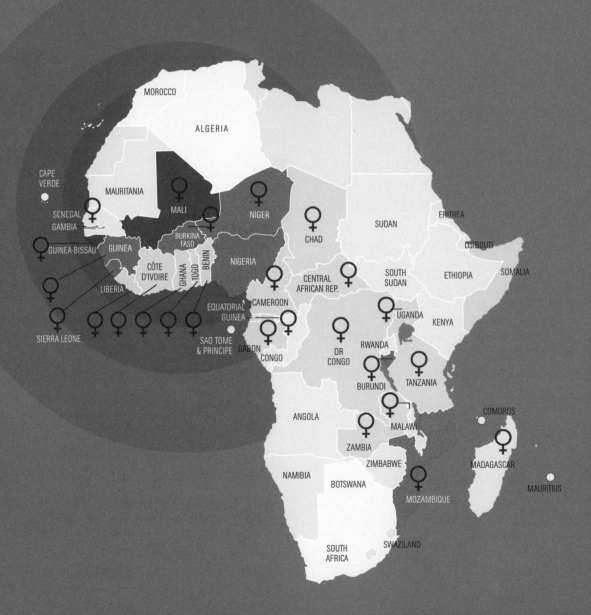

No-go zone

2015

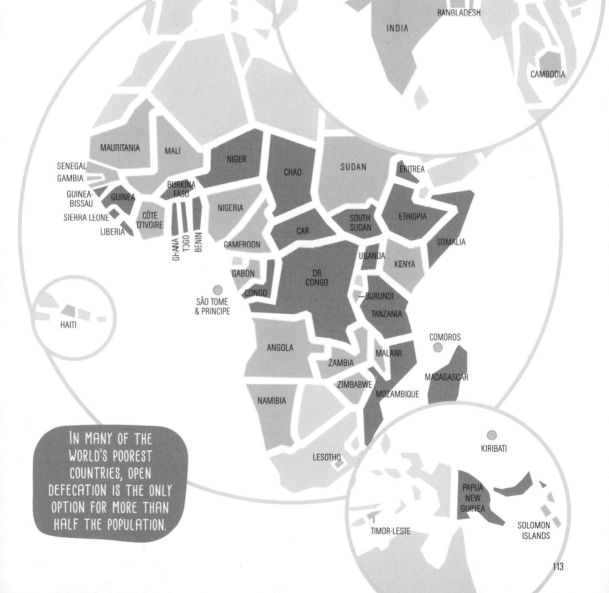

26% – 50% of the population has "basic sanitation"

fewer than 26% of the population has "basic sanitation"

"Basic sanitation" means that excreta is separated from direct human contact, and includes covered pit latrines and pour-latrines.

AFGHANISTAN

NEPAL

BANGLADESH

INDIA

CAMBODIA

MAURITANIA

MALI

SENEGAL

GAMBIA

GUINEA-BISSAU

GUINEA

SIERRA LEONE

LIBERIA

CÔTE D'IVOIRE

BURKINA FASO

NIGER

CHAD

SUDAN

ERITREA

NIGERIA

GHANA

TOGO

BENIN

CAMEROON

CAR

SOUTH SUDAN

ETHIOPIA

SOMALIA

GABON

CONGO

DR CONGO

UGANDA

KENYA

SÃO TOME & PRINCIPE

BURUNDI

TANZANIA

HAITI

ANGOLA

ZAMBIA

MALAWI

COMOROS

MADAGASCAR

ZIMBABWE

MOZAMBIQUE

NAMIBIA

LESOTHO

KIRIBATI

IN MANY OF THE WORLD'S POOREST COUNTRIES, OPEN DEFECATION IS THE ONLY OPTION FOR MORE THAN HALF THE POPULATION.

PAPUA NEW GUINEA

TIMOR-LESTE

SOLOMON ISLANDS

Drink up

Pesticides contaminate water supplies throughout the USA: at least 12 million people drink water contaminated by high levels of 1,2,3-Trichloropropane (TCP); chromium-6 – an **industrial chemical** made famous by the activism of Erin Brockovich – is present in the drinking water supplies of more than 250 million Americans across all 50 states; 1,4-dioxane – an industrial solvent – is in the drinking water used by more than 7 million people at levels above the Environmental Protection Agency "negligible cancer risk" threshold.

HAITI

Chemicals from plastics, many of them endocrine disruptors that are suspected agents of breast cancer and "gender-bending" estrogenic effects, are a constant part of our daily diet. In 2017, **micro-plastic fibers** were found in 83% of drinking water samples worldwide.

Pesticide contamination of surface water threatens water safety globally. In 2015, agricultural insecticide concentrations above regulatory thresholds were found in more than half of sediment and surface water samples in 73 countries.

MAURITANIA   MALI   NIGE

BURKINA FASO

GUINEA-BISSAU   GUINEA   CÔTE   NIGERIA
SIERRA LEONE   D'IVOIRE
LIBERIA

TOGO   BENIN

CAMEROON

EQUATORIAL — GUINEA

C

AN

NAM

213,725

Southeast
Asia

181,476   Africa   186,130

150,179

Dirty water

● fewer than 75% of the population have access to basic (improved) water supplies
2015

Access to an "improved" drinking water source has dramatically increased in the past two decades. Still, an estimated 600–800 million people, mostly poor and in rural areas of developing countries, don't have improved water supplies. Of these, almost half live in Sub-Saharan Africa.

Drinking water, even from an "improved" source is not always safe. Fecal contamination of drinking water kills hundreds of thousands of people a year. And new chemical threats are multiplying rapidly. Even advanced water treatment systems are unable to remove many pesticide and other chemical residues that are becoming ubiquitous.

TAJIKISTAN
AFGHANISTAN
MYANMAR

SUDAN   ERITREA YEMEN
SOUTH SUDAN   ETHIOPIA
AR
SOMALIA
DR CONGO   UGANDA   KENYA
RWANDA
BURUNDI
TANZANIA
ZAMBIA   MALAWI
ZIMBABWE
MADAGASCAR
SWAZILAND
LESOTHO

KIRIBATI

PAPUA NEW GUINEA
TIMOR-LESTE
SOLOMON ISLANDS

Deaths from diarrhea

2014

women ●   men ●

Eastern Mediterranean low- and middle-income
39,838   41,227

Western Pacific low- and middle-income
6,536   7,626

Americas low- and middle-income
5,525   6,021

Europe low- and middle-income
1,675   1,890

Toilets

Only 27% of the global population has access to the highest-standard sanitation: private sanitation facilities that are connected to sewers from which wastewater is treated.
2.3 billion people still don't have basic sanitation facilities such as toilets or latrines. About a billion people have to defecate in the open – in street gutters, behind bushes or into open bodies of water. For women, open defecation is particularly humiliating, especially during menstruation; it also compels women to seek isolated places where they are vulnerable to rape and abuse. Pregnancy without safe sanitation is precarious.

Access, use, and control of toilets are important social indicators. The availability of toilets reflects – and shapes – gender norms. Public toilet provision for women everywhere in the world lags behind that for men, as any woman knows who has stood in a long queue for public toilets while men breeze in and out of theirs. The absence or inadequate provision of public toilets for women reflects and reinforces women's exclusion from public power and public spaces generally: it is hard to participate fully in civil society if there's nowhere to pee. Girls' schooling is affected. Many schools in poorer countries or districts don't have safe or private toilet facilities; without them, girls can't go to school, especially as they reach puberty.

In many parts of the world, gay rights and transgender rights movements prominently include demands to appropriately meet the toilet needs of sexual minorities and trans people. Predictably, this has become a flash point for conservative groups and politicians. Many feminists raise a more complicated political challenge: where right-to-toilets activism has become a push for creating gender-mixed facilities, the dismantling of women's spaces in favor of "gender neutral" spaces is not necessarily liberatory for everyone.

In 2015, more than 500,000 households in the USA – accounting for about 1.3 million people – did not have "complete plumbing facilities". These rates are especially high in counties containing Indian reservations – in one county in South Dakota, for example, 14% of households lacked complete plumbing in 2014, and in Apache County, Arizona, 17% lacked complete plumbing.

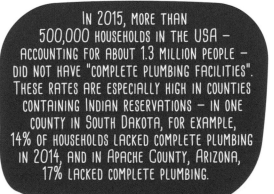

Right to pee!

Right to pee activism, Mumbai, India, 2017

Pollution planet

Pollution takes its economic toll

THE GLOBAL ECONOMIC COST OF DISEASE, DISABILITY, AND IMPAIRMENT CAUSED BY POLLUTION LIKELY EXCEEDS 10% OF THE GLOBAL GDP. THE WORLD PAYS THE PRICE OF ILLNESS, HEALTH CARE, LOST WAGES AND LOST PRODUCTIVITY CAUSED BY EXPOSURE TO AIR POLLUTANTS, ENDOCRINE DISRUPTING CHEMICALS, LEAD, MERCURY, PESTICIDES, NEUROTOXINS, AND OTHER UBIQUITOUS HUMAN-CREATED POLLUTION.

"We could be the agents that cause our own extinction as well as much of the rest of life on earth...we have so altered the nature of nature that earth becomes inhospitable."

Dr. Sylvia Earle, Marine Biologist, 2017

"We should no longer accept the counsel of those who tell us that we must fill our world with poisonous chemicals."

Rachel Carson,
Biologist and Conservationist,
"Silent Spring", 1962

Pollution takes its health toll

POLLUTION-RELATED DISEASES RESULTED IN AN ESTIMATED 9 MILLION PREMATURE DEATHS IN 2015: 16% OF ALL DEATHS WORLDWIDE, AND ALMOST 3 TIMES THE NUMBER OF DEATHS FROM AIDS, TUBERCULOSIS, AND MALARIA COMBINED. IN THE MOST HEAVILY POLLUTED PLACES, POLLUTION-RELATED DISEASES ARE RESPONSIBLE FOR MORE THAN 1 DEATH IN 4.
POLLUTION DISPROPORTIONATELY KILLS THE POOR AND THE VULNERABLE. EVERYWHERE, DISEASES CAUSED BY POLLUTION ARE MOST PREVALENT AMONG MINORITIES AND SOCIALLY MARGINALIZED GROUPS, AND POLLUTION HOTSPOTS ARE DISPROPORTIONATELY CONCENTRATED IN POOR COMMUNITIES.

Autism
The risk of having a child with Autism Spectrum Disorder doubles for mothers who live near a freeway during pregnancy. Children are 60% more likely to develop ASD if their mothers lived near agricultural fields where organophosphate pesticides were applied during their pregnancy.

Premature Births
Every year in the USA, about 16,000 premature births – putting both mother and infant at risk – are attributable to air pollution.

Lead
Children in 4 million American households may be exposed to high levels of lead.

"Pollution can no longer be viewed as an isolated environmental issue, but is a transcendent problem that affects the health and wellbeing of entire societies."

Lancet Commission, 2017

In the USA

Deadly dust

In much of the world, especially rich-world, high-consumption, industrialized, and urbanized places, people conduct their everyday lives in a fog of synthetic chemicals. Modern Western homes, often sealed against the elements, can be particularly dense with chemicals that are known to be toxic, carcinogenic, or strongly suspected of being carcinogenic. Of the roughly 80,000 chemicals used in everyday goods in the USA, about 1,300 are known endocrine disruptors, strongly associated with men's and women's reproductive disorders and hormone-sensitive breast cancers.

Indoor toxic chemicals

Chemicals with hazardous health traits were found in more than 90% of samples of dust in US homes in 2016. Chemicals included those with likely reproductive system toxicity, fetal/child developmental toxicity, cancer-causing associations and hormone disruption.

PESTICIDE RESIDUES ARE WIDESPREAD IN AMERICAN HOMES. 75% OF AMERICAN HOUSEHOLDS USED AT LEAST ONE PESTICIDE PRODUCT INDOORS IN 2016.

DEHP
DEHA
BBzP
DnPB
DiPB
MeP
HHCB
TPHP
TDCIPP
HBCDD
PFCs

PHTHALATES — VINYL FLOORING, FOOD PACKAGING, NAIL POLISH, PAINTS, PERSONAL CARE AND BEAUTY PRODUCTS

PHENOL — COSMETICS, LOTIONS, DEODORANTS

FRAGRANCE — SCENTED PRODUCTS

FLAME RETARDANT — TREATED FURNITURE, BABY PRODUCTS, BUILDING INSULATIONS, CARPET PADDING

PERFLUORINATED COMPOUNDS — WATERPROOF OUTDOOR APPAREL, STAIN RESISTANT CARPETING AND TEXTILES, CIRCUIT BOARDS, NON-STICK COOKWARE

Deadly air

Around 3 billion people cook and heat their homes using "solid fuels" such as wood, charcoal, coal, dung, or crop wastes, burned on open fires or in traditional stoves. More than 4 million people a year die from the resulting household air pollution. Women experience longer and more frequent exposure to household air pollution due to their greater involvement in daily household and cooking activities, but more men die from household air pollution because they have higher underlying disease rates, especially from smoking. Improved low-fuel-use cookstoves, long in development, might lessen the impact of particulate emissions from burning solid fuels, but the evidence to date on their actual benefits is mixed.

Regional deaths from household air pollution

Regions with the greatest numbers of deaths from household air pollution, mostly attributable to burning solid fuels
2012

- Africa
- Western Pacific
- South-East Asia
- Eastern Mediterranean

Global deaths

- women, aged 25+
- men aged 25+
- children aged 0 – 4

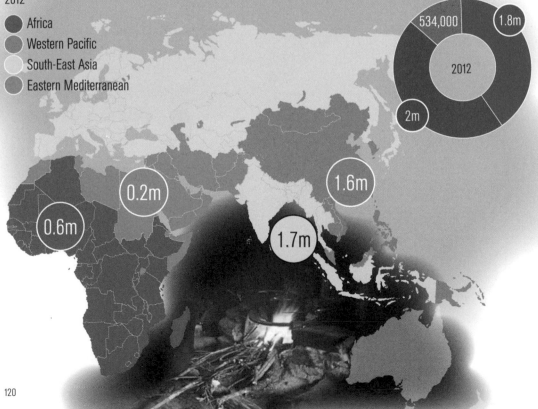

534,000

1.8m

2012

2m

0.2m

0.6m

1.6m

1.7m

Don't eat the fish!

Mercury, a powerful neurotoxin, accumulates in the marine food chain. Pregnant women have long been warned about the dangers of eating certain fish. In addition to the hazards facing the woman herself, mercury consumption can cause severe developmental disorders in the fetus. High fish-consumption cultures and communities are at particular risk.

HOW MUCH FISH TO EAT?
PER WEEK

8oz
12oz = 2–3 SERVINGS

LOW LEVELS OF MERCURY

Salmon Pollock Cod Shrimp Tuna (Light Canned) Tilapia Catfish

HIGH LEVELS OF MERCURY

Tilefish (From the Gulf of Mexico) Swordfish 6oz Shark White (Albacore) Tuna King Mackerel

Source: U.S. Food and Drug Administration

Inuit (Canada):

of Nunavik (northern Quebec) and one community had blood mercury levels above the Canadian recommended maximum. In 2004, 28% of the general population and 72% of women of reproductive age in Nunavut had mercury levels equal to or higher than the WHO recommendation. In a 2007–2008 study, 25% of children in recommendation.

USA

2.4% of women and 3.7% of men in the USA in 2010–2011 had methyl mercury levels higher than the EPA recommended threshold. But results varied considerably by race/ethnicity:

MEXICAN AMERICAN	0.4%
BLACK NON-HISPANIC	2.1%
WHITE NON-HISPANIC	2.8%
ASIAN	15.6%

Minimata

THE DANGERS OF MERCURY EXPOSURE WERE FIRST REVEALED IN THE 1950s IN MINIMATA, JAPAN. FOR DECADES, A CHEMICAL COMPANY HAD DUMPED MERCURY-CONTAMINATED WASTEWATER DIRECTLY INTO MINIMATA BAY. THE HEAVY METAL BIOACCUMULATED IN THE SEAFOOD CHAIN, CAUSING THOUSANDS OF DEFORMITIES, DEATHS, AND CONGENITAL DEFECTS AMONG THE LOCAL POPULATION.

Danger zones

Percentage of women of childbearing age with mercury levels (in hair samples) above EPA recommendations
2017

Kiribati	Marshall Islands	Cook Islands	Tuvalu	Japan	Spain	Mauritius	Côte d'Ivoire	Bangladesh	Tajikistan
100%	96%	95%	93%	71%	64%	36%	23%	5%	0%

Work

Unpaid work looms larger in women's lives than in men's.

One of the major shifts in the world of work is that women everywhere are entering the waged workforce in unprecedented numbers. On the one hand, this can bring significant empowerment and autonomy. For women to control their own economic destiny is a foundation on which all other rights rest. Without paid work, women have a much harder time leaving an abusive relationship, exploring sexual identities, securing the means to make reproductive decisions, or planning for a future for themselves and their children.

On the other hand, the terms under which women participate in the waged workforce are typically very different from men's: women universally get paid less for equal and equivalent work (a gap magnified by age and race/ ethnicity); workforces do not generally accommodate women's reproductive roles; and, women are both "concentrated" in certain job sectors and "segregated" into jobs defined as women's work. Feminists often describe women as being caught between the "sticky floor and the glass ceiling" – concentrated in low-pay, low-status job sectors, and prevented from breaking into the top ranks of workplace power and authority.

Much of women's and men's total "work" goes unnoticed and uncounted in official reckonings. Informal work, unpaid labor, childcare, "volunteer" work, household work – all are made invisible. Unpaid work looms larger in women's lives than in men's: when the totality of the work needed to support households and individuals, including household chores and caring for children, are taken into account, women work an estimated 60% more than men everywhere in the world.

Segregated work

most recent data since 2010

Women are both "concentrated" and "segregated" in the workforce. Everywhere in the world, there are "men's jobs" and "women's jobs," although the definitions of these change over time and from place to place. The jobs that women and men are allowed or encouraged to do reflect cultural norms of appropriate femininity and masculinity as well as a status spectrum. When women are in the majority in a specific sector, the jobs they do are less valued and lower paid.

Women's work, almost everywhere in the world

Nursing and midwifery professionals:
mostly women in UK (89%) and Bangladesh (88%)

Primary school teachers:
mostly women in UK (89%), Mongolia (96%), New Zealand (84%), and Bolivia (66%)
BUT mostly men in Liberia (87%) and Nepal (58%)

Call-center workers:
mostly women in Malaysia, Philippines, and Latvia

Dental hygienists:
mostly women in Europe (97%), USA (97%), and Canada (97%)

Men's work, almost everywhere in the world

Surgeons:
mostly men in Austria (90%, general surgeons), UK (09%, consultant surgeons), and New Zealand (91%, all surgical specialties)

Airline pilots:
mostly men in USA (93%), Finland (88%), Japan (93%), and Brazil (98%); 93% worldwide

Road construction unskilled laborers:
mostly men in USA, Brazil, and France **BUT** mostly women in India and Nepal

Taxi drivers:
mostly men in UK (98%), Hong Kong (85%), and Australia (94%) **BUT** "Uber promises to create 100,000 jobs for women drivers worldwide by 2020 as part of a global partnership with UN Women."

Changing places?

Dentistry:
USA: women as a percentage of first-year dental students: 1978: 16%; 2014: 48%

Veterinarians:
USA: women as a percentage of students in veterinary medical schools: 1986: 50%; 2017: 80%

Women in the workforce
Percentage of women aged 15–64 who work for pay

most recent data since 2012

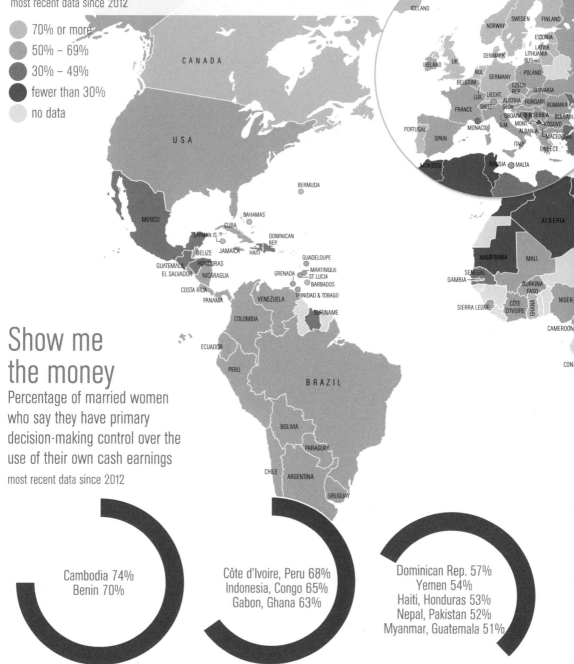

- 70% or more
- 50% – 69%
- 30% – 49%
- fewer than 30%
- no data

Show me the money

Percentage of married women who say they have primary decision-making control over the use of their own cash earnings

most recent data since 2012

Cambodia 74%
Benin 70%

Côte d'Ivoire, Peru 68%
Indonesia, Congo 65%
Gabon, Ghana 63%

Dominican Rep. 57%
Yemen 54%
Haiti, Honduras 53%
Nepal, Pakistan 52%
Myanmar, Guatemala 51%

Worldwide, more and more women are working outside the home for pay, but they typically do so under different circumstances than men – for less pay, in different jobs, and under different constraints. Data on workforce participation must be treated with caution. What is counted as "work" in official statistics makes much of the world's labor, especially that of women, invisible.

Kenya 49%
Philippines 46%
Afghanistan 41%
Angola 40%

Jordan 39%
Kyrgyzstan 35%
Tajikistan 33%
Bangladesh, Zimbabwe 32%
Ethiopia, Liberia 30%

DR Congo, Egypt 29%
Malawi 28%

The earnings gap

Everywhere women's earnings are lower than men's, and everywhere the gap is magnified by race and age. One of the primary drivers of this gap is sheer discrimination: despite recent equal-pay laws in many countries, it is still the case that women routinely get paid less than men for the same work, and they are not given the same promotion and advancement opportunities. The overall gap is more complex than this alone and the concept of a gender gap is a broader one. Women are caught between the sticky floor and the glass ceiling.

Their overall earning share is smaller because: women are concentrated and segregated into feminized (typically low-wage) jobs, and the highly-paid occupations are highly masculinized; women have a higher rate of part-time work; and the gender-skewed demands of family care interrupt women's waged work trajectory, sometimes for many years. When women retire, the pay gap follows them in the form of pension and social safety net gaps.

BBC

THE REVELATION IN 2017 OF A YAWNING GENDER GAP IN PAY AT THE BBC PROVOKED GOVERNMENT INQUIRIES, PUBLIC OUTRAGE, AND AN INTERNAL CRISIS OF CONFIDENCE.

BBC, UK, 2017

HIGHEST PAID MALE PRESENTER:
£2.2 MILLION
HIGHEST PAID FEMALE PRESENTER:
£450,000 – £500,000

WALMART, USA

IN 2001, A GENDER DISCRIMINATION LAWSUIT BY WOMEN WORKING AT WALMART REVEALED SYSTEMATIC PAY DISCRIMINATION: WOMEN HOURLY WORKERS EARNED ABOUT $1,100 LESS A YEAR THAN THEIR MALE EQUIVALENTS, $14,500 LESS AMONG MANAGEMENT WORKERS. THE US SUPREME COURT DISMISSED THE CASE IN 2011 ON THE GROUNDS THAT THE "CLASS" – 1.6 MILLION WOMEN WORKERS – WAS NOT PROPERLY CONSTITUTED. SEVEN WOMEN FROM THE ORIGINAL SUIT RE-FILED THEIR CASE IN 2017. THE STORY CONTINUES.

Race, ethnicity, pay, USA

Women's earnings as a proportion of white men's earnings

2016

90%	77%	63%	59%	57%	54%
Asian	white non-Hispanic	Black	Native Hawaiian/ Pacific Islander	American Indian/ Alaska Native	Hispanic/Latina

Euro gap

Women's average gross hourly
earnings as a percentage of men's

2014–15

A GLOBAL FIRST

THE ICELANDIC GOVERNMENT HAS MADE THE
GENDER PAY GAP ILLEGAL. AS OF 2018, THE ONUS IS
ON EMPLOYERS TO PROVE THAT THEY PAY MEN AND
WOMEN IN THE SAME JOBS EQUALLY. EMPLOYERS STILL
CAN PAY WORKERS DIFFERENTLY BASED ON EXPERIENCE,
PERFORMANCE AND OTHER CRITERIA; HOWEVER, THEY
MUST SHOW THAT DIFFERENCES IN WAGES ARE NOT
DUE TO GENDER. THE ICELANDIC GOVERNMENT HAS
COMMITTED TO CLOSING THE GENDER PAY GAP
BY 2022.

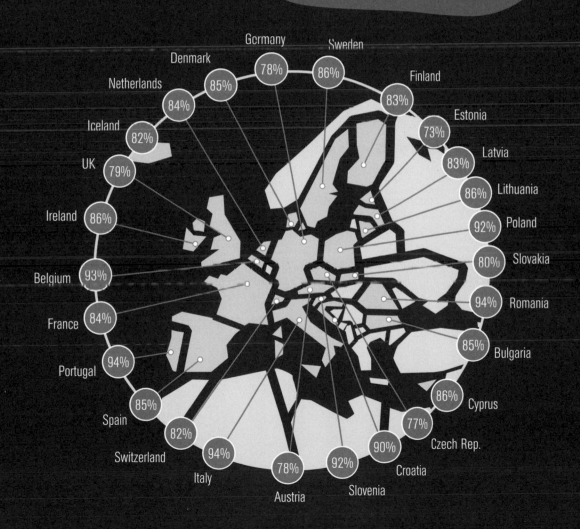

- Germany 78%
- Sweden 86%
- Denmark 85%
- Finland 83%
- Netherlands 84%
- Estonia 73%
- Iceland 82%
- Latvia 83%
- UK 79%
- Lithuania 86%
- Ireland 86%
- Poland 92%
- Belgium 93%
- Slovakia 80%
- France 84%
- Romania 94%
- Portugal 94%
- Bulgaria 85%
- Spain 85%
- Cyprus 86%
- Switzerland 82%
- Czech Rep. 77%
- Italy 94%
- Croatia 90%
- Austria 78%
- Slovenia 92%

Women's work

Informal work

Percentage of women's non-agricultural work for pay that takes place in the informal sector (often in addition to formal employment)

most recent data since 2012

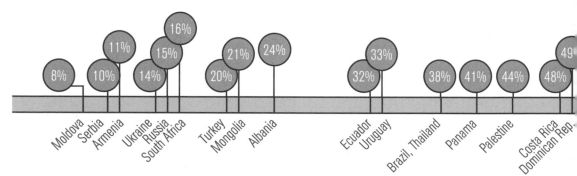

8% Moldova
10% Serbia
11% Armenia
14% Ukraine
15% Russia
16% South Africa
20% Turkey
21% Mongolia
24% Albania
32% Ecuador
33% Uruguay
38% Brazil, Thailand
41% Panama
44% Palestine
48% Costa Rica
49% Dominican Rep.

The global assembly line

Percentage of women among all workers in Export Processing Zones (EPZs)
2006

● women
● men

EPZs are tax-free industrial areas for foreign companies. Labor laws are often suspended and workers unprotected. In 2006 there were EPZs in 130 countries.

Morocco 20%
India 32%
Jordan 33%
Fiji 35%
Macedonia, Vietnam 45%
Malawi 51%
Dominican Rep. 53%
Malaysia 54%
Kenya, Mexico 60%
Haiti 69%
Guatemala, Panama, S. Korea 70%
Madagascar 71%
Philippines 74%

The "informal sector" comprises jobs that are not registered, not waged, and usually not regulated. The informal sector includes street vending, selling of home-made goods, and home-based services such as sewing or paid childcare. A larger share of women's work than men's is in the informal economy.

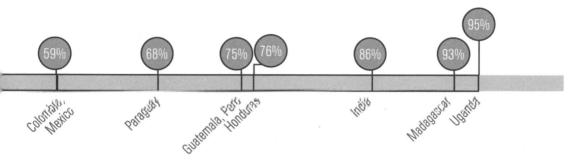

59% Colombia, Mexico
68% Paraguay
75% Guatemala, Peru
76% Honduras
86% India
93% Madagascar
95% Uganda

Export Processing Zones

There are about 3,500 EPZs in the world employing over 66 million people, more than 85% of whom are in Asia. A conspicuous feature of EPZ employment is that it is highly feminized.

EPZs offer new opportunities for women to enter the waged workforce, but for employers the "appeal" of women workers – almost all young – is that they can be paid less and are seen as a disposable workforce. Cheap manufacturing for export production extracts a high price from the workers.

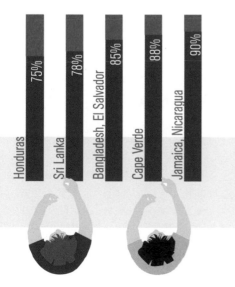

75% Honduras
78% Sri Lanka
85% Bangladesh, El Salvador
88% Cape Verde
90% Jamaica, Nicaragua

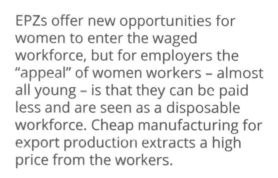

IN 2012, A GARMENT FACTORY FIRE AT TAZREEN FASHIONS IN DHAKA KILLED 117 PEOPLE AND INJURED SEVERAL HUNDRED MORE. IN 2013, THE RANA PLAZA GARMENT FACTORY BUILDING IN DHAKA COLLAPSED, KILLING 1,134 GARMENT WORKERS AND INJURING 2,000 MORE. IN BOTH CASES, BOSSES AND OWNERS HAD IGNORED UNSAFE CONDITIONS, EVEN WHEN WORKERS EXPRESSED THEIR CONCERNS. 85% – 90% OF WORKERS IN BANGLADESH'S EXPORT GARMENT INDUSTRY ARE WOMEN.

It's lonely at the top

Women's share of seats on boards of the largest publicly listed companies

selected examples, 2016

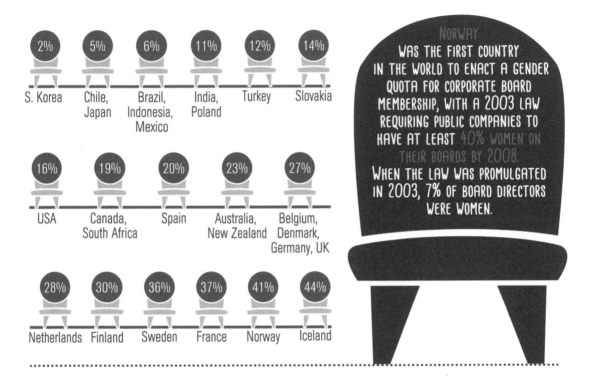

2%	5%	6%	11%	12%	14%
S. Korea	Chile, Japan	Brazil, Indonesia, Mexico	India, Poland	Turkey	Slovakia
16%	19%	20%	23%	27%	
USA	Canada, South Africa	Spain	Australia, New Zealand	Belgium, Denmark, Germany, UK	
28%	30%	36%	37%	41%	44%
Netherlands	Finland	Sweden	France	Norway	Iceland

NORWAY WAS THE FIRST COUNTRY IN THE WORLD TO ENACT A GENDER QUOTA FOR CORPORATE BOARD MEMBERSHIP, WITH A 2003 LAW REQUIRING PUBLIC COMPANIES TO HAVE AT LEAST 40% WOMEN ON THEIR BOARDS BY 2008. WHEN THE LAW WAS PROMULGATED IN 2003, 7% OF BOARD DIRECTORS WERE WOMEN.

 6% of the 500 largest companies (by revenue) in the USA in 2017 had a woman CEO

 80% of the 5,089 executive and senior officials in the Fortune 500 companies are men.

...and 73% are white, 21% are Asian, 3% Latino/a, 2% Black, 0.2% Native American, and 0.1% Native Hawaiian or Pacific Islander.

#JUST SAYIN'

New companies are no better than old in terms of gender balance, and often worse. In the USA in 2017, 68% of "unicorn" technology companies – high-flyers with billion dollar-plus valuations – had no women on their boards. As of late 2017, Twitter had 3 women on their 9-person board; Apple and Facebook each had 2 of 8; Alphabet (parent company of Google) had 3 of 12.

Maternity and paternity leave
Legal requirements and paid support

In most countries without government funding, employers are required to provide paid support

2013

- ● maternity leave in days (maximum shown)
- ● paternity leave in days
- % percentage of previous earnings paid during maternity leave

> THE US GOVERNMENT IS THE ONLY ONE IN THE DEVELOPED WORLD THAT NEITHER MANDATES NOR PROVIDES FOR PAID MATERNITY LEAVE.

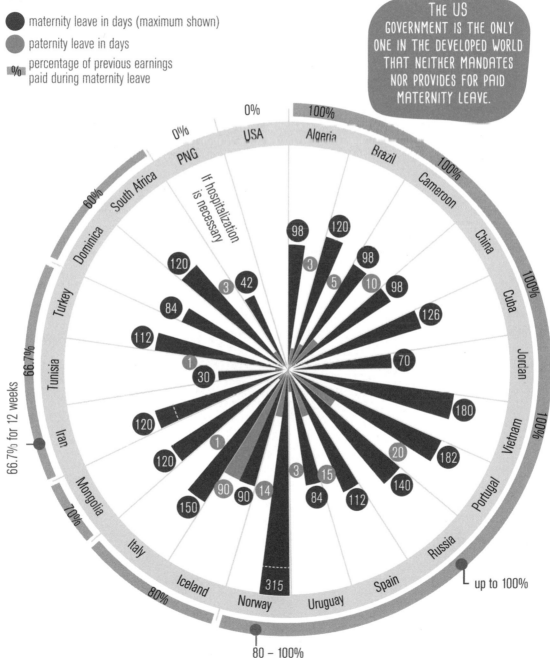

0% USA
0% PNG
100% Algeria
100% Brazil
Cameroon
China
100% Cuba
Jordan
100% Vietnam
Portugal
up to 100% Russia
Spain
80 – 100% Uruguay
Norway
80% Iceland
Italy
70% Mongolia
Iran
66.7% for 12 weeks
66.7% Tunisia
Turkey
Dominica
60% South Africa

If hospitalization is necessary

Maternity/paternity values: 98, 120, 3, 98, 5, 10, 98, 126, 70, 180, 182, 20, 140, 112, 84, 15, 3, 14, 90, 90, 150, 120, 1, 120, 30, 1, 112, 84, 120, 3, 42, 315

131

Unemployment

Percentages of men and women aged 25+
officially counted as unemployed

2016

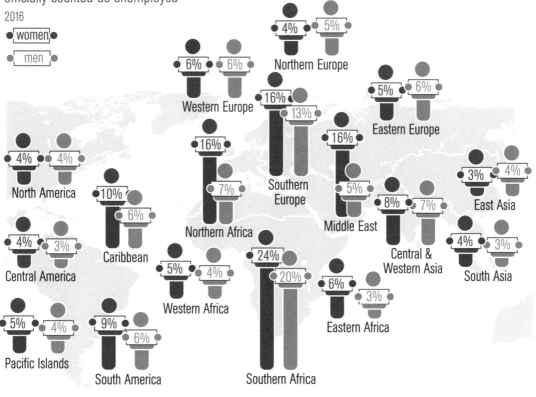

women
men

Northern Europe 4% / 5%

Western Europe 6% / 6%

Eastern Europe 5% / 6%

Southern Europe 16% / 13%

North America 4% / 4%

Caribbean 10% / 6%

Northern Africa 16% / 7%

Middle East 16% / 5%

East Asia 3% / 4%

Central America 4% / 3%

Western Africa 5% / 4%

Central & Western Asia 8% / 7%

South Asia 4% / 3%

Pacific Islands 5% / 4%

South America 9% / 6%

Southern Africa 24% / 20%

Eastern Africa 6% / 3%

Race and gender: intersectionality at work

women
men

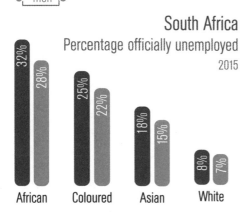

South Africa
Percentage officially unemployed
2015

African 32% / 28%
Coloured 25% / 22%
Asian 18% / 15%
White 8% / 7%

USA
Percentage officially unemployed aged 16+
2017 (first quarter)

Black 7% / 9%
Hispanic 6% / 6%
white 4% / 5%
Asian 3% / 4%

Part-time work

women
men

Underemployed
Percentage aged 14+ working part-time
and wanting more hours
2016

In marginal part-time work
Percentage aged 15+
working 14 hours per week or fewer
2014

	Underemployed		In marginal part-time work	
Austria	7%	3%	10%	3%
Czech Rep.	1%	0.3%	2%	1%
France	12%	8%	6%	3%
Germany	6%	3%	13%	5%
Italy	6%	4%	6%	2%
Ireland	8%	7%	8%	4%
Netherlands	9%	4%	17%	9%
Spain	14%	7%	7%	2%
Sweden	5%	3%	7%	5%
UK	9%	5%	10%	4%
USA	4%	4%	5%	4%

Domestic & care work
Unpaid Work

Average number of hours a day spent
on unpaid domestic and care work

most recent data since 2012

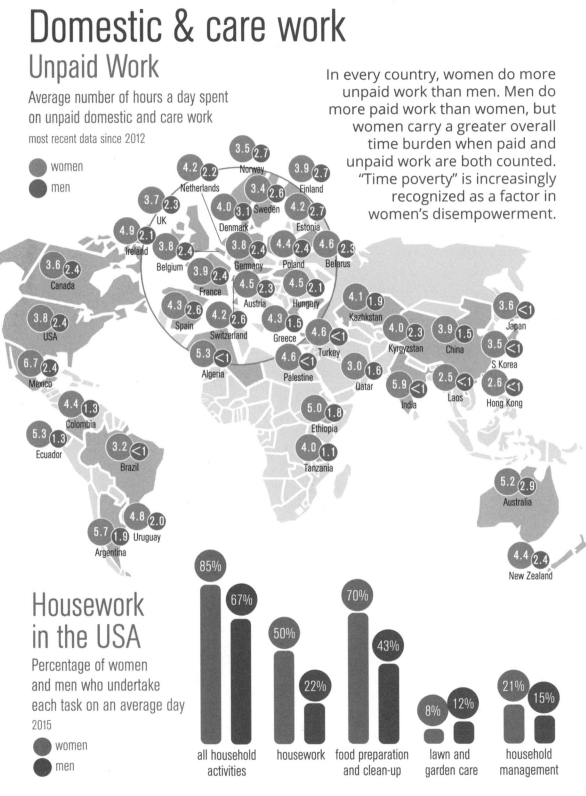

● women
● men

In every country, women do more
unpaid work than men. Men do
more paid work than women, but
women carry a greater overall
time burden when paid and
unpaid work are both counted.
"Time poverty" is increasingly
recognized as a factor in
women's disempowerment.

Norway 3.5 / 2.7
Netherlands 4.2 / 2.2
Finland 3.9 / 2.7
Sweden 3.4 / 2.6
UK 3.7 / 2.3
Denmark 4.0 / 3.1
Estonia 4.2 / 2.7
Ireland 4.9 / 2.1
Belgium 3.8 / 2.4
Germany 3.8 / 2.4
Poland 4.4 / 2.4
Belarus 4.6 / 2.3
France 3.9 / 2.4
Austria 4.5 / 2.3
Hungary 4.5 / 2.1
Kazhkstan 4.1 / 1.9
Spain 4.3 / 2.6
Switzerland 4.2 / 2.6
Greece 4.3 / 1.5
Turkey 4.6 / <1
Kyrgyzstan 4.0 / 2.3
China 3.9 / 1.5
Japan 3.6 / <1
Algeria 5.3 / <1
Palestine 4.6 / <1
S Korea 3.5 / <1
Qatar 3.0 / 1.6
India 5.9 / <1
Laos 2.5 / <1
Hong Kong 2.6 / <1
Canada 3.6 / 2.4
USA 3.8 / 2.4
Mexico 6.7 / 2.4
Colombia 4.4 / 1.3
Ecuador 5.3 / 1.3
Brazil 3.2 / <1
Ethiopia 5.0 / 1.8
Tanzania 4.0 / 1.1
Australia 5.2 / 2.9
Uruguay 4.8 / 2.0
Argentina 5.7 / 1.9
New Zealand 4.4 / 2.4

Housework in the USA

Percentage of women
and men who undertake
each task on an average day

2015

● women
● men

	all household activities	housework	food preparation and clean-up	lawn and garden care	household management
women	85%	50%	70%	8%	21%
men	67%	22%	43%	12%	15%

- Liaising with school/nursery over everyday issues
- Liaising with school/nursery over trips
- Being the first person called if there's a problem at school/nursery
- Packing schoolbags
- Doing/supervising homework
- Arranging childcare
- Arranging applications for primary/secondary school
- Arranging play dates
- Taking children to clubs
- Organizing birthday parties
- Buying clothes
- Organizing Christmas
- Buying family presents/cards
- Managing doctor/dentist/optician appointments
- Looking after children at evenings and weekends
- Preparing activities for your partner to look after the children at evenings and weekends
- Reading bedtime stories
- Looking after poorly children
- Taking time off work to look after poorly children
- Settling children who wake in the night
- Organizing birthday presents for family members
- Booking holidays

"Mercy, it's the revolution and I'm in my bathrobe."

"Over the past ten years, men have increased their participation in household tasks... by six minutes."

Who does the laundry?
UK, 2014

Household chores for which men have primary responsibility:
- Putting out trash bins
- Do It Yourself (DIY) building/repair projects
- Changing lightbulbs

Household chores for which women have primary responsibility:
- Weekly clean
- Daily clean
- Vacuuming
- Cleaning kitchen/bathroom
- Heavy duty kitchen cleaning (oven/fridge)
- Tidying up
- Washing clothes
- Washing bedding
- Changing sheets
- Ironing
- Managing the family budget
- Organizing car insurance
- Organizing home insurance
- Organizing payment of utility bills, and...

Household decision-makers

Percentage of married women aged 15–49 who say they participate in decisions on major
household purchases – either making the decision by themselves or jointly with husband

most recent data since 2012

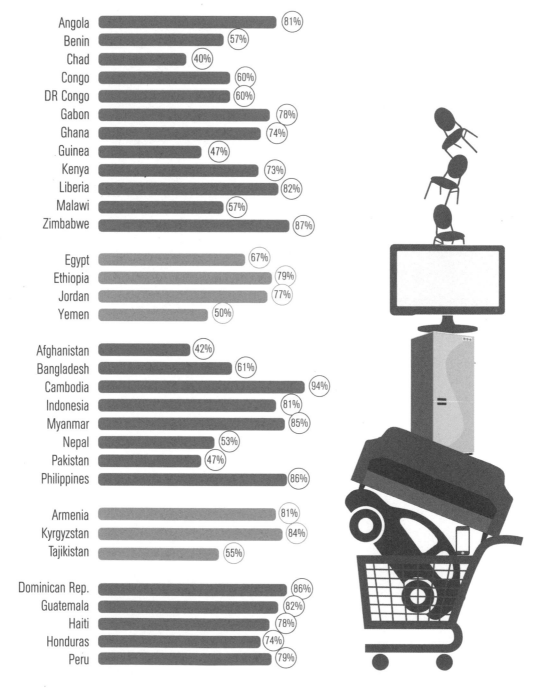

Country	%
Angola	81%
Benin	57%
Chad	40%
Congo	60%
DR Congo	60%
Gabon	78%
Ghana	74%
Guinea	47%
Kenya	73%
Liberia	82%
Malawi	57%
Zimbabwe	87%
Egypt	67%
Ethiopia	79%
Jordan	77%
Yemen	50%
Afghanistan	42%
Bangladesh	61%
Cambodia	94%
Indonesia	81%
Myanmar	85%
Nepal	53%
Pakistan	47%
Philippines	86%
Armenia	81%
Kyrgyzstan	84%
Tajikistan	55%
Dominican Rep.	86%
Guatemala	82%
Haiti	78%
Honduras	74%
Peru	79%

Child labor

Everywhere in the world, children provide free labor for households, girls more so than boys, and often for so many hours that they aren't able to participate in school, play, or paid economic activities. Household work is not counted in most official child labor statistics.

Each day, about 152 million children aged 5–17 are engaged in child labor; 42% are girls, 58% boys.

Most work on family farms or in family enterprises.

73 million of them are doing hazardous work such as working in mines or on fishing boats.

Not just a few chores

Girls aged 5–17 as a proportion of all children who perform housework, by hours per week
2016

50%
62%
65%
68%
70%

fewer than 14 hours | 14–20 | 21–27 | 27–42 | 43 hours and more

Lost childhoods

20% or more of girls aged 5–17 are engaged in child labor where known, 2010–16

KYRGYZSTAN
AFGHANISTAN
NEPAL
HAITI
MALI
NIGER
CHAD
SUDAN
YEMEN
GUINEA-BISSAU
GUINEA
SIERRA LEONE
LIBERIA
BURKINA FASO
COTE D'IVOIRE
GHANA
TOGO
BENIN
NIGERIA
CAMEROON
CAR
ETHIOPIA
SOMALIA
EQUATORIAL GUINEA
KENYA
DR CONGO
RWANDA
BURUNDI
SÃO TOME & PRINCIPE
TANZANIA
COMOROS
ANGOLA
ZAMBIA
MALAWI
MADAGASCAR
SOLOMON ISLANDS
BOLIVIA
PARAGUAY
MOZAMBIQUE
LESOTHO

Walking for water

Where water needs to be collected outside the home, the task falls mostly on the shoulders of women and girls. This is a physically arduous job, often dangerous as the search for water can take women into isolated areas, the water itself is often unclean and unsafe, and water collecting is a key contributor to "time poverty": the unpaid time spent collecting water deprives women and girls of opportunities to participate in other activities, whether schooling, paid work, or even just leisure.

Who is collecting water?
In Sub-Saharan African households without piped water
2006–09

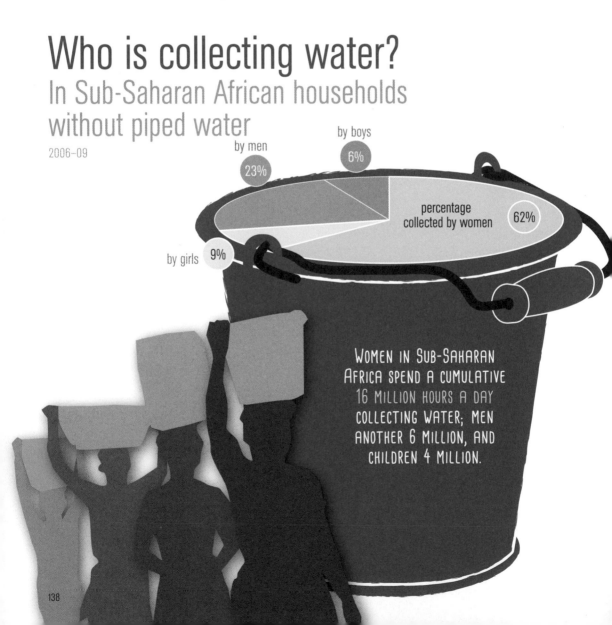

by men
23%

by boys
6%

percentage collected by women
62%

by girls 9%

WOMEN IN SUB-SAHARAN AFRICA SPEND A CUMULATIVE 16 MILLION HOURS A DAY COLLECTING WATER; MEN ANOTHER 6 MILLION, AND CHILDREN 4 MILLION.

Women in agriculture

The world's agricultural labor force is shrinking, year by year.

Worldwide, about 30% of women's "counted" economic activity is in agriculture, down from 41% in 2000. In the least developed countries, it's just over 60%.

The drop in the agricultural labor force reflects changes in the way food is produced. While small farms predominate in poorer countries, the global trend is towards mechanization and consolidation, with food increasingly produced by fewer people on larger farms – often working for transnational agricultural conglomerates.

Mechanization and consolidation produce a masculinization of farming, while women still constitute the majority of the agricultural labor force in small-scale and subsistence farming.

Cash and export crops are frequently regarded as "men's crops" and subsistence crops as "women's crops".

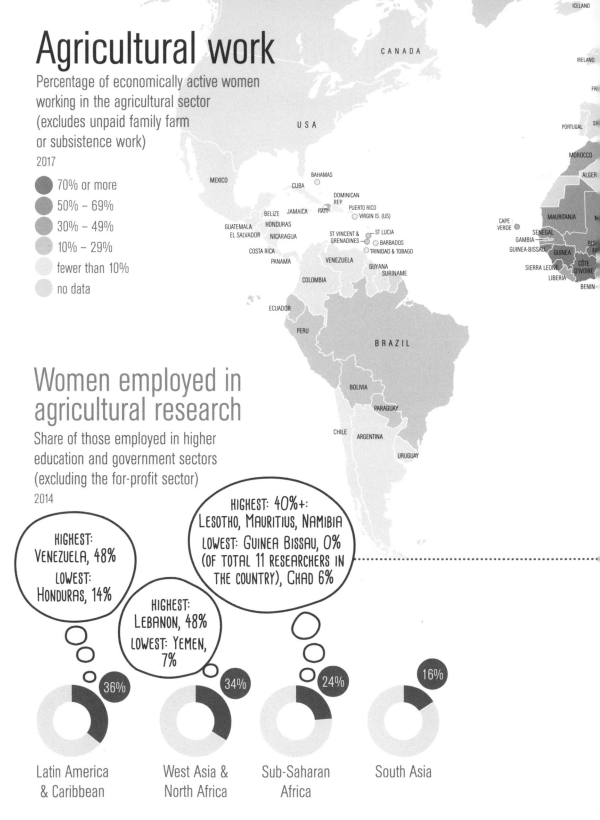

Agricultural work

Percentage of economically active women
working in the agricultural sector
(excludes unpaid family farm
or subsistence work)

2017

- 70% or more
- 50% – 69%
- 30% – 49%
- 10% – 29%
- fewer than 10%
- no data

Women employed in agricultural research

Share of those employed in higher
education and government sectors
(excluding the for-profit sector)

2014

HIGHEST:
VENEZUELA, 48%
LOWEST:
HONDURAS, 14%

HIGHEST: 40%+:
LESOTHO, MAURITIUS, NAMIBIA
LOWEST: GUINEA BISSAU, 0%
(OF TOTAL 11 RESEARCHERS IN
THE COUNTRY), CHAD 6%

HIGHEST:
LEBANON, 48%
LOWEST: YEMEN,
7%

36%
Latin America
& Caribbean

34%
West Asia &
North Africa

24%
Sub-Saharan
Africa

16%
South Asia

Agricultural extension services

In developing countries on average, women comprise **43%** of the agricultural labor force and account for an estimated two-thirds of the world's 600 million poor livestock keepers. Yet only **15%** of the world's extension agents are women, and only **5%** of women farmers benefit from extension services.

Farmers' access to extension workers

2015

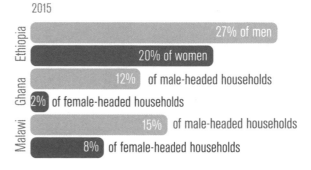

Ethiopia
- 27% of men
- 20% of women

Ghana
- 12% of male-headed households
- 2% of female-headed households

Malawi
- 15% of male-headed households
- 8% of female-headed households

Primary responsibility for farm tasks

Labor allocation and decision-making responsibility on farms vary widely over place and time, but almost always reflect prevailing cultural norms of femininity and masculinity.

Organic farming

Ontario, Canada
on heterosexual-couple farms
2007

mostly men
- equipment maintenance
- purchasing seeds & supplies
- manure management
- applying fertilizer
- mechanized field work
- planting

mostly women
- book-keeping

mostly joint
- care of livestock
- hand weeding & harvesting

Post-harvest rice production

Eastern Uganda
2016

mostly men
- harvesting, cutting & bundling
- beating to thresh rice
- checking rice for dryness
- bagging for storage
- decisions on harvesting technology

mostly women
- cooking food for harvesting laborers
- turning and 'scare-crowing' drying rice

mostly joint
- carrying rice to drying tarpaulins
- spreading rice in sun to dry
- winnowing
- decisions on winnowing technology

Coffee farming

Narino, Colombia
2015

mostly men
- pesticide application
- planting
- seed selection
- shade management
- stumping
- fertilizing
- harvesting
- sales

mostly women
there is no coffee-related activity that is primarily women's work
- raising livestock

mostly joint
- wet milling
- drying

Gendered pathways of pesticide exposure

Eastern Europe
2015

  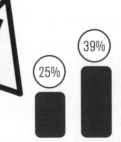 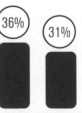

4% Belarus
15% Armenia
37% Georgia
56% Kyrgyzstan

Percentage of women farmers who handle pesticides directly

25% Belarus
39% Armenia
36% Georgia
31% Kyrgyzstan

Percentage of women farmers who do NOT handle pesticides directly, but who hand-wash pesticide-contaminated clothes

Capture fishing

Percentage of women in total fishing workforce,
including fishing and post-harvest jobs

global average, 2012

Capture fishing is male dominated,
but women make up **47%** of the
total global fisheries workforce
when all parts of the cycle are
counted. Women are more heavily
involved than men in post-
production activities such as
processing and selling fish.

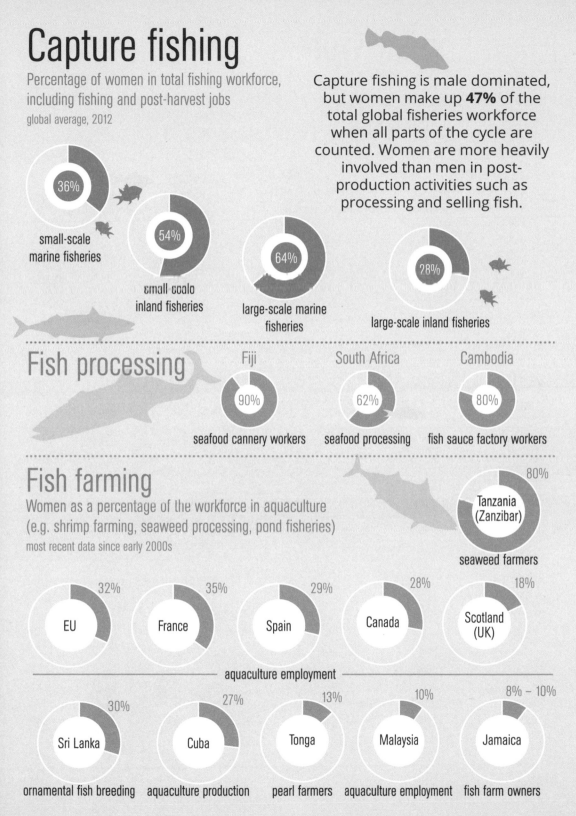

36%

small-scale
marine fisheries

54%

small-scale
inland fisheries

64%

large-scale marine
fisheries

28%

large-scale inland fisheries

Fish processing

Fiji

90%

seafood cannery workers

South Africa

62%

seafood processing

Cambodia

80%

fish sauce factory workers

Fish farming

Women as a percentage of the workforce in aquaculture
(e.g. shrimp farming, seaweed processing, pond fisheries)

most recent data since early 2000s

80%
Tanzania
(Zanzibar)

seaweed farmers

32%
EU

35%
France

29%
Spain

28%
Canada

18%
Scotland
(UK)

—————————————— aquaculture employment ——————————————

30%
Sri Lanka

27%
Cuba

13%
Tonga

10%
Malaysia

8% – 10%
Jamaica

ornamental fish breeding | aquaculture production | pearl farmers | aquaculture employment | fish farm owners

Migrating for work

In 2015 about **3%** of the global population was on the move, most crossing international borders.

48% of all international migrants are women, many looking for new economic opportunities.

NURSES

Shortages of nurses in rich countries are fueling new flows of women migrants. International recruiters are actively seeking nurses from poor countries, especially in Africa, Asia, and the Caribbean. In many cases, this is producing an acute health-provider shortage in those countries.

17,000 to 22,000 health professionals leave the Philippines to work abroad every year, most of them nurses. In 2010, 12,100 nurses from the Philippines, 85% women, were newly hired overseas. They went to: ▶

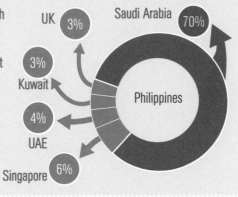

UK 3%
Saudi Arabia 70%
3%
Kuwait
4%
UAE
Singapore 6%
Philippines

Main countries sending and receiving nurses

SENDING		RECEIVING			BOTH
Philippines	Zimbabwe	Australia	Switzerland	UAE	Ireland
Guyana	Uganda	New Zealand	USA	Oman	Spain
Jamaica	Poland	UK	Canada	Bahrain	
China	Lithuania	Germany	Israel	Qatar	
India		Norway	Saudi Arabia	Singapore	
		Netherlands	Kuwait	Brunei	
		Belgium	Libya		

IN THE USA IN 2015, OF THE FOREIGN-BORN WOMEN WHO WERE EMPLOYED IN HEALTH-CARE OCCUPATIONS, MOST WERE WORKING AS NURSING, PSYCHIATRIC, OR HOME HEALTH AIDES (28%), OR AS REGISTERED NURSES (27%). IN CONTRAST, THEIR MALE COUNTERPARTS WERE MOST LIKELY TO WORK AS PHYSICIANS AND SURGEONS (30%), OR AS TECHNOLOGISTS AND TECHNICIANS (20%).

IN 2017, 15% OF NURSES IN THE UK WERE INTERNATIONAL MIGRANTS: 7% CAME FROM OTHER EU COUNTRIES, THE LARGEST SHARES FROM IRELAND, PORTUGAL, AND SPAIN; ANOTHER 8% CAME FROM COUNTRIES OUTSIDE THE EU, THE LARGEST SHARE FROM INDIA, THE PHILIPPINES, AND ZIMBABWE.

Percentage of foreign-born nurses
2010–11

Switzerland 29%
Australia 25%
New Zealand 23%
Canada 17%
USA 14%

Domestic work

There are 11.5 million migrant domestic workers in the world: nannies, cleaners, and in-home health-care workers. About 73% of them are women.

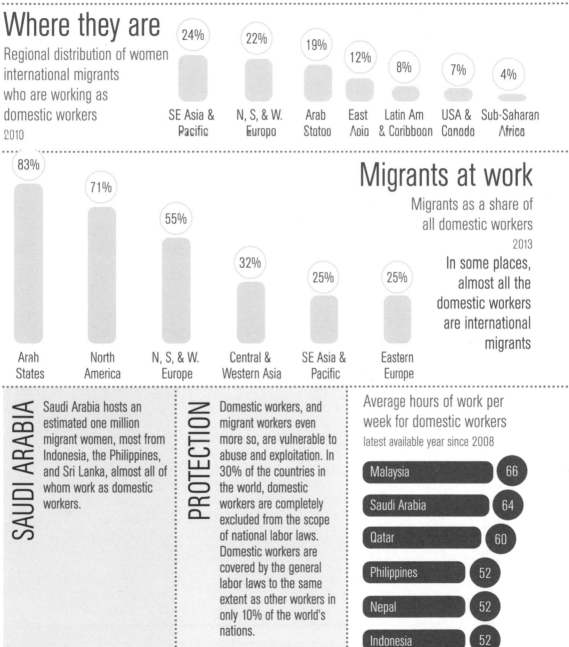

Where they are

Regional distribution of women international migrants who are working as domestic workers
2010

24%	22%	19%	12%	8%	7%	4%
SE Asia & Pacific	N, S, & W. Europe	Arab States	East Asia	Latin Am & Caribbean	USA & Canada	Sub-Saharan Africa

Migrants at work

Migrants as a share of all domestic workers
2013

In some places, almost all the domestic workers are international migrants

83%	71%	55%	32%	25%	25%
Arab States	North America	N, S, & W. Europe	Central & Western Asia	SE Asia & Pacific	Eastern Europe

SAUDI ARABIA

Saudi Arabia hosts an estimated one million migrant women, most from Indonesia, the Philippines, and Sri Lanka, almost all of whom work as domestic workers.

PROTECTION

Domestic workers, and migrant workers even more so, are vulnerable to abuse and exploitation. In 30% of the countries in the world, domestic workers are completely excluded from the scope of national labor laws. Domestic workers are covered by the general labor laws to the same extent as other workers in only 10% of the world's nations.

Average hours of work per week for domestic workers
latest available year since 2008

Malaysia	66
Saudi Arabia	64
Qatar	60
Philippines	52
Nepal	52
Indonesia	52

Education and connectivity

> **"** I said to myself, 'Malala, be brave. You must not be afraid of anyone. You are only trying to get an education. You are not committing a crime.' **"**

Malala Yousafzai

In Pakistan in 2012, a 15-year old schoolgirl was shot in the head by Taliban gunmen. They were trying to silence Malala Yousafzai because she had become an outspoken and highly visible advocate for girls' rights to education. And in attempting to kill her, they were trying to intimidate all girls. She survived and prevailed, becoming a global advocate for girls' education and the youngest Nobel Peace Prize laureate.

Average years of schooling

Attained by women, aged 25+
2010

- 10 – 13
- 7 – 9
- 4 – 6
- fewer than 4
- no data

<1 less than one year of schooling

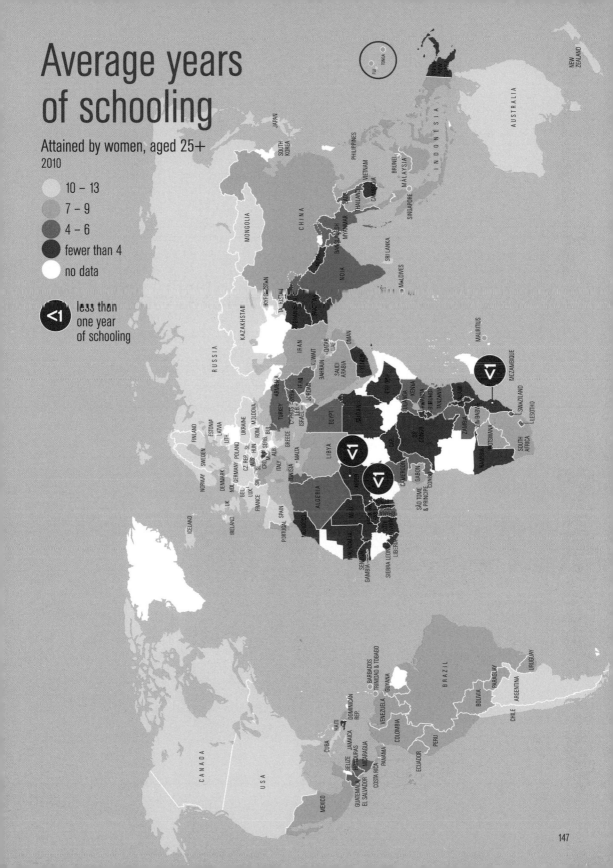

NEW ZEALAND

AUSTRALIA

FIJI   TONGA

JAPAN

SOUTH KOREA

PHILIPPINES

VIETNAM

BRUNEI

MALAYSIA

I N D O N E S I A

SINGAPORE

CAMBODIA

THAILAND

LAOS

MYANMAR

SRI LANKA

MALDIVES

CHINA

MONGOLIA

BANGLADESH

INDIA

NEPAL

BHUTAN

PAKISTAN

KYRGYZSTAN

TAJIKISTAN

AFGHANISTAN

KAZAKHSTAN

RUSSIA

MAURITIUS

MOZAMBIQUE

TANZANIA

SWAZILAND

LESOTHO

SOUTH AFRICA

BOTSWANA

ZIMBABWE

ZAMBIA

MALAWI

BURUNDI

KENYA

TANZANIA

UGANDA

SOMALIA

ETHIOPIA

SUDAN

CHAD

CONGO

GABON

CAMEROON

SÃO TOMÉ & PRINCIPE

IRAN

OMAN

QATAR
UAE

KUWAIT

BAHRAIN

SAUDI ARABIA

IRAQ

JORDAN

EGYPT

LIBYA

ARMENIA

TURKEY

SYRIA
LEB.
ISRAEL

CYPRUS

GREECE

MALTA

ITALY

ALB.

TUNISIA

ALGERIA

MOROCCO

MAURITANIA

SENEGAL

GAMBIA

SIERRA LEONE

LIB-RIA

FINLAND

NORWAY

SWEDEN

DENMARK

ESTONIA

LATVIA

LITH.

BEL.

NDL.

GERMANY

POLAND

CZ. REF.

AUS.

HUN.

SL.

CRO.

SERB.

BUL.

ROM.

MOLDOVA

UKRAINE

UK

IRELAND

ICELAND

FRANCE

SW.

LUX.

PORTUGAL

SPAIN

CANADA

USA

MEXICO

CUBA

HAITI

DOMINICAN REP.

JAMAICA

BELIZE

HONDURAS

GUATEMALA

EL SALVADOR

NICARAGUA

COSTA RICA

PANAMA

BARBADOS

TRINIDAD & TOBAGO

GUYANA

VENEZUELA

COLOMBIA

ECUADOR

PERU

BRAZIL

BOLIVIA

PARAGUAY

URUGUAY

ARGENTINA

CHILE

147

Not making the grade
Low primary school completion rates for girls

2015, where known
completion rates below 75%

● 50% – 75%

● fewer than 50%

More girls are in primary school than ever before, but in many countries even basic education is beyond reach. Globally, proportionally fewer girls than boys are enrolled in school in the first place, and they are removed at an earlier age. If hardship strikes or intensifies – war, deepening poverty, declining donor assistance – girls will be pulled from school first as families or governments make cuts. Further, girls often leave school at puberty if adequate sanitation facilities are not provided for them.

SYRIA
LEBANON
AFGHANISTAN
PAKISTAN
MAURITANIA
MALI
NIGER
SENEGAL
GAMBIA
BURKINA FASO
CHAD
SUDAN
ERITREA
YEMEN
DJIBOUTI
GUINEA
SIERRA LEONE
LIBERIA
BENIN
CÔTE D'IVOIRE
EQUATORIAL GUINEA
CAMEROON
CAR
SOUTH SUDAN
ETHIOPIA
DR CONGO
UGANDA
RWANDA
BURUNDI
PAPUA NEW GUINEA
MADAGASCAR
MOZAMBIQUE

Gender gaps in primary school completion

selected examples, 2015

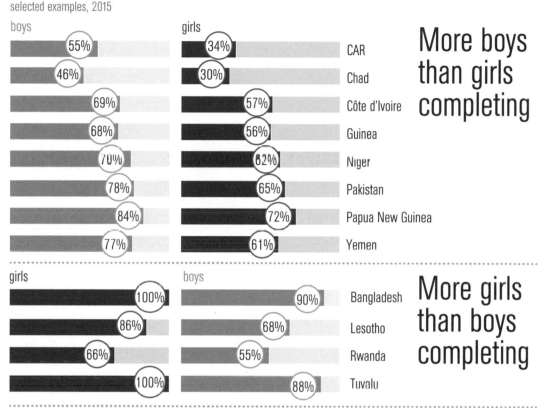

boys | girls

55%	34%	CAR
46%	30%	Chad
69%	57%	Côte d'Ivoire
68%	56%	Guinea
70%	62%	Niger
78%	65%	Pakistan
84%	72%	Papua New Guinea
77%	61%	Yemen

More boys than girls completing

girls | boys

100%	90%	Bangladesh
86%	68%	Lesotho
66%	55%	Rwanda
100%	88%	Tuvalu

More girls than boys completing

Income and school completion

Percentage of children completing primary school from the richest and poorest income quintiles (richest 20% and poorest 20% of population)

selected examples, most recent data since 2011

	richest	poorest		richest	poorest		richest	poorest
Afghanistan	69%	21%	Dominican Rep	98%	74%	Laos	97%	28%
Bangladesh	89%	62%	Ethiopia	73%	20%	Nepal	92%	68%
Bhutan	90%	43%	Guinea	72%	12%	Nigeria	96%	21%
Cambodia	90%	48%	Honduras	98%	61%	South Sudan	44%	7%
Cameroon	91%	18%	Kenya	94%	58%	Tanzania	92%	51%

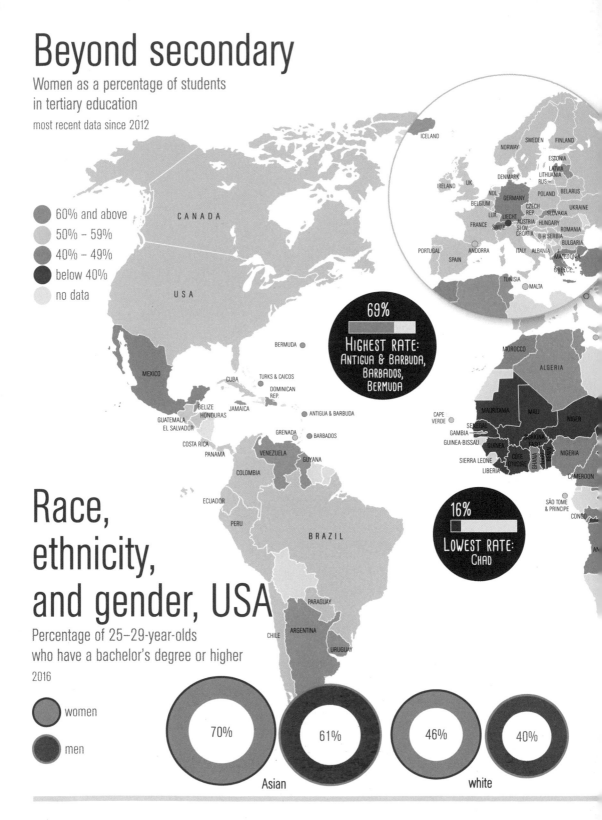

Beyond secondary

Women as a percentage of students
in tertiary education

most recent data since 2012

- 60% and above
- 50% – 59%
- 40% – 49%
- below 40%
- no data

69%
HIGHEST RATE:
ANTIGUA & BARBUDA,
BARBADOS,
BERMUDA

16%
LOWEST RATE:
CHAD

Race,
ethnicity,
and gender, USA

Percentage of 25–29-year-olds
who have a bachelor's degree or higher

2016

- women
- men

| 70% | 61% | 46% | 40% |
| Asian | | white | |

RUSSIA

KAZAKHSTAN

MONGOLIA

KYRGYZSTAN

UZBEKISTAN

TURKMENISTAN

NORTH KOREA

JAPAN

SOUTH KOREA

CHINA

GEORGIA

ARMENIA   AZER.

TURKEY

CYPRUS

LEB.

SYRIA

ISRAEL

PALESTINE

JORDAN

IRAN

AFGHANISTAN

KUWAIT

BAHRAIN

QATAR

UAE

OMAN

SAUDI
ARABIA

EGYPT

SUDAN

PAKISTAN

NEPAL

BHUTAN

INDIA

BANGLADESH

MARSHALL ISLANDS

ERITREA

YEMEN

DJIBOUTI

LAOS

THAILAND

VIETNAM

PHILIPPINES

ETHIOPIA

CAMBODIA

SRI LANKA

COOK
ISLANDS

MALDIVES

BRUNEI

UGANDA

MALAYSIA

SINGAPORE

DR
CONGO

RWANDA

BURUNDI

TANZANIA

SEYCHELLES

I N D O N E S I A

COMOROS

TIMOR-LESTE

ZAMBIA   MALAWI

MADAGASCAR

MAURITIUS

ZIMBABWE

BOTSWANA

MOZAMBIQUE

AUSTRALIA

SOUTH
AFRICA

SWAZILAND

LESOTHO

NEW
ZEALAND

25%	20%	22%	16%	12%	8%
Black		Hispanic		American Indian/Alaska Native	

Progress by degrees

When women were allowed admission to undergraduate degree-awarding programs in universities on an equal basis with men

At some universities, affiliated women's colleges admitted women earlier but the degrees were not issued (nor, in some cases, recognized) by the primary university until the dates shown

selected examples

	Year university opened (to men)	When women admitted
University of Melbourne (Australia)	1853	1881
University of Toronto (Canada)	1843	1884
Heidelberg University (Germany)	1385	1900
Oxford University (UK)	1167	1920
Cairo University (Egypt)	1908	1928
Makerere University (Uganda)	1922	1945
University of Tokyo (Japan)	1877	1946
Cambridge University (UK)	1209	1948
Yale College (USA)	1701	1969
Brown University (USA)	1764	1971
Dartmouth College (USA)	1769	1972
Harvard University (USA)	1636	1977

Higher education

The history of higher education, until recently, has been one of female exclusion. In the most elite universities, hundreds of years elapsed between their founding as men's clubs and when they – often over fierce opposition – admitted women.

From this inauspicious start, **one of the most remarkable changes in global education patterns is the current shift to the "feminization" of higher education.** In the 1990s, more men than women attended post-secondary education, almost universally.

By the early 2000s, in most of the world, the gender disparity in higher education had shifted: more women than men now participate in tertiary education, in many countries by a considerable margin. While this tilt to feminization is found in most of the world, it is still not the case in many countries in Sub-Saharan Africa and Southern Asia.

Various explanations for this shift have been offered: as a general rule, men perform less well in exams and other success measures in secondary schooling, which may discourage them from enrolling in tertiary institutions; having greater economic opportunities than their female counterparts, men may see advantages in joining the waged workforce without the delay of tertiary education; as higher education becomes more associated with women, men may be even more deterred.

The shift to female advantage in tertiary enrollments emerged at the same time as tertiary education opportunities started to expand overall.

#JUST SAYIN'

In most countries, higher education is still a preserve of the elite.

520 million women can't read this

Illiteracy rates of 50% or more for women aged 15+

most recent data, 2013–15

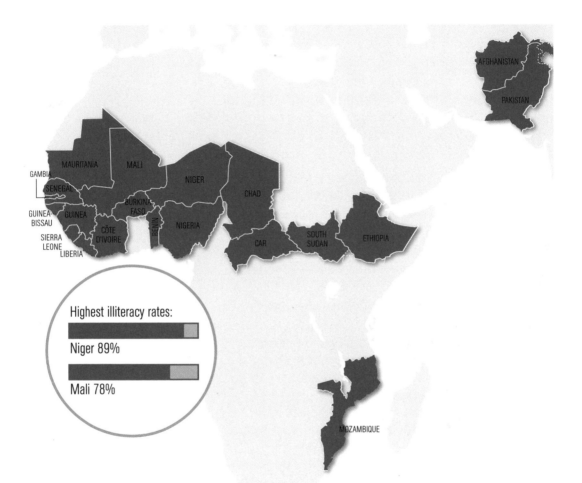

AFGHANISTAN

PAKISTAN

MAURITANIA

MALI

GAMBIA

SENEGAL

NIGER

CHAD

GUINEA-
BISSAU

GUINEA

BURKINA
FASO

BENIN

NIGERIA

CÔTE
D'IVOIRE

SIERRA
LEONE

LIBERIA

CAR

SOUTH
SUDAN

ETHIOPIA

MOZAMBIQUE

Highest illiteracy rates:

Niger 89%

Mali 78%

Improvements in literacy have shifted the map in the last two decades. Still, about **780 million adults in the world remain illiterate. Nearly two-thirds of them are women**, a proportion that has remained unchanged for two decades. In 2015, 20 countries reported an illiteracy rate for women of 50% or more; for men, 8 countries.

Generalized illiteracy is mostly a function of poverty and limited educational opportunity, but higher rates for women suggest entrenched gender discrimination. Gender-specific contributory factors include: the time overburdening of women, especially in rural areas (see page 134); the restriction of girls and women to the domestic sphere; and resistance from men who fear losing their domestic power if women become literate. Literacy improves women's economic wellbeing, deceases their dependency on men, and increases their ability to control or understand their own property, wealth, health, and legal rights. The good news is that illiteracy rates have been steadily declining over the past three decades, largely as the result of efforts to increase basic educational opportunities for girls.

Looking good

Percentage of adult women who are literate

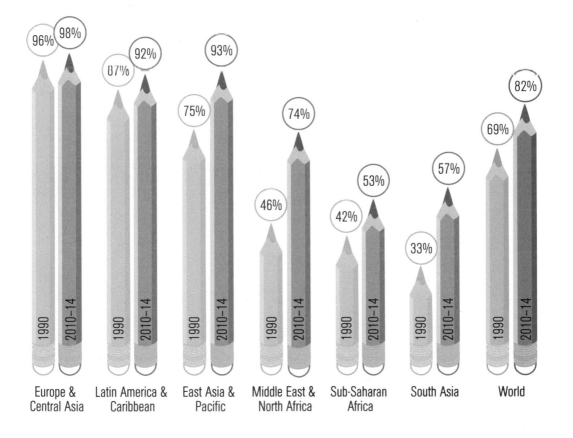

	1990	2010–14
Europe & Central Asia	96%	98%
Latin America & Caribbean	87%	92%
East Asia & Pacific	75%	93%
Middle East & North Africa	46%	74%
Sub-Saharan Africa	42%	53%
South Asia	33%	57%
World	69%	82%

Big leaps forward

Percentage of adult women who are literate

selected examples

1988–91 ⭐ 2010–15

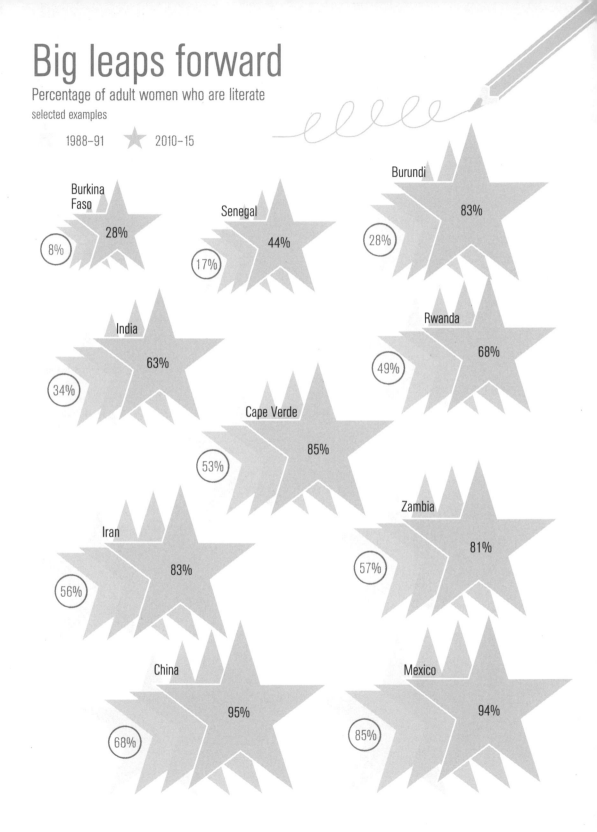

Burkina Faso
28%
8%

Senegal
44%
17%

Burundi
83%
28%

India
63%
34%

Rwanda
68%
49%

Cape Verde
85%
53%

Iran
83%
56%

Zambia
81%
57%

China
95%
68%

Mexico
94%
85%

Functional illiteracy

Illiteracy in the USA

Percentage of adults aged 16–65
scoring very low levels of literacy

2014

THE USA, LIKE
MOST RICH COUNTRIES,
OFFICIALLY REPORTS NEAR-ZERO
RATES OF ILLITERACY TO
INTERNATIONAL DATA
COLLECTION AGENCIES.

19%

10%

35%

43%

18%

19%

overall   white   Black   Hispanic   women   men

#JUST SAYIN'

About 36 million adults in the USA
cannot read, write, or do basic math
above a third grade level.

Illiteracy internationally

Percentages of women and men with low literacy skills

selected OECD countries, 2014

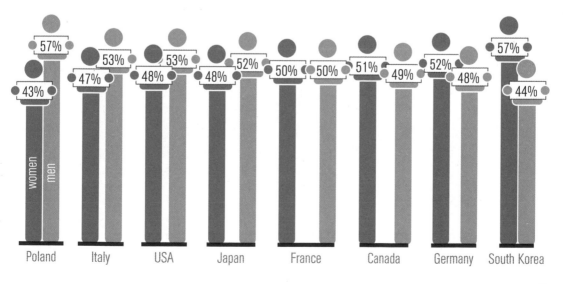

	women	men
Poland	43%	57%
Italy	47%	53%
USA	48%	53%
Japan	48%	52%
France	50%	50%
Canada	51%	49%
Germany	52%	48%
South Korea	57%	44%

When computers were women

In the late 1950s, American **Grace Hopper** was one of the first programmers in modern computing, leading the team that invented **COBOL**. Her principle that programming languages should be as easily understood as English influenced the development of "if/then" programming architecture, instead of 1s and 0s. In 1969, Hopper was awarded the inaugural Data Processing Management Association **"Man of the Year"** award.

Austrian **Hedy Lamarr**, while known primarily as an actress, was also a computer inventor. In the 1940s, to help the Allied war effort, she invented a frequency-hopping system that was the precursor of many contemporary wireless technologies including Bluetooth, GPS, and cellphone networks.

The ENIAC 6: In 1946, 6 women programmed the first all-electronic, programmable computer, the ENIAC, in a secret World War II project run by the US Army in Philadelphia. They learned to program without programming languages or tools (none existed) – only logical diagrams. When the ENIAC was unveiled to the press and the public in 1946, the women were never mentioned.

Hidden figures:

Starting in World War II, women mathematicians, many African-American, were the **"hidden figures"** that calculated flight trajectories and developed critical algorithms for the American NASA space program. They were among the earliest FORTRAN programmers and managers as the space program shifted computing to machines.

Mathematician **Ada Lovelace** (1815–52) is often credited as the world's first computer programmer, developing the algorithms and instructions for Charles Babbage's computing machine. His machine was never built.

Boys' own world

Percentage of computer science bachelor's degrees
conferred on women, USA

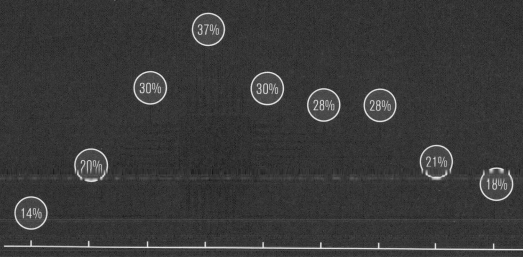

In the USA, modern computer science is dominated by men. But it hasn't always been this way. In addition to the women who were computer pioneers, for several decades the number of women studying computer science was growing faster than the number of men. But in 1984, that changed.

The share of women in computer science started falling at roughly the same time that personal computers started showing up in American homes in significant numbers. These early personal computers weren't much more than toys – marketed almost entirely to men and boys. Computers entered the category of "boys' toys". Having access to and familiarity with these machines gave boys an advantage in entry-level programming classes.

BUT!

NOT IN INDIA, WHERE WOMEN
CONSTITUTED 42% OF
UNDERGRADUATE STUDENTS
IN COMPUTER SCIENCE AND
COMPUTER ENGINEERING
IN 2011.

Percentage of households with a computer

2017

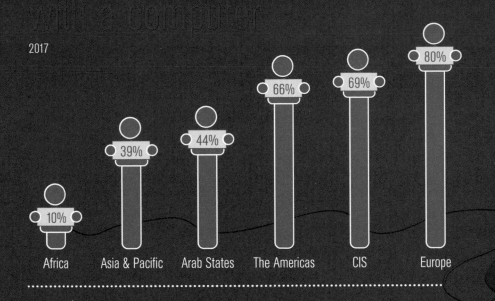

Africa	Asia & Pacific	Arab States	The Americas	CIS	Europe
10%	39%	44%	66%	69%	80%

Percentage of American households with a desktop or laptop computer

most recent data since 2015

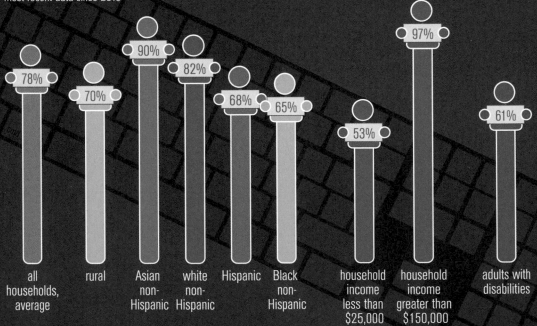

all households, average	rural	Asian non-Hispanic	white non-Hispanic	Hispanic	Black non-Hispanic	household income less than $25,000	household income greater than $150,000	adults with disabilities
78%	70%	90%	82%	68%	65%	53%	97%	61%

Gender divide by country

Percentage using the internet, most recent data since 2015

- ● women
- ● men

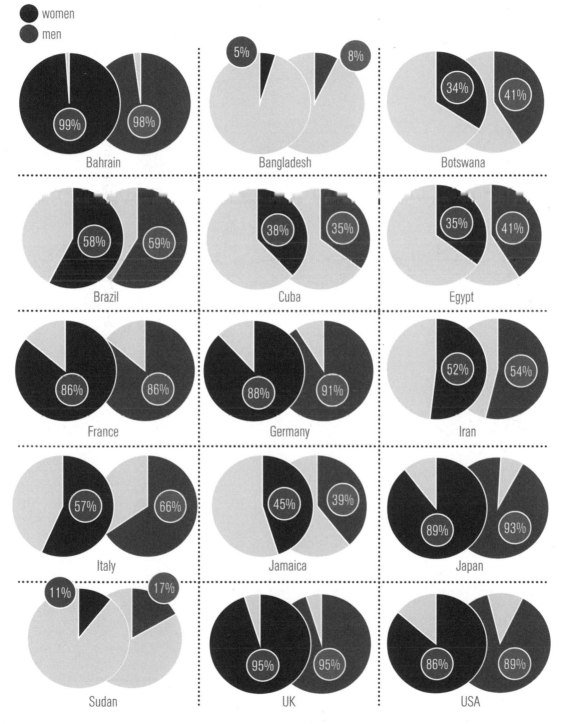

Bahrain — 99% / 98%

Bangladesh — 5% / 8%

Botswana — 34% / 41%

Brazil — 58% / 59%

Cuba — 38% / 35%

Egypt — 35% / 41%

France — 86% / 86%

Germany — 88% / 91%

Iran — 52% / 54%

Italy — 57% / 66%

Jamaica — 45% / 39%

Japan — 89% / 93%

Sudan — 11% / 17%

UK — 95% / 95%

USA — 86% / 89%

Digital divide

Percentage of internet users

2016

- 50% or more
- less than 50%

Gender divide by region

Percentage using the internet

2017

- men
- women

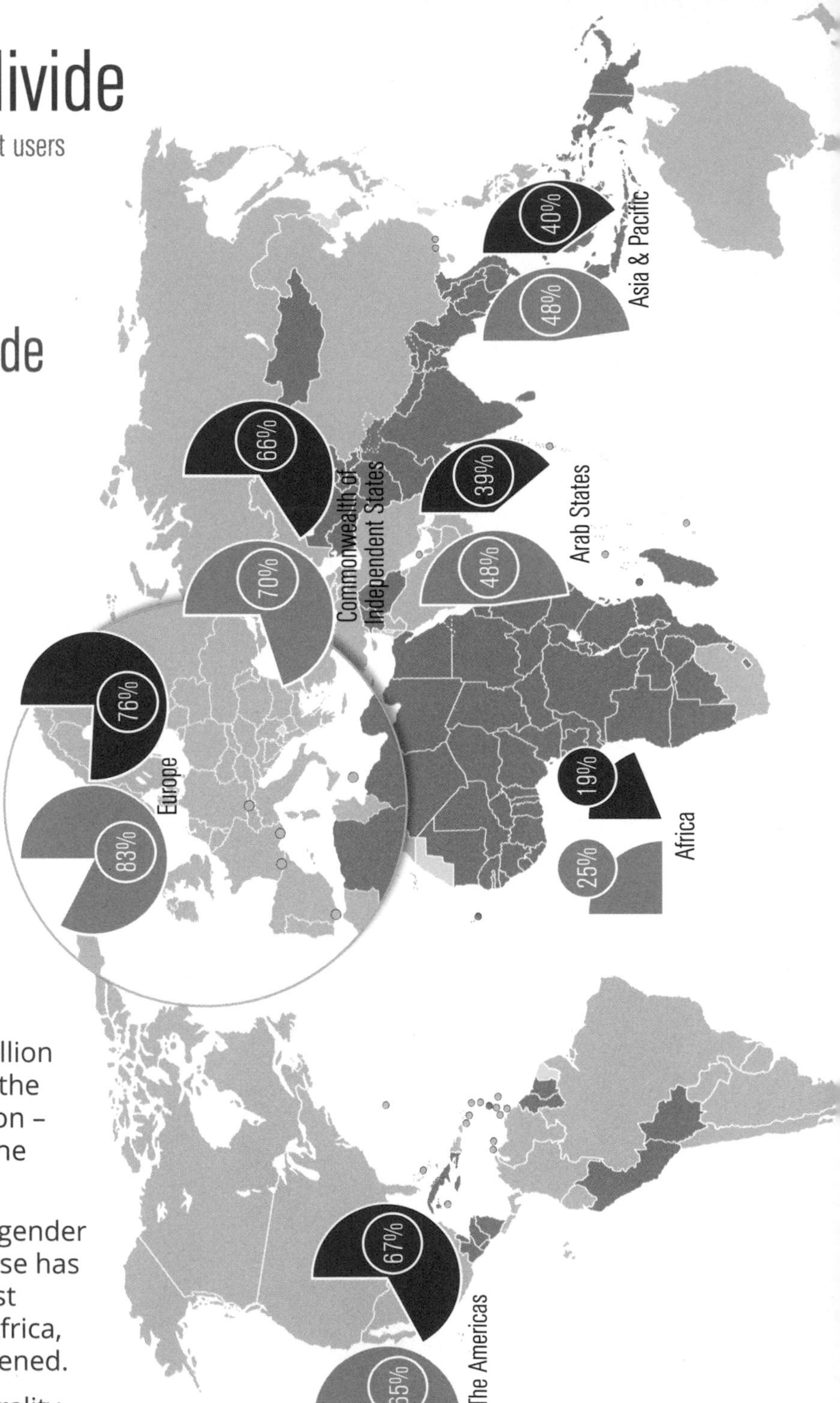

Asia & Pacific

40%

48%

Commonwealth of Independent States

66%

70%

Arab States

39%

48%

Europe

76%

83%

Africa

19%

25%

The Americas

67%

65%

Late 2016: 3.9 billion people – 53% of the world's population – were not using the internet.

Since 2013: The gender gap in internet use has narrowed in most regions except Africa, where it has widened.

Overall, class, rurality, education, and gender shape access.

Keeping up
with the news

Adult internet users who used
the internet to get political news
in the previous year

2014

women ●
men ●

	0	20	40	60	80	100
Brazil						
China						
Colombia						
El Salvador						
Indonesia						
Malaysia						
Nigeria						
Peru						
Poland						
Ukraine						
Venezuela						
Vietnam						

Keeping up
with health

More women than men use the
internet for health information

2013–15

women ●
men ●

	0	20	40	60	80	100
Bangladesh						
Brazil						
Colombia						
France						
Germany						
Japan						
S. Korea						
Morocco						
Poland						
Qatar						
Ukraine						
UK						

Women and social media

Online activism can support and catalyze social action. Social media facilitates trans-community and transnational feminist solidarity.

Women's online organizing can help movements leap beyond the local. Overall, almost everywhere in the world, women are more active social media users than men.

MEXICO

In 2016, tens of thousands of women gathered in Mexico City and across the country to protest a rising wave of femicides and sexual harassment. The march was the culmination of weeks of social media activism, with several hashtags emerging to draw attention to sexual harassment and assault. #NoEsNo #primaveravioleta

POLAND

In October 2016, Polish women organized a nation-wide strike and protest to oppose proposed legislation that would have made abortion almost entirely illegal. "Black Monday" brought tens of thousands of women to the streets across Poland and in solidarity marches across Europe. #czarnyprotest #BlackMonday

HAWAII

The January 2017 Women's Marches that brought millions of women into the streets around the world started with a Facebook post. The night that Donald Trump putatively won the US Presidential election in November 2016, a Hawaiian woman, Teresa Shook, posted a Facebook plea for a women's rights march. Within hours, organizing was underway. #womensmarch

BRAZIL

In October 2015, more than 50,000 Black women from across Brazil converged on the capital to rally against racism, sexism, and genocide. #MarchaDasMulheresNegras

EGYPT, JORDAN, NEPAL

HarassMap is a crowd-sourced web platform in Egypt to report and map sexual harassment and interventions; in Jordan it's 7arkashat; in Nepal, FightVAWG.

#Online harassment

... On the other hand, the web can be a dangerous place. Digital tools and online platforms provide new ways and outlets for harassment, bullying, threats, stalking, trafficking, racism, homophobia, and toxic misogyny. Troll attacks on women are fierce and unrelenting.

Attitudes toward online harassment

USA, 2017

women   men

70%   54%

Online harassment is a "major problem"

21% OF WOMEN, AGED 18–29, SAY THEY HAVE EXPERIENCED ONLINE SEXUAL HARASSMENT; 53% HAVE BEEN SENT EXPLICIT IMAGES THEY DIDN'T ASK FOR.

women   men

49%   64%

Offensive content online is taken too seriously

women   men

50%   35%

Offensive content online is too often excused as no big deal

women   men

36%   56%

It is more important for people to be able to speak their minds freely online

women   men

63%   43%

It is more important for people to feel welcome and safe online

#JUST SAYIN'

2016: 74% of Twitter's leadership and 73% of Facebook's senior leadership were men.

2017: 75% of Google's leadership were men.

The myth of the connected world

Low- and middle-income regions
2015

- ⬤ percentage of women who do **not** own a mobile phone
- ⬤ gender gap: how much less likely a woman is to own a mobile phone than a man

IN 2015, 52% OF MEN AND 59% OF WOMEN IN LOW- AND MIDDLE-INCOME COUNTRIES DID NOT OWN A MOBILE PHONE.

Europe & Central Asia
42% 4%

East Asia & Pacific
54% 3%

Middle East & North Africa
48% 8%

64% 13%

South Asia
72% 38%

49% 5%

Latin America & Caribbean

Sub-Saharan Africa

For some women, the gap is bigger still

The gap between women and men in access to mobile phones, by wealth and education
2015

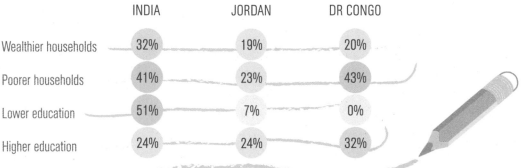

	INDIA	JORDAN	DR CONGO
Wealthier households	32%	19%	20%
Poorer households	41%	23%	43%
Lower education	51%	7%	0%
Higher education	24%	24%	32%

Closing the gap
Latin America & the Caribbean

Percentage using a mobile phone

2016

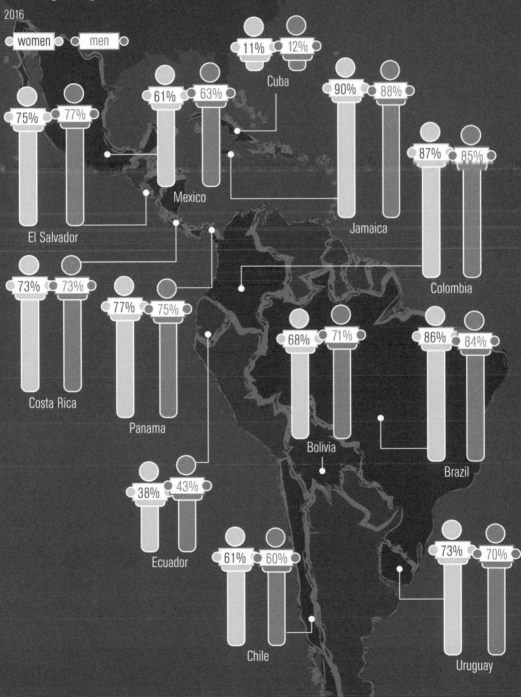

women   men

El Salvador
women 75% men 77%

Mexico
women 61% men 63%

Cuba
women 11% men 12%

Jamaica
women 90% men 88%

Colombia
women 87% men 85%

Costa Rica
women 73% men 73%

Panama
women 77% men 75%

Bolivia
women 68% men 71%

Brazil
women 86% men 84%

Ecuador
women 38% men 43%

Chile
women 61% men 60%

Uruguay
women 73% men 70%

Can't afford it

Percentage who say that cost of the handset is a barrier to owning and using mobile phones, 2015

Jordan	Colombia	Mexico	Niger	India	Kenya	DR Congo	Indonesia
76%	66%	66%	57%	50%	50%	44%	40%

Harassment goes mobile

Percentage of women reporting that fear of phone harassment from strangers is an impediment to owning or using a phone, 2015

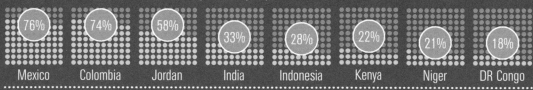

Mexico	Colombia	Jordan	India	Indonesia	Kenya	Niger	DR Congo
76%	74%	58%	33%	28%	22%	21%	18%

Mobile autonomy

Percentage of women who say that owning a phone makes them feel more autonomous or independent, 2015

Jordan	Indonesia	Kenya	Colombia	India	Mexico	DR Congo	Niger
89%	80%	78%	78%	74%	74%	71%	69%

Families disapprove

Percentage of women reporting that their families are or would be uncomfortable with them using a mobile phone, 2015

> IN INDIA, 114 MILLION MORE MEN THAN WOMEN HAVE CELLPHONES, EXACERBATING AN ALREADY DEEP GENDER INEQUALITY. SEVERAL VILLAGE COUNCILS IN GUJARAT AND UTTAR PRADESH HAVE ISSUED DECREES BANNING UNMARRIED WOMEN FROM USING CELLPHONES.

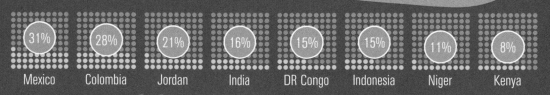

Mexico	Colombia	Jordan	India	DR Congo	Indonesia	Niger	Kenya
31%	28%	21%	16%	15%	15%	11%	8%

" Mobile phones are really dangerous for women. Girls are more susceptible to bringing shame upon themselves. " Male village elder in Gujarat, India, 2016

Property and poverty

Global economic inequality is intertwined with gender inequality.

In most of the world's countries, women either don't have equal rights under the law to own and control property, or their legal rights are trumped by customary practices that keep tangible assets out of their hands. Globalization has tended to deepen property disadvantage as access to communal or household-based land has been displaced by the cash economy.

The World Economic Forum estimates that at current pace the gender gap in economic participation and opportunity will not be closed for another 217 years.

This conclusion doesn't only reflect women's position in the workforce. A significant driver of the gender gap in economic disadvantage is women's limited control of assets, property, and financial reserves.

Economic inequality defines this decade. In 2017, the wealthiest top 10% of adults in the world owned 88% of all global assets; the top 1% owned half of all global assets. Of the 1,810 billionaires on the 2016 Forbes World Billionaires list, 89% are men.

These billionaires together own as much wealth as the bottom 70% of humanity. That they are men is neither incidental nor inconsequential.

Property

Women's rights to own, use, and control land

As delineated in 116 developing countries, 2014

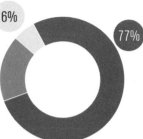

law does not guarantee equal rights **6%**

77% equal rights in law, but prevailing customary laws and traditional practices typically inhibit these rights

17%

equal rights in both law and practice

Ownership of "household owned" land in Africa

most recent data since 2010

- solely men-owned
- solely women-owned
- owned jointly

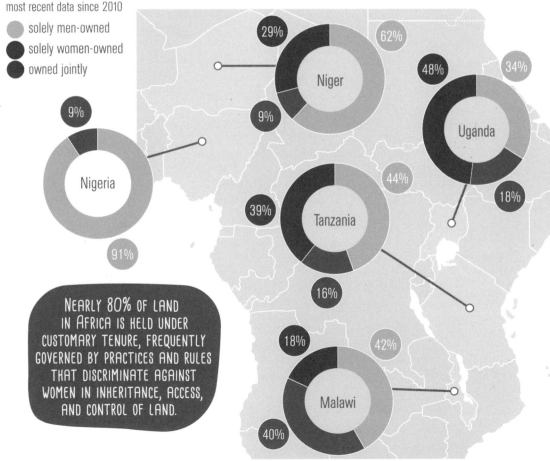

29% Niger **62%**

48% Uganda **34%**

9%

9%

39% Tanzania **44%**

Nigeria

18%

16%

91%

18% **42%**

Malawi

40%

NEARLY 80% OF LAND IN AFRICA IS HELD UNDER CUSTOMARY TENURE, FREQUENTLY GOVERNED BY PRACTICES AND RULES THAT DISCRIMINATE AGAINST WOMEN IN INHERITANCE, ACCESS, AND CONTROL OF LAND.

Women as a proportion of agricultural landholders

In rich countries, most recent since 2010

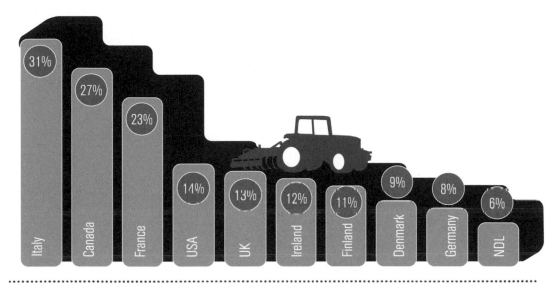

Italy	Canada	France	USA	UK	Ireland	Finland	Denmark	Germany	NDL
31%	27%	23%	14%	13%	12%	11%	9%	8%	6%

Home ownership in the USA

2017

US average: 64%

50%
female single person households

47%
male single person households

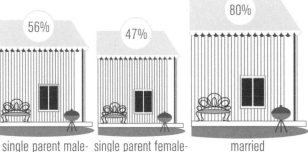
56%
single parent male-headed households

47%
single parent female-headed households

80%
married couple families

72%
white non-Hispanic

57%
Asian/Hawaiian/Pacific Islander

53%
American Indian/Alaska Native

47%
Hispanic

43%
Black, non-Hispanic

Inheritance

The legal system in more than 35 countries does not give women the same inheritance rights as men when their spouses die, nor girl children the same rights of inheritance from parents as boys.

In dozens more countries, by traditional practice and customary law women and girls are often pressured to give up their inheritance in favor of a male relative.

Not in line
as of 2016

women and girls do not have the same inheritance rights as men and boys

MOROCCO
TUNISIA
SYRIA
LEBANON
IRAQ
IRAN
AFGHANISTAN
ALGERIA
JORDAN
PALESTINE
KUWAIT
PAKISTAN
NEPAL
BAHRAIN
EGYPT
QATAR
UAE
MAURITANIA
SAUDI ARABIA
OMAN
BANGLADESH
SENEGAL
GAMBIA
GUINEA
CHAD
SUDAN
YEMEN
DJIBOUTI
NIGERIA
TONGA
UGANDA
BRUNEI
MALAYSIA
KENYA
BURUNDI
TANZANIA
INDONESIA
SWAZILAND
LESOTHO

#JUST SAYIN'

UK law dictates that in most circumstances hereditary peerages and the estates that come with them pass only to male heirs, even distant ones, regardless of whether there are daughters who should be first in line by age or family status. While a daughter cannot inherit the title, she could be left her fair share of the property and money if her father chose to do so in his will. So far, the majority haven't.

No reserves

Percentage of women who would find it impossible
to come up with emergency funds if needed

2014

25% – 35%

36% – 50%

50% and higher

PHILIPPINES

INDONESIA

BANGLADESH

INDIA

SRI LANKA

THAILAND

PAKISTAN

GEORGIA

ARMENIA

IRAN

KUWAIT

SAUDI
ARABIA

YEMEN

SOMALIA

MAURITIUS

MADAGASCAR

TURKEY

IRAQ

JORDAN

ETHIOPIA

KENYA

TANZANIA

MALAWI

CYPRUS

PALESTINE

EGYPT

CONGO

BURUNDI

ZIMBABWE

SOUTH
AFRICA

CAMEROON

GABON

CONGO

ANGOLA

NAMIBIA

LITHUANIA

HUNGARY

ROMANIA

BULGARIA

GREECE

SERBIA

CROATIA

ALBANIA

ITALY

TUNISIA

BENIN

TOGO

GHANA

SENEGAL

GUINEA

SIERRA LEONE

PORTUGAL

BRAZIL

URUGUAY

ARGENTINA

PUERTO RICO

HAITI

JAMAICA

COLOMBIA

PERU

CHILE

ECUADOR

MEXICO

HONDURAS

NICARAGUA

GUATEMALA

EL SALVADOR

COSTA RICA

173

Living on the edge

Percentage of households living in multidimensional poverty,
a combined index of both monetary and non-monetary deprivations

developing countries, most recent data since 2011

- 50% and over
- 30% – 49%
- 10% – 29%
- fewer than 10%
- no data

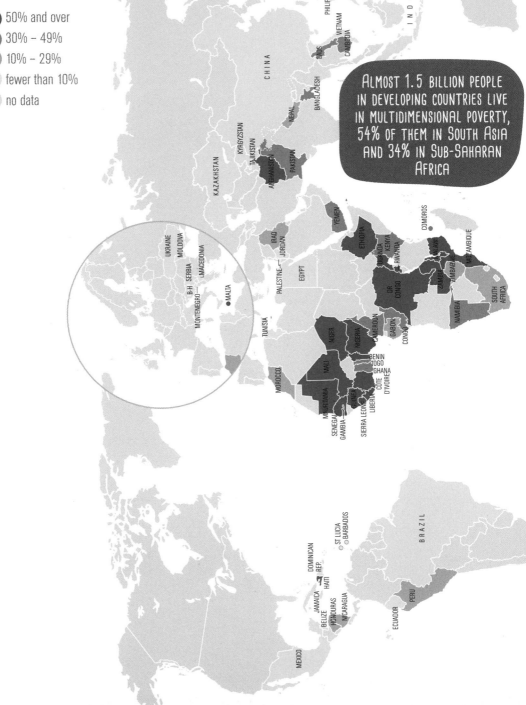

ALMOST 1.5 BILLION PEOPLE IN DEVELOPING COUNTRIES LIVE IN MULTIDIMENSIONAL POVERTY, 54% OF THEM IN SOUTH ASIA AND 34% IN SUB-SAHARAN AFRICA

Extreme poverty

2016

 more than 50% of the population lives on less than $1.90 a day
(purchasing power parity terms)

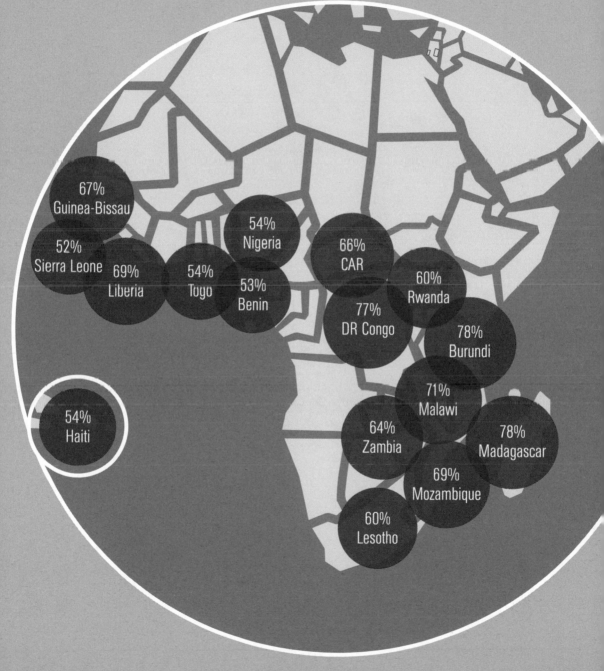

67%
Guinea-Bissau

52%
Sierra Leone

69%
Liberia

54%
Togo

53%
Benin

54%
Nigeria

66%
CAR

60%
Rwanda

77%
DR Congo

78%
Burundi

54%
Haiti

71%
Malawi

64%
Zambia

78%
Madagascar

69%
Mozambique

60%
Lesotho

At risk of poverty in Europe

Percentage of women and men "at risk" of poverty

most recent data since 2015

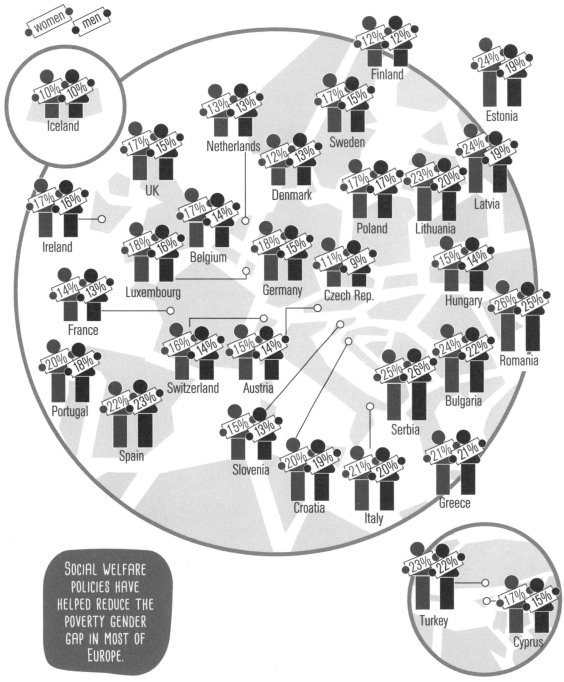

women • men •

Iceland 10% 10%

Finland 12% 12%

Estonia 24% 19%

UK 17% 15%

Netherlands 13% 13%

Sweden 17% 15%

Denmark 12% 13%

Latvia 24% 19%

Ireland 17% 16%

Belgium 17% 14%

Poland 17% 17%

Lithuania 23% 20%

Luxembourg 18% 16%

Germany 18% 15%

Czech Rep. 11% 9%

Hungary 15% 14%

France 14% 13%

Switzerland 16% 14%

Austria 15% 14%

Romania 26% 25%

Portugal 20% 18%

Bulgaria 25% 26%

Spain 22% 23%

Slovenia 15% 13%

Serbia 24% 22%

Croatia 20% 19%

Italy 21% 20%

Greece 21% 21%

SOCIAL WELFARE POLICIES HAVE HELPED REDUCE THE POVERTY GENDER GAP IN MOST OF EUROPE.

Turkey 23% 22%

Cyprus 17% 15%

Penniless in Latin America

Percentage of women and men aged 15+
without their own income

combined averages, 17 Latin American countries

2013

lowest
income quintile

highest
income quintile

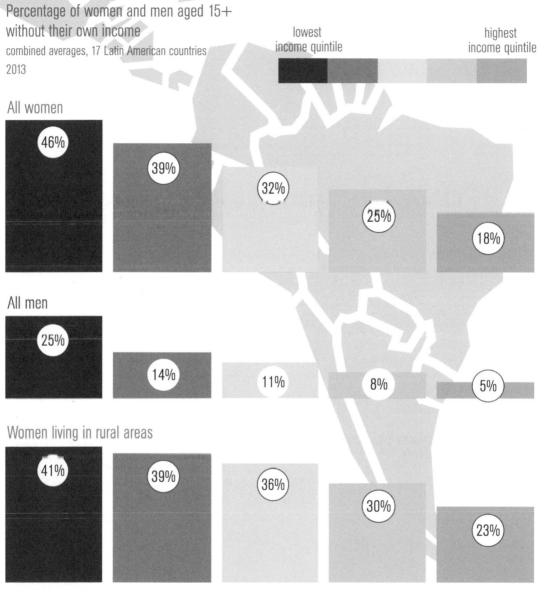

All women

46%   39%   32%   25%   18%

All men

25%   14%   11%   8%   5%

Women living in rural areas

41%   39%   36%   30%   23%

Men living in rural areas

31%   16%   13%   11%   6%

Profile of poverty, USA

Official poverty rate for different populations

2016

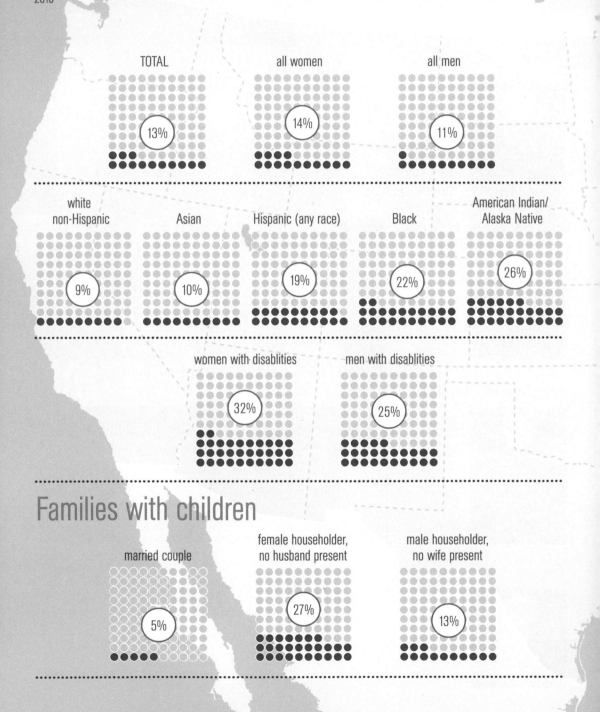

TOTAL — 13%

all women — 14%

all men — 11%

white non-Hispanic — 9%

Asian — 10%

Hispanic (any race) — 19%

Black — 22%

American Indian/ Alaska Native — 26%

women with disablities — 32%

men with disablities — 25%

Families with children

married couple — 5%

female householder, no husband present — 27%

male householder, no wife present — 13%

Profile of wealth, USA

The racial wealth gap

Median household worth in dollars

2013

(the value of all assets, minus debts,
including real estate, cars, bank accounts,
retirement accounts)

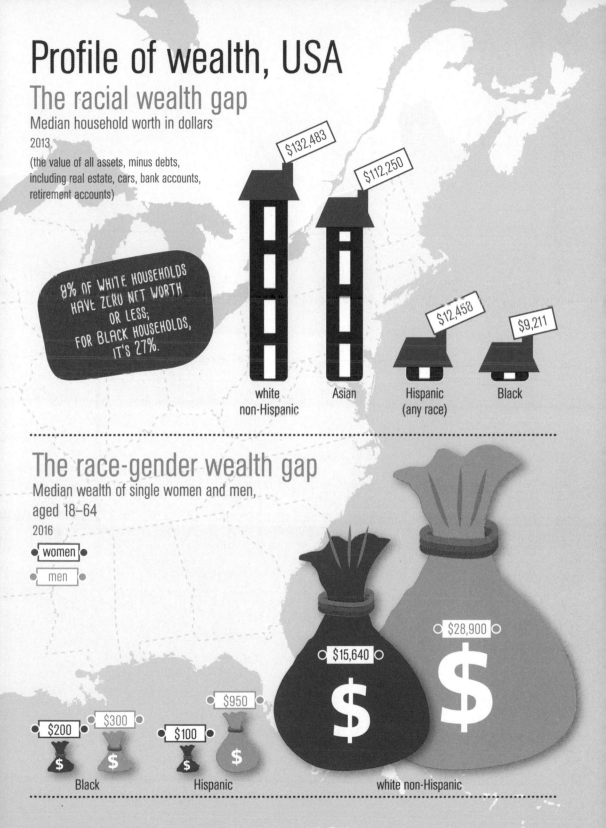

8% OF WHITE HOUSEHOLDS
HAVE ZERO NET WORTH
OR LESS;
FOR BLACK HOUSEHOLDS,
IT'S 27%.

$132,483

$112,250

$12,458

$9,211

white
non-Hispanic

Asian

Hispanic
(any race)

Black

The race-gender wealth gap

Median wealth of single women and men,
aged 18–64

2016

● women ●

● men ●

$200

$300

$100

$950

$15,640

$28,900

Black

Hispanic

white non-Hispanic

Rich world / poor world

Men on top

Wealth is concentrating upwards, into fewer and fewer hands – mostly men's. Even the International Monetary Fund warns that inequality undermines economic and social sustainability and stability. In 2017 the World Economic Forum identified rising income and wealth disparity as the top risk to global stability.

In 2017, 42 people held as much wealth as the poorer HALF of the world's population – 3.7 billion people.
In 2016, it was 61 people; in 2009, 380.

In 2017, the word's 2,043 billionaires – 90% of them men – saw their fortunes grow by $762 billion. At the same time, women provided $10 trillion in unpaid care to support the global economy.

INDONESIA: The 4 richest people (all men) own more wealth than the bottom 100 million people.

USA: The 3 richest people (all men) own the same wealth as the bottom half of the US population, roughly 160 million people.

The world's Top 10 billionaires

2017

■■■■■■■■ Bill Gates

■■■■■■■■ Warren Buffet

■■■■■■■■ Jeff Bezos

■■■■■■■■ Armancio Ortega

■■■■■■■■ Mark Zuckerberg

■■■■■■■■ Carlos Slim Helu

■■■■■■■■ Larry Ellison

■■■■■■■■ Charles Koch

■■■■■■■■ David Koch

■■■■■■■■ Michael Bloomberg

Does a rising tide lift all boats?

"Inclusive development" measures the extent to which all members of society benefit from economic growth and rising standards of living.

Advanced economies, 2018

Top 10 most inclusive:
Norway, Iceland, Luxembourg, Switzerland, Denmark, Sweden, Netherlands, Ireland, Australia, Austria

Bottom 10 least inclusive:
Greece, Portugal, Italy, Spain, Israel, Japan, USA, Estonia, UK, Slovak Republic

10 highest-paid CEOS

UK, 2015

- Sir Martin Sorrell
- Tony Pidgeley
- Rakesh Kapoor
- Jeremy Darroch
- Flemming Ornsjov
- Bob Dudley
- Erik Engstrom
- Mike Wells
- Michael Dobson
- Antonio Horta-Osorio

10 highest-paid CEOS

USA, 2016

- Marc Lore
- Tim Cook
- John Weinberg
- Sundar Pichai
- Elon Musk
- Virginia Rometty
- Mitch Garber
- Philippe Dauman
- Leslie Moonves
- Mario Gabelli

total compensation, includes stocks and bonuses

IN THE UK, THE AVERAGE CEO OF A FTSE100 COMPANY NOW RECEIVES £5.5 MILLION A YEAR, WHICH MEANT THAT BY ABOUT NOON ON JANUARY 3, 2017, THE AVERAGE FTSE 100 BOSS HAD ALREADY EARNED MORE THAN THE AVERAGE WORKER IN HIS COMPANY WOULD EARN IN THAT WHOLE YEAR - AN AVERAGE SALARY OF £28,200.

IT TAKES JUST FOUR DAYS FOR A CEO FROM ONE OF THE TOP FIVE GLOBAL FASHION BRANDS TO EARN WHAT A BANGLADESHI GARMENT WORKER WILL EARN IN HER ENTIRE LIFETIME.

Ratio of CEO pay to the average person's income

selected examples, 2010

541:1	South Africa
483:1	India
299:1	USA
229:1	UK
203:1	Canada
176:1	Germany
101:1	Norway
68:1	France
43:1	China

Banking on it

Percentage of adults, aged 15+ with an account at a formal financial institution

selected examples, 2014

For women more so than men, informal social and family networks provide financial security. But making the leap to participating in formal financial institutions and processes can reduce poverty, help protect against financial shocks and enhance financial security. The most basic entry point for "financial inclusion" in formal systems is having a bank account. Mobile money is changing the nature of financial inclusion, especially in Sub-Saharan Africa.

THE USE OF M-PESA, THE DOMINANT MOBILE MONEY SYSTEM IN KENYA, IN ITS FIRST 10 YEARS ALONE, LIFTED ALMOST 200,000 HOUSEHOLDS OUT OF EXTREME POVERTY; FEMALE-HEADED HOUSEHOLDS WERE PREDOMINANT AMONG THEM.

2% OF ADULTS GLOBALLY USE A MOBILE MONEY ACCOUNT, BUT IN SUB-SAHARAN AFRICA 12% OF ADULTS HAVE MOBILE MONEY ACCOUNTS. IN KENYA, 96% OF HOUSEHOLDS HAVE AT LEAST ONE MEMBER WHO USES MOBILE MONEY.

men	gap	women
Morocco 52%	25	27% Morocco
UAE 90%	24	66% UAE
Bahrain 90%	23	67% Bahrain
India 63%	20	43% India
Myanmar 29%	12	17% Myanmar
Afghanistan 16%	12	4% Afghanistan
Bhutan 39%	11	28% Bhutan
Pakistan 14%	11	3% Pakistan
Nicaragua 24%	10	14% Nicaragua
Sudan 20%	10	10% Sudan
Iran 97%	10	87% Iran
world average 64%	7	57% world average
Brazil 72%	7	65% Brazil
Kenya 59%	7	52% Kenya
Botswana 53%	7	46% Botswana
Bolivia 44%	6	38% Bolivia
Thailand 81%	6	75% Thailand
China 81%	5	76% China
Cambodia 15%	4	11% Cambodia
France 98%	3	95% France
Jamaica 79%	1	78% Jamaica
Japan 97%	1	96% Japan
Singapore 97%	1	96% Singapore
UK 99%	0	99% UK
Sweden 100%	0	100% Sweden

women	gap	men
Sri Lanka 83%	+1	82% Sri Lanka
Argentina 51%	+1	50% Argentina
Indonesia 37%	+2	35% Indonesia
USA 95%	+3	92% USA
Russia 70%	+6	64% Russia
Philippines 34%	+12	22% Philippines

 See The myth of the connected world, page 166

Power

THEY TRIED TO
BURY US...
THEY DIDN'T
KNOW WE WERE
SEEDS...

Votes for women
Date of universal suffrage for women
On equal terms with men in national elections

GREENLAND

ICELAND

CANADA

NORWAY SWEDEN

EST

LA

LITH.

DENMARK

RUSSIA

IRELAND UK

NDL POLAND

BEL. GERMANY CZ

LIECHT. REP. SL

LUX SLO AUS HUM

FRANCE SWITZ. CRO. B-H SE

ANDORRA MONACO ITALY ALB.

SPAIN MAC-

PORTUGAL GRE

MALTA

TUNISIA

MOROCCO

USA

ALGERIA LIBYA

MEXICO

BAHAMAS

CUBA

DOMINICAN
REP.

JAMAICA HAITI

PUERTO RICO

BELIZE ANTIGUA & BARBUDA

GUATEMALA HONDURAS ST KITTS & NEVIS DOMINICA

EL SALVADOR NICARAGUA GRENADA ST LUCIA

COSTA RICA PANAMA BARBADOS

ST VINCENT & GRENADINES

TRINIDAD & TOBAGO

VENEZUELA

GUYANA

COLOMBIA SURINAME

FRENCH GUIANA

ECUADOR

PERU

BRAZIL

BOLIVIA

PARAGUAY

CHILE ARGENTINA

URUGUAY

CAPE
VERDE

MAURITANIA MALI NIGER CHA

SENEGAL

GAMBIA BURKINA

GUINEA- GUINEA FASO NIGERIA

BISSAU CÔTE CAI

SIERRA LEONE D'IVOIRE

LIBERIA GHANA TOGO BENIN

CAMEROON

EQUATORIAL
GUINEA

SÃO TOME GABON

& PRINCIPE CONGO DR
CON

ANGOLA

NAMIBIA

BOTSWANA

SOUTH
AFRICA

1893–1919
1920–44
1945–59
1960–79
since 1980
voter restrictions
no data

RUSSIA

KAZAKHSTAN
MONGOLIA
UZBEKISTAN
GEORGIA
AZER.
KYRGYZSTAN
NORTH KOREA
TURKEY ARMENIA TURKMEN.
TAJIKISTAN
JAPAN
SOUTH KOREA
CYPRUS
NON-ISRAELI
JORDAN
SYRIA
IRAQ
IRAN
AFGHANISTAN
CHINA
KUWAIT
EGYPT
BAHRAIN
QATAR
U.A.E.
PAKISTAN
NEPAL
BHUTAN
TAIWAN
SAUDI ARABIA
OMAN
BANGLADESH
MYANMAR
Hong Kong
MARSHALL IS.
MICRONESIA
NAURU
SUDAN
YEMEN
INDIA
LAOS
KIRIBATI
ERITREA
THAILAND
TUVALU
DJIBOUTI
VIETNAM
SAMOA
SOUTH SUDAN
ETHIOPIA
CAMBODIA
PHILIPPINES
VANUATU
FIJI
TONGA
UGANDA
SOMALIA
SRI LANKA
PALAU
KENYA
MALDIVES
BRUNEI
RWANDA
BURUNDI
MALAYSIA
SINGAPORE
TANZANIA
SEYCHELLES
INDONESIA
PAPUA NEW GUINEA
ZAMBIA
COMOROS
TIMOR-LESTE
MALAWI
ZIMBABWE
MAURITIUS
MOZAMBIQUE
MADAGASCAR
SWAZILAND
LESOTHO

Saudi Arabia
Women are denied the vote in national elections (but were allowed to vote in municipal elections in 2015)

AUSTRALIA

NEW ZEALAND

185

Beyond the official story
When "universal suffrage" doesn't really mean universal

USA

The Nineteenth Amendment to the United States Constitution, passed in 1920, is touted as the official date of women's voting liberation: "The right of citizens of the United States to vote shall not be denied or abridged by the United States or by any State on account of sex."

BUT!

NATIVE AMERICAN MEN AND WOMEN WHO LIVED ON RESERVATIONS WERE NOT GRANTED CITIZENSHIP, AND THUS THE RIGHT TO VOTE, UNTIL 1924. IN PUERTO RICO, A TERRITORY OF THE USA, WOMEN DID NOT WIN THE VOTE UNTIL 1929, WHEN IT WAS GRANTED ONLY TO LITERATE WOMEN. THEY WON UNIVERSAL SUFFRAGE ONLY IN 1935.

SOUTH AFRICA

White women won the vote in 1930.

BUT!

INDIAN AND "COLOURED" WOMEN WERE ONLY GRANTED THE RIGHT TO VOTE IN 1984 AND BLACK WOMEN IN 1994.

AUSTRALIA

White women won the vote in 1902.

BUT!

ABORIGINAL WOMEN AND MEN HAD TO WAIT UNTIL 1962 WHEN THEY WERE GRANTED THE RIGHT TO VOTE IN FEDERAL ELECTIONS.

Years apart
Gap between men's and women's suffrage

in selected countries

men's vote   women's vote

years' gap
Denmark 1915 0 1915 Denmark
Netherlands 1917 2 1919 Netherlands
UK 1918   10   1928 UK
Japan 1925   20   1945 Japan
Italy 1919   26   1945 Italy
USA 1870   50   1920 USA
Belgium 1893   55   1948 Belgium
Spain 1869   62   1931 Spain
France 1848   96   1944 France
Switzerland 1848   123   1971 Switzerland

Militaries
Women as percentage of active armed forces
most recent data since 2016

- ● fewer than 5%
- ● 5% – 9%
- ● 10% – 14%
- ● 15% and higher
- ● present in the armed forces, proportion unknown
- ● no data

#MeToo in militaries:

Assault on women in militaries by their fellow soldiers is widespread. Women in North Korea report that in the military "rape is a fact of life". In the US military, 8,600 women and 6,300 men reported being sexually assaulted in 2016, most more than once, giving a total of 41,000 reported assaults. 21% of active duty women and 6% of men faced severe and persistent sexual harassment. Open LGBT members have much higher rates of assault and harassment.

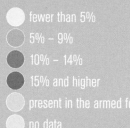

#JUST SAYIN'

Shifting 10% of global military spending to agriculture and infrastructure in poor countries could eliminate extreme hunger and poverty by 2030; to provide universal primary and early secondary education would take about 3% of global military spending.

CANADA

USA

CUBA

BELIZE
JAMAICA
HONDURAS
NICARAGUA

VENEZUELA
GUYANA
COLOMBIA

ECUADOR

PERU

BRAZIL

BOLIVIA

CHILE
ARGENTINA

To the extent that militaries are sources of employment, political clout, and social prestige, women should not be excluded from those opportunities. But many feminists argue that increasing women's participation in masculinized institutions of organized violence harms the long-term interests of all women, and that the feminist task is to dismantle militaries and militarism rather than bolstering them with women's participation.

Saudi Arabia 2018

The government will allow women to serve in non-combat security positions in the military in certain provinces. Women will need permission from their male guardian to apply and enlist.

22 COUNTRIES IN THE WORLD HAVE NO STANDING MILITARIES, INCLUDING ICELAND, COSTA RICA, SAMOA, MAURITIUS AND SEVERAL STATES IN THE CARIBBEAN.

NORWAY SWEDEN FINLAND
ESTONIA
DENMARK LITHUANIA
LATVIA
RUS.
IRELAND UK
NDL. POLAND
GERMANY
BELGIUM CZECH UKRAINE
LUX. REP.
FRANCE SWITZ. AUSTRIA HUNGARY MOLDOVA
SLO. ROMANIA
ITALY CROATIA
MONT. BULGARIA
SPAIN ALBANIA
GREECE TURKEY

RUSSIA

GEORGIA

NORTH KOREA
JAPAN
SOUTH KOREA

SYRIA
ISRAEL IRAQ
CHINA

ALGERIA LIBYA SAUDI UAE
ARABIA PAKISTAN NEPAL
INDIA
THAILAND PHILIPPINES
VIETNAM

GHANA NIGERIA
SRI LANKA

KENYA

TANZANIA

ANGOLA MALAWI

NAMIBIA ZIMBABWE
BOTSWANA
MOZAMBIQUE
AUSTRALIA

SOUTH AFRICA

NEW ZEALAND

Women in national government

As a proportion of elected representatives in national government

in lower house if a two-house legislature
June 2017

- 40% and over
- 30% – 39%
- 20% – 29%
- 10% – 19%
- under 10%
- no women in government
- no data

FIRST FEMALE PRESIDENT OF THE UNITED STATES?

NOT YET...

CANADA

USA

MEXICO
CUBA
BAHAMAS
DOMINICAN REP.
JAMAICA
HAITI
BELIZE
HONDURAS
ST KITTS & NEVIS
ANGUILLA
DOMINICA
ST LUCIA
GUATEMALA
EL SALVADOR
NICARAGUA
GRENADA
ST VINCENT & GRENADINES
BARBADOS
TRINIDAD & TOBAGO
COSTA RICA
PANAMA
VENEZUELA
GUYANA
SURINAME
COLOMBIA
ECUADOR
PERU
BRAZIL
BOLIVIA
PARAGUAY
CHILE
ARGENTINA
URUGUAY

NORWAY
ICELAND
FINLAND
SWEDEN
ESTONIA
UK
LATVIA
LITHUANIA
DENMARK
RUS
IRELAND
BELARUS
NDL
GERMANY
POLAND
BELGIUM
CZECH REP.
SLOVAKIA
LUX
LIECHT
AUSTRIA
HUNGARY
FRANCE
SWITZ
SLOV
ROMANIA
MONACO
CROATIA
B-H
SERBIA
BULGA.
PORTUGAL
ANDORRA
S. M
MONT.
MACEDONIA
ALBANIA
SPAIN
ITALY
GREECE
TUNISIA
MALTA
MOROCCO

ALGER
CAPE VERDE
MAURITANIA
MAL
SENEGAL
GAMBIA
BUR
GUINEA-BISSAU
GUINEA
FA
SIERRA LEONE
CÔTE D'IVOIRE
LIBERIA

Slow progress

World average of women in national governments

in lower house if a two-house legislature

3%	8%	8%	11%	12%	12%	16%	23%
1945	1955	1965	1975	1985	1995	2005	2017

Women in ministerial positions

Percentage, where 30% and over

2015

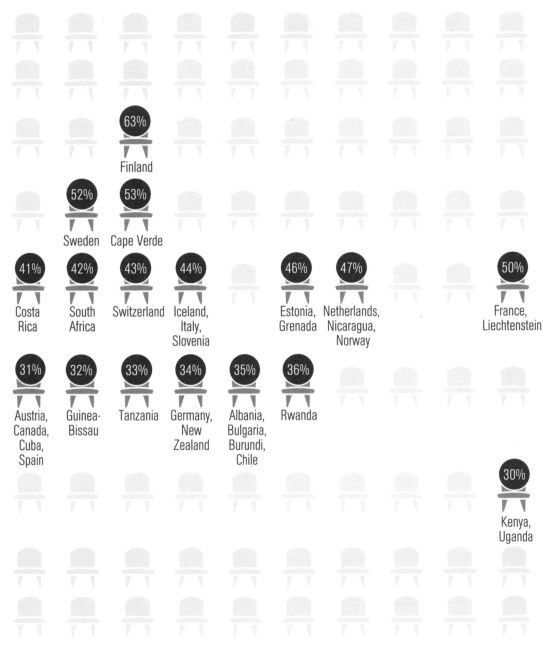

63% Finland

52% Sweden   53% Cape Verde

41% Costa Rica   42% South Africa   43% Switzerland   44% Iceland, Italy, Slovenia   46% Estonia, Grenada   47% Netherlands, Nicaragua, Norway   50% France, Liechtenstein

31% Austria, Canada, Cuba, Spain   32% Guinea-Bissau   33% Tanzania   34% Germany, New Zealand   35% Albania, Bulgaria, Burundi, Chile   36% Rwanda

30% Kenya, Uganda

European Parliament

Percentage of women elected to the European Parliament by national delegation

February 2017

67% Malta

62% Finland

55% Croatia, Ireland

50% Austria, Estonia, Latvia, Sweden

46% Spain

43% UK

42% France, Netherlands

38% Italy, Slovenia

37% Germany

33% Belgium, Luxembourg

31% Denmark, Slovakia

29% Portugal

28% Romania

26% Poland

24% Bulgaria, Czech Rep, Greece

19% Hungary

18% Lithuania

17% Cyprus

Quotas for national government

Gender quotas are used to improve women's representation in national governments
2017

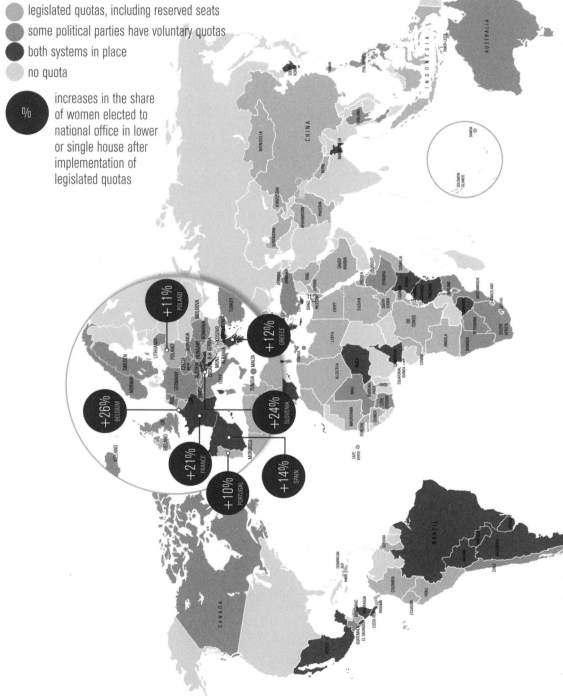

- legislated quotas, including reserved seats
- some political parties have voluntary quotas
- both systems in place
- no quota

% increases in the share of women elected to national office in lower or single house after implementation of legislated quotas

+11% POLAND

+12% GREECE

+26% BELGIUM

+24% SLOVENIA

+21% FRANCE

+10% PORTUGAL

+144% SPAIN

Women at the United Nations

As a percentage of senior managers
(D1 and above) in the UN system
2015

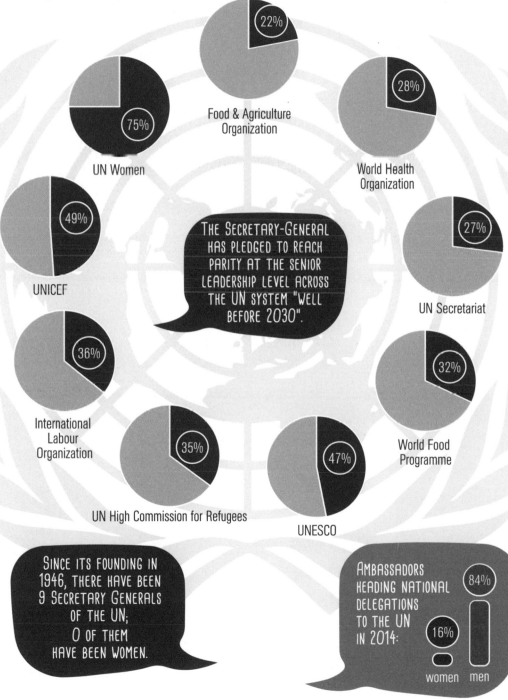

Food & Agriculture
Organization — 22%

World Health
Organization — 28%

UN Women — 75%

UNICEF — 49%

UN Secretariat — 27%

THE SECRETARY-GENERAL HAS PLEDGED TO REACH PARITY AT THE SENIOR LEADERSHIP LEVEL ACROSS THE UN SYSTEM "WELL BEFORE 2030".

International
Labour
Organization — 36%

UN High Commission for Refugees — 35%

UNESCO — 47%

World Food
Programme — 32%

SINCE ITS FOUNDING IN 1946, THERE HAVE BEEN 9 SECRETARY GENERALS OF THE UN; 0 OF THEM HAVE BEEN WOMEN.

AMBASSADORS HEADING NATIONAL DELEGATIONS TO THE UN IN 2014:

84%

16%

women   men

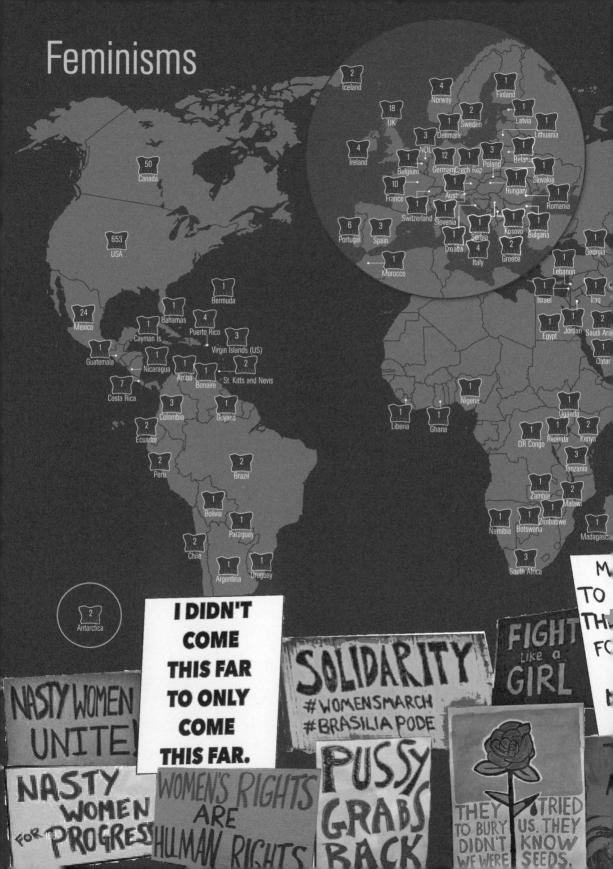

Women on the march, January 21, 2017

estimated number of marches in each country

Women press for social justice and advocate for their rights every day: in election booths, in workplaces, in personal relationships, in art, prose and poetry, through analysis and teaching, in the courts. And, often, in the streets.

On January 21, 2017, 5–6 million people around the world took to the streets. Mobilized initially by women's reaction against the election of Donald Trump to the US presidency, it soon ballooned into a global demonstration of broad support for anti-fascist and anti-racist women's rights. Some of the marches consisted, bravely, of only 2 or 3 people; in many cities, hundreds of thousands filled the streets.

1 Russia

2 Japan

3 South Korea

1 China

1 Laos

1 Macau

1 HK

21 India

1 Myanmar

2 Thailand

3 Vietnam

1 Cambodia

1 Philippines

1 Singapore

2 Indonesia

1 Timor-Leste

1 Mauritius

4 Australia

5 New Zealand

1 Guam

1 Micronesia

1 Fiji

He Waka Eke Noa

UNEXPLAINED LAUGHTER DISRUPTS THE PATRIARCHY

WE'RE IN THIS TOGETHER, OR NOT AT ALL

GIRL POWER

OCEANS SING AND RE WE!

FEMINISM THE RADICAL NOTION THAT WOMEN ARE PEOPLE

I CANT BELIEVE I STILL HAVE TO PROTEST THIS F***ING

WHITE SILENCE COSTS LIVES

CT TS CH RS HT

Sources

Part One WOMEN IN THE WORLD

12–13 Ending discrimination

CEDAW – United Nations Treaty Collection; Hearing before the subcommittee on human rights and the law. Committee on the Judiciary. Nov 18, 2010. US Senate Hearing *111–1143*; Poso ML. Palau takes time to ratify the CEDAW. April 19, 2010. www.mvariety.com; WUNRN. Tonga – Ongoing debate over CEDAW ratification, reflects US CEDAW challenges on a smaller scale. Feb 1, 2016. wunrn.com; Women's Committee of the National Council of Resistance of Iran. CEDAW: Why the Iranian Regime does not join the CEDAW. March 2016. http://women. ncr-iran.org; Sudan: Bahsir says Sudan will not sign CEDAW Convention. Jan 14, 2001. allafrica.com

14–15 Measuring discrimination • The global gender gap

World Economic Forum. *The Global Gender Gap Report 2017*.

16 Discrimination against women

OECD. *Social Institutions and Gender Index, Synthesis Report 2014*. 2015.

17 Life expectancy

UNDP. *Human Development Report, 2016*; UN. *The World's Women 2015: Trends and Statistics*.

18–19 Lesbian rights • Beyond the binary

Ahnam T. Transgender rights, Bangladesh style. July 2, 2015. www. nytimes.com; Amnesty International. Gender, Sexuality, and Identity. www.amnestyusa.org/issues/ gender-sexuality-identity/; Amnesty International Report 2016/17. *State of the World's Human Rights*; Chiam Z et al. *Trans Legal Mapping Report 2016: Recognition before the law*. Geneva: ILGA, Nov 2016; Eddy M and Bennett J. Germany must allow third gender category. Nov 8, 2017. www.nytimes. com

20–21 Legal status of gays • Latecomers

Carroll A. and Mendos LR. *State Sponsored Homophobia 2017: A world survey of sexual orientation laws: criminalisation, protection and recognition*. Geneva: ILGA. May 2017; International Lesbian and Gay Association. Sexual Orientation Laws. http://ilga.org/what-we-do/maps-sexual-orientation-laws/

22–23 Getting married

UN Population Division. *World Marriage Data 2015*.

23 Waiting longer

UN Economic Commission for Europe. Statistical Tables. http://w3.unece. org/PXWeb2015/pxweb/en/STAT/ STAT__30-GE__02-Families_households

24 Breaking up is hard to do

Eurostat Divorce Indicators. 2017; Yau N. Never Been Married. Data Underload. www.flowingdata.com/2016/03/10/ never-been-married/; NCHS. Cohabitation, Marriage, Divorce, and Remarriage in the United States. Series Report 23, Number 22; Raley RK et al. *The Growing Racial and Ethnic Divide in US Marriage Patterns.* The Future of children / Center for the Future of Children, the David and Lucile Packard Foundation. 2015, 25(2):89-109; US Bureau of Labor Statistics. Marriage and divorce: patterns by gender, race, and educational attainment. October 2013.

25 Same-sex marriage • Same-sex civil partnerships

Marriage equality law passes Australia's parliament in landslide vote. Dec 7, 2017. www.theguardian.com; Pew Research Center. Gay Marriage Around the World. June 30, 2017.

26 Child marriage in the USA

Kristof N. 11 years old, a mom, and pushed to marry her rapist. May 26, 2017. www.nytimes.com; Massachusetts Law Updates. Child Brides. https://blog.mass.gov/ masslawlib/legal-topics/child-brides/; Morris A. New Hampshire House kills bill that would raise minimum marriage age to 18. 9 March 2017. www.concordmonitor.com; Tahirih Justice Center. Understanding state statues on minimum marriage age and exceptions. Updated July 11, 2017. http://www.tahirih.org; Tsui A et al. Child marriage in America by the Numbers. July 6, 2017. www. Frontline.org; McClendon D. and Sandstrom A. Child marriage is rare in the US, although this varies by state. Nov 1, 2016. www.pewresearch. org; Unchained at Last. www. unchainedatlast.org

27 Global child marriages

Girls Not Brides. www.girlsnotbrides. org/about-child-marriage/; UN. *The World's Women 2015: Trends and Statistics*; UNICEF. *Ending Child Marriage: Progress and Prospects*. 2014; UNICEF Data. Monitoring the situation of children and women. data.unicef. org/topic/child-protection/child-marriage/

28–29 Household size • One-person Europe

Asia Foundation. A Survey of the Afghan People. 2015; Chamie J. The rise of one-person households. Feb 22, 2017. www.ipsnews.net; China. Statistical Yearbook. 2016; ESRI Demographic Data Release Notes: Botswana. Average Household size; EUROSTAT. Household Composition Statistics. 2016; Government of Canada. 2016 Census Topic: Families, households and marital status; Government of Hong Kong. Living Arrangement and Household Characteristics; Government of Nepal. Central Bureau of Statistics. 2016; Iran Census. 2016; Living alone EUROSTAT. Household Composition Statistics. 2016; OECD Family Database; Office for National Statistics, UK. Families and Households: 2017; UNFPA. Lao People's Democratic Republic. http:// lao.unfpa.org/en

30 Not all households are equal

Eurostat Statistics Explained. Quality of Life in Europe. 2015; US Census Bureau. Income and Poverty in the United States: 2016. Table B-1.

31 Refugees

UNHCR. *Global Report 2016*; UNHCR. Syria Regional Refugee Response. Feb 22, 2018. UNHCR. Statistical Database; UNRWA In Figures 2017; UNHCR. Iraq Refugee Crisis; UNHCR. Inside the world's 10 largest refugee camps; UNHCR. Dadaab – Kenya: Camp Population Statistics (31 Jan 2017); UNHCR. South Sudan Situation; Where are the Syrian refugees? May 4, 2017. www.aljazeera.com

32–33 Crisis zones

Human Rights Watch. World Report 2018; ReliefWeb. www.reliefweb. int/countries; UN Office for the Coordination of Humanitarian Affairs. *Global Humanitarian Overview 2018*; UN General Assembly. Human Rights Council. Report of the commission of inquiry on human rights in the Democratic People's Republic of Korea. Feb 7, 2014.

34 Peacemakers

Council on Foreign Relations. Women's Roles in Peace Processes.

34 Peacekeeping

Saghal quote is from: Jordan M. Sex charges haunt UN forces. Nov 26, 2004. www.csmonitor.com; Taylor S. Dispatches: A Year of Reckoning on Sexual Abuse by UN Peacekeepers. Human Rights Watch. Dec 22, 2015; United Nations Peacekeeping: Gender.

Part Two KEEPING WOMEN IN THEIR PLACE

38–39 Kingdom of boxes

Begum R. The brave female activists who fought to lift Saudi Arabia's driving ban. Sept 29, 2017. www.hrw.org; Hubbard B. Once shunned as "drivers", women who fought ban now celebrate. Oct 7, 2017. www.nytimes.com; Human Rights Watch. Women's Rights. Boxed In: Women and Saudi Arabia's Male Guardianship System. July 16, 2016; Saudi police "stopped" fire rescue. March 15, 2002. www.bbc.co.uk/news; Saudi women will need permission from male "guardians" to drive. Sept 27, 2017. www.alaraby.co.uk; World Bank. *Women, Business and the Law.*

40 Legally bound

DR Congo: Women's Situation. www.thekvinnatillkvinnafoundation.org/country/dr-congo/womens-situation/; Human Rights Watch. Letter regarding the human rights situation in Sudan during the 36th session of the UH Human Rights Council. Sept 21, 2017; Moaddel M. *The birthplace of the Arab spring: values and perceptions of Tunisians and a comparative assessment of Egyptian, Iraqi, Lebanese, Pakistani, Saudi, Tunisian, and Turkish publics.* College Park, MD: University of Maryland, 2013.

41 Dress offensive • Public opinion

Bruce-Lockhart A. Five countries with the strictest dress codes. World Economic Forum. Jan 7, 2016; Pew Research Center. Restrictions on Women's Religious Attire. Sept 21, 2017.

42 "Honor" killings

Honor Based Violence Awareness Network. www.hbv-awareness.com; Honor Killings: Tradition and Law. www.sites.tufts.edu/anth27h/honor-killing-today; Nasrullah M et al. The epidemiological patterns of honour killing of women in Pakistan, *European Journal of Public Health*, Volume 19, Issue 2, April 1, 2009, 193–197; US Department of State. Country Reports on Human Rights Practices.

43 "Justified" beatings • Telling, or not

UN. *The World's Women 2015: Trends and Statistics.*

44 Domestic violence by country

UN. *The World's Women 2015: Trends and Statistics.*

45 Domestic violence by region

Bunch C. Women's Rights as Human Rights: Toward a Re-Vision of Human Rights. *Human Rights Quarterly*, Vol. 12, No. 4, Nov. 1990: 486–498; WHO.

Global Health Observatory. Intimate Partner Violence Prevalence. Data by WHO region.

46 Focus on intimate partner abuse

Breiding M. et al. Prevalence and Characteristics of Sexual Violence, Stalking, and Intimate Partner Violence Victimization – National Intimate Partner and Sexual Violence Survey, United States 2011. CDC. Sept 5, 2014; Chauhan R. and Baraik VK. Mapping Crime against Women in India: Spatio-Temporal Analysis, 2001–2012. *Development*, 246. 2016; National Coalition Against Domestic Violence. *Facts about domestic violence.* www.ncadv.org/statistics; National Crimes Record Bureau. Chapter 5 Crime Against Women. www.ncrb.gov.in/StatPublications/CII/CII2015/chapters/Chapter%205 15.11.16.pdf; Office for National Statistics. Domestic abuse in England and Wales, year ending March 2016; Rauhala E. Despite a new law, China is failing survivors of domestic violence. Feb 7, 2017. www.washingtonpost.com

48–49 Marry-your-rapist laws

www.abaadmena.org; Barad E et al. Gender-Based Violence Laws in Sub-Saharan Africa. 2007; Equality Now. *The World's Shame: The global rape epidemic*; Sengupta S. One by One, Marry-Your-Rapist Laws Are Falling in the Middle East. *July 22, 2017. www.nytimes.com;* World Bank. Women, Business, and the Law. 2016.

50–51 Rape

Institute for Security Studies. Rape and other forms of sexual violence in South Africa. 2014; Middleton L. Corrective Rape: Fighting a South African Scourge. March 8, 2011. www.time.com; Raj A. et al. Sexual violence and rape in India. *The Lancet*, Volume 383, Issue 9920, 865; Smith SG. et al. The National Intimate Partner and Sexual Violence Survey (NISVS): 2010–2012 State Report. National Center for Injury Prevention and Control. 2017; South African Medical Research Council. *Understanding men's health and the use of violence;* United Nations, 2015. *The World's Women 2015: Trends and Statistics;* World Health Organization. *Global and regional estimates of violence against women: prevalence and health effects of intimate partner violence and non-partner sexual violence.* 2013.

52 Rape in war zones

Goetz AM. Inciting soldiers to rape in the Philippines. June 6, 2017; www.opendemocracy.net; Enloe C. *Maneuvers: The international politics of militarizing women's lives.* Berkeley:

University of California Press, 2000; Human Rights Watch. *"They said we are their slaves".* Oct 5, 2017; Report of the UN Secretary-General on Conflict-Related Sexual Violence. April 15, 2017; Storr W. The rape of men: the darkest secret of war. July 16, 2011. www.theguardian.com; Thomas DQ and Regan ER. Rape in War: Challenging the Tradition of Impunity. *SAIS Review* 1994, 82–99; Women's Media Centre. Women Under Siege. Witness Reports: Bosnia.

53 The rapist at home

Centers for Disease Control. Intersection of intimate partner violence and HIV in women; Equality Now. *The Global Rape Epidemic.* 2017; Kentish B. Indian government files legal papers to try to stop marital rape being outlawed. Sept 1, 2017. www.independent.co.uk; Sarkar M and Torre I. Marital rape: Where in the world is it legal? May 2, 2015. www.edition.cnn.com; United Nations, 2015. *The World's Women 2015: Trends and Statistics;* UN Office on Drugs and Crime (UNODC). Statistics on justice and prison reform; Women Living Under Muslim Laws. *Iran: Gender discrimination at its worst.* 2014.

54–55 Murder of women

Refuge. www.refuge.org.uk/get-help-now/what-is-domestic-violence/domestic-violence-the-facts/; National Coalition against Domestic Violence; Petrosky E. et al. Racial and Ethnic Differences in Homicides of Adult Women and the Role of Intimate Partner Violence – United States, 2003–2014. MMWR Morbidity and mortality weekly report 2017. 66 (28), 741–746; Salfati C. et al. Prostitute homicides: A descriptive study. *Journal of Interpersonal Violence* 23.4 (2008): 505–543; Small Arms Survey. Nov 2016. A Gendered analysis of violent deaths. Number 63. November 2016; Statistics Canada. Prostitution Offences in Canada: Statistical Trends; The silent nightmare of domestic violence in Russia. March 1, 2013. www.bbc.com; US Department of State. Country Reports on Human Rights Practices; Vagianos A. 30 Shocking domestic violence statistics that remind us it's an epidemic. June 12, 2017. www.huffingtonpost.com; Violence Policy Center. When Men Murder Women: An analysis of 2015 homicide data. 2017; Waiselfisz JJ. Mapa da Violência 2015: Homicídio de mulheres no Brasil. www.flasco.org.br

56 Dowry deaths

24,771 dowry deaths reported in last 3 years. July 31, 2015. www.

indianexpress.com; Corraya, S. In Bangladesh, 87 per cent of women victims of domestic violence. 02/03/2014. www.asiannews.it; Nigam, C. 21 lives lost to dowry every day across India: conviction rate less than 35 per cent. April 22, 2017. www.indiatoday.in; Rao, H. The wedding ritual that kills 2,000 brides in Pakistan every year. Dec 30, 2016. www.en.dailypakistan.com; Violence against women: Dowry. www.askbd. org/ask/2017/01/08/dowry-january-december-2016/

57–58 Fundamentalist wars on women

Abdelaziz S. ISIS states its justification for the enslavement of women. Oct 13, 2014. www.cnn.com; Amnesty International. Iraq: Yezidi survivors of horrific abuse in IS captivity neglected by international community. Oct 10, 2016. www.amnesty.org; Amnesty International. Escape from Hell: Torture and sexual slavery in Islamic State captivity in Iraq. 2014. www. amnesty.org.uk; Human Rights Watch. April 5, 2016. Iraq: Women suffer under ISIS. www.hrw.org; Mahmood M. Double-layered veils and despair... women describe life under ISIS. Feb17, 2015. www.theguardian.com; Otten C. The Long Read: Slaves of ISIS. July 25, 2017. www.theguardian. com; The Crisis Group. Women and the Boko Haram Insurgency; UNICEF. Use of children as "human bombs" rising in north east Nigeria. August 22, 2017; Warner J and Matfess H. Exploding Stereotypes: The unexpected operational and demographic characteristics of Boko Haram's suicide bombers. Combatting Terrorism Center. www.ctc.usma.edu

Part Three BIRTHRIGHTS
60–61 Births

World Bank. Data. Fertility Rate, Total.

62 Age at first birth

CIA World Factbook. Mother's mean age at first birth.

62 Changing expectations

World Bank. Data. Fertility Rate, Total.

63–65 Contraception is still women's responsibility • Types of contraception • Use of contraception

UN/ DESA. Population Division. World Contraceptive Use 2017.

64 Changing contraceptive use

Contraception and family planning around the world – interactive. www. theguardian.com

66 Family Planning 2020 Initiative

Clinton Foundation. Family Planning Market Report. August 2016.

67 Unmet need

UN/DESA. Population Division. World Contraceptive Use 2017; Guttmacher Institute. Adding It Up: Investing in Contraception and Maternal and Newborn Health, 2017. July 13, 2017.

68–69 Dying to give birth

Amnesty International. Deadly Delivery: The Maternal Health Care Crisis in America. 2010; CDC. Reproductive Health; Creanga AA. et al. Maternal Mortality and Morbidity in the United States: Where Are We Now? Journal of Women's Health. January 2014, 23(1): 3-9.

69 Danger zones

WHO. GHO data. Skilled attendants at birth; WHO. Health Service Coverage, data by country; UNICEF. Maternal Mortality.

70 Race, place, ethnicity and death

Amnesty International. Deadly Delivery: The Maternal Health Care Crisis in America. 2010; Australia Institute Health and Welfare. Humphrey MD. et al. Maternal deaths in Australia 2008–2012. Maternal deaths series no. 5. Canberra: AIHW; CDC. Reproductive Health; Creanga AA. et al. Maternal Mortality and Morbidity in the United States: Where Are We Now? Journal of Women's Health. January 2014, 23(1): 3-9; Creanga AA. et al. Pregnancy-related mortality in the United States, 2006–2010. Obstetrics and Gynecology, 125(1): 5-12. 2015; Knight M. Maternal mortality and severe morbidity in the UK: Trends and key messages for care. 2015. www.iss.it/binary/moma/cont/Knight.pdf; Morrison J. Race and Ethnicity by the Numbers. Americas Quarterly. 2012; Singh GK. Maternal Mortality in the United States, 1935–2007. Rockville, MD: US Department of Health and Human Services. 2010.

72–73 Abortion laws

Australia: Children by Choice. www. childrenbychoice.org.au; Guttmacher Institute. International abortion: Legality and Safety; Sedgh G. et al. Abortion incidence between 1990 and 2014: Global, regional, and subregional levels and trends. The Lancet, 2016; World Abortion Laws 2017. Center for Reproductive Rights.

72 Male approval, again

WHO. Global Abortion Policies Database; Gynopedia. Taiwan; Women on Waves. Abortion Law: Malawi.

74 Who's having abortions?

Guttmacher Institute. www.data. guttmacher.org/regions; Sedgh G. et al. Abortion incidence between 1990 and 2014: Global, regional, and subregional levels and trends. The Lancet, 2016.

75 Safety and availability

Boseley S. Almost half of all abortions performed worldwide are unsafe, reveals WHO. Sept 27, 2017. www. theguardian.com; Ganatra B. et al. Global, regional, and subregional classification of abortions by safety, 2010–14. The Lancet. Sept 27, 2017; WHO. Fact Sheet. www.who.int/ mediacentre/factsheets/fs388/en/

76 Bringing back the coathanger

Feminist Majority Foundation. 2016 National Clinic Violence Survey. February 2017; Guttmacher Institute. United States: Abortion; Holter L. Abortion Apocalypse: 7 states have just one abortion clinic and some are in danger of closing. Aug 11, 2017. www.refinery29.com

77 Son preference

Newport F. Americans prefer boys to girls, just as they did in 1941. June 23, 2011. www.news.gallup.com

78 India: Fewer girls than boys

Census of India.

79 China: more boys born than girls

UNICEF. Children in China: An Atlas of Social Indicators. 2014.

78–79 Missing women

Bongaarts J. and Guilmoto CZ. How many more missing women? Excess female mortality and prenatal sex selection, 1970–2050. Population and Development Review 41.2 (2015): 241-269.

80 Unnatural selection

Alkema L. et al. National, regional, and global sex ratios of infant, child, and under-5 mortality and identification of countries with outlying ratios: a systematic assessment. The Lancet Global Health 2.9 (2014): e521-e530; Brink S. Selecting Boys over Girls is a Trend in More and More Countries. Aug 25, 2015. www.npr.org; Bongaarts J and Christophe ZG. How many more missing women? Excess female mortality and prenatal sex selection, 1970–2050. Population and Development Review 41.2 (2015): 241-26; Hudson V. and Den Boer A. When a boy's life is worth more than his sister's. Foreign Policy. July 30, 2015. Foreignpolicy.com; UNFPA. Gender-biased sex selection: Overview; UNFPA. Sex Imbalances at Birth. 2012.

Part Four BODY POLITICS

82–83 Women in the Olympics

Center for Human Rights in Iran. Iranian women made history at Rio Olympics. Sept 5, 2016; Factsheet, Women in the Olympic movement, update – January 2016. www.olympic.org; Mooallem J. Once prohibited, women's ski jumping set to take flight. Feb 1, 2018. www.nytimes.com; Shepherd S. *Kicking Off: How Women in Sport Are Changing the Game.* Bloomsbury, 2016; Think Again Graphics. 2016. The Gender Games.

84–85 One step forward...

Acosta V. and Carpenter L. Women in Intercollegiate Sport. A Longitudinal, National Study, Thirty-Seven Year Update. 1977–2014. Unpublished manuscript. www.acostacarpenter.org; Allen, S. John McEnroe: Serena Williams world's best woman tennis player, but would rank "like 700" among men. June 25, 2017. www.chicagotribune.com; Caple, N. et al. Gender, race, and LGBT inclusion of head coaches of women's collegiate teams. A special collaborative report on select NCAA Division I conferences for the 45th anniversary of Title IX. June 2017; How women won the fight for equal prize money. www.weforum.org/agenda/2017/07/wimbledon-women-equal-prize-money/; Isidore C. Women world cup champs win way less money. July 7,2015. www.money.cnn.com; Lines A. FA in twitter storm over "sexist" tweet after welcoming back Lionesses from Women's World Cup. July 6, 2015. www.mirror.co.uk; Longman J. Number of women coaching in college has plummeted in Title IX era. Mar 30, 2017. www.nytimes.com; Press Association. Peter Alliss: Women who want to play at Muirfield should marry a member. May 20, 2016. www.theguardian.com; Rothenberg B. Roger Federer $731,000, Serena Williams $495,000. April 12, 2016. www.nytimes.com; Stark R. Where are the women? NCAA. *Champion Magazine;* Top 20 tennis earners. www.totalsportek.com/tennis/atp-career-prize-money-leaders

86–87 The global beauty beat

The Great Pageant Community. thegreatpageantcommunity.com; Miss Universe. www.missuniverse.com/about; Miss World. www.missworld.com

88–89 The big business of beauty

Abraham M. The complicated ethics of being a dermatologist in a country where many people want whiter skin. Quartz India. September 8, 2017. www.qz.com; Biakolo K. Skin Lightening is a $10 billion industry and Ghana wants nothing to do with it. July 11, 2016. www.qz.com; Bocca B. et al. Toxic metals contained in cosmetics: A status report. *Regulatory Toxicology and Pharmacology* 68(3): 447-467. 2014; Brown A. Americans' Desire to Shed Pounds Outweighs Effort. Nov 29, 2013. www.news.gallup.com; Campaign for Safe Cosmetics. www.safecosmetics.org/get-the-facts/chem-of-concern/; Environmental Working Group. Skin Deep Cosmetics Database. www.ewg.org/skindeep/; Gallup News. Personal weight Situation. www.news.gallup.com/poll/7264/personal-weight-situation.aspx; Moss R. Two Thirds of Brits Are on a Diet "Most Of The Time", Study Shows. 10/3/2016. www.huffingtonpost.co.uk/; PR Newswire. Europe Weight Loss and Weight Management Diet Market expected to grow to $3120 million by 2025. July 13, 2017. www.prnewswire.com; The Beauty Economy Special Report. Global Cosmetics Market. www.res.cloudinary.com/yumyoshojin/image/upload/v1/pdf/the-beauty-economy-2016.pdf; Top 20 Global Beauty Companies. www.beautypackaging.com/issues/2016-10-01/view_features/top-20-global-beauty-companies-688974; Twigg M. Where plastic is fantastic. July 5, 2007. www.businessoffashion.com; Westervelt A. Not so pretty: women apply an average of 168 chemicals every day. April 30, 2015. www.theguardian.com; Women in Europe for a Common Future (WECF) *Women and chemicals: The impact of hazardous chemicals on women.* 2016; WWD's Top 10 Beauty Companies of 2016. www.wwd.com; UNEP 2016. Global Gender and Environment Outlook.

90 Shaping the elusive body beautiful

American Society of Plastic Surgeons. *2016 Plastic Surgery Statistics Report;* Wolpow N. Plastic surgeons are mostly men, but their patients are mostly women. Aug 16, 2017.www.racked.com; International Society of Aesthetic Plastic Surgery. International Study on Aesthetic/Cosmetic Procedures Performed in 2016.

91–94 FGM • Under the knife

Center for Reproductive Rights. www.reproductiverights.org/document/female-genital-mutilation-fgm-legal-prohibitions-worldwide; Lubis AM and Jong HN. FGM in Indonesia hits alarming level. Feb 6, 2016. www.thejakartapost.com; UNICEF. Female Genital Mutilation/Cutting Country Profiles. August 2016; UNFPA. For many girls, school holidays means FGM cutting season. Aug 10, 2017; UNFPA. Female Genital Mutilation; UNICEF. Female Genital Mutilation/Cutting: A Global Concern. 2016; UNFPA-UNICEF Joint Programme on Female Genital Mutilation/Cutting. *Accelerating Change: By the Numbers.* 2016 report. July 2017; WHO. Female Genital Mutilation; Why is Malaysia still practising female genital mutilation? Feb 6, 2018. www.themalaysianinsight.com

95 Police-recorded sexual offences against children

UNODC. Total Sexual Offences Against Children.

95 Forced sex

WHO. Violence against women; UN. *The World's Women 2015: Trends and Statistics.*

96 Sex tourism

Child sex tourism in the world – countries. Meldkindersekstoerisme.nl; ECPAT International. www.ecpat.org/; ECPAT. Offenders on the Move: Global Study on Sexual Exploitation of Children in Travel and Tourism 2016. May 2016; UN. Report of the Special Rapporteur on the sale of children, child prostitution and child pornography. December 2, 2016.

97 Prostitution

Garfinkel R. A new twist on the world's oldest profession: Nab the Johns, not the prostitutes. March 13, 2017. www.washingtontimes.com; Marian J. Prostitution Laws in Europe. www.jakubmarian.com; UK House of Commons. Home Affairs Committee. Prostitution. Third Report of session 2016–17.

98–99 Sex trafficking

Maiti Nepal. maitinepal.org/; Nazish K. Women and Girls, A Commodity: Human Trafficking in Nepal. Feb 22, 2014. www.thediplomat.com; South China Morning Post. Twin earthquakes in Nepal made it easier for traffickers to sell women into slavery. April 25, 2017. www.scmp.com; UN Treaties Depository; UNODC, *Global Report on Trafficking in Persons 2016;* US State Department. *Trafficking in Persons Report, 2017.*

100 Pornography

Darling K. IP Without IP? A Study of the Online Adult Entertainment Industry. *Stanford Technology Law Review.* 655 (2014)D; Dugan A. Men, Women Differ on Morals of Sex, Relationships. *Social and Policy Issues* June 19, 2015. www.news.gallop.com; EDsmart. Internet Pornography Stats. www.edsmart.org/pornography-stats/; PornHub Insights. 2017 Year in Review; Ruvolo

J. How Much of the Internet is Actually for Porn? *Forbes*. Sept 7, 2011; Levine LS. Feminist Debates: Pornography. Ms. Magazine Blog. June 10, 2014. www.msmagazine.com; Wright PJ. US Males and Pornography, 1973–2010: Consumption, Predictors, Correlates. *Journal of Sex Research*. 2013.

Part Five HEALTH

102–103 Breast cancer

Data – world age-standardized rate per 100,000 women.

Ferlay J et al. Cancer incidence and mortality worldwide: Sources, methods and major patterns in GLOBOCAN 2012. *International Journal of Cancer*. 136: E359–E386. 2015; IARC. Global Cancer Observatory. www.gco.iarc.fr/today/home; World Cancer Research Fund International. Breast cancer statistics. www.wcrf.org

102 Weekly death toll

IARC. Global Cancer Observatory. Estimated number of deaths, breast cancer, worldwide in 2012. www.gco.iarc.fr

104 Breast cancer: The regional lottery

Data – age-standardized rate per 100,000 women.

Ferlay J. et al. Cancer incidence and mortality worldwide: Sources, methods and major patterns in GLOBOCAN 2012. *International Journal of Cancer*. 136: E359–E386. 2015.

104 Race, ethnicity, and breast cancer

Data – age-standardized rate per 100,000 women.

CDC. USA. Breast Cancer rates by race and ethnicity. www.cdc.gov

105 HIV in East and Southern Africa

AVERT. www.avert.org/professionals/hiv-around-world; UNAIDS. AIDsInfo. www.aidsinfo.unaids.org/; UNAIDS. *Global AIDS Update 2016.*

106–107 Living with HIV

UNAIDS. AIDsInfo. aidsinfo.unaids.org/; UNAIDS. *Global AIDS Update 2016*; CCD. HIV in the USA: At a glance. New HIV diagnoses in the USA. www.cdc.gov

107 Weekly toll

AVERT. HIV Around the World. www.avert.org; CDC. HIV in the United States at a Glance. www.cdc.gov; UNAIDS. AIDsInfo. www.aidsinfo.unaids.org/; UNAIDS. *Global AIDS Update 2016.*

108 Treatment for HIV

AVERT. HIV Around the World. www.avert.org; UNAIDS. AIDsInfo. www.

aidsinfo.unaids.org/; UNAIDS. *Global AIDS Update 2016.*

109 New HIV infections and young women

AVERT. HIV Around the World. www.avert.org; UNWomen. Facts and Figures: HIV and AIDS. www.unwomen.org/en; UNAIDS. AIDsInfo. www.aidsinfo.unaids.org/; UNAIDS. *Global AIDS Update 2016.*

110 Tuberculosis

CDC. USA. Tuberculosis: Data and Statistics. 2016. www.cdc.gov; TB Facts.Org. www.tbfacts.org/tb-statistics/; WHO. Gender and Tuberculosis. January 2002. apps.who.int/iris/bitstream/10665/68891/1/a85584.pdf; WHO. *Global Tuberculosis Report 2017*; WHO. Tuberculosis Factsheets. October 2017. www.who.int

111–112 Malaria • Annual malaria mortality

Murray CJL et al. Global malaria mortality between 1980 and 2010: A systematic analysis. *The Lancet*. Volume 379, 9814: 413–431; Roll Back Malaria. Gender and Malaria. September 2015. Factsheet on Gender and the SDGs. www.rollbackmalaria.org; UNDP. December 2015. Discussion Paper: Gender and Malaria. www.undp.org; Wang H. et al. Global, regional, and national under-5 mortality, adult mortality, age-specific mortality, and life expectancy, 1970–2016: A systematic analysis for the Global Burden of Disease Study 2016. *The Lancet*, Volume 390, 10100: 1084–1150; WHO. Gender, Health and Malaria. Gender and Health Information sheet. June 2007; WHO. *World Malaria Report 2015*; WHO. *World Malaria Report 2017*; WHO. *World Malaria Report 2016.*

113 No-go zone

UNICEF and WHO. *Progress on drinking water, sanitation and hygiene: 2017 update and SDG baselines.*

114–115 Water • Drink up • Dirty water

Environmental Working Group's Tap Water Database. www.ewg.org/tapwater/#.Wu7rVZoh3IU; Prüss-Ustün A. et al. Burden of disease from inadequate water, sanitation and hygiene in low- and middle-income settings: A retrospective analysis of data from 145 countries. *Tropical Medicine and International Health*, 2014, 19(8): 894–905; UNEP 2016; Stehle S. and Schulz R. Agricultural insecticides threaten surface waters at the global scale. *Proceedings of the National Academy of Sciences*, 2015,

112(18): 5750–5755; UN Environment. Global Gender and Environment Outlook. web.unep.org/ggeo; UNICEF and WHO. *Progress on drinking water, sanitation and hygiene: 2017 update and SDG baselines.*

116–117 Toilets • Right to pee!

Ingraham C. 1.6 million Americans don't have indoor plumbing. April 23, 2014. www.washingtonpost.com; Mundy K. et al. No girl left behind – education in Africa. 2015. www.globalpartnership.org; OECD. Housing Quality Database. HC2.3.A1. Share of households without exclusive flushing toilet, by poverty status and year. Roma E. and Pugh I. *Toilets for Health.* London School of Hygiene and Tropical Medicine in collaboration with Domestos. London. 2012; UN Environment. Global Gender and Environment Outlook. www.web.unep.org/ggeo; UNICEF and WHO. *Progress on drinking water, sanitation and hygiene: 2017 update and SDG baselines;* United States Census. American Community Survey. 2015; WHO. Sanitation Fact Sheet. July 2017.

118 Pollution planet

Grandjean P. and Martine B. Calculation of the disease burden associated with environmental chemical exposures: application of toxicological information in health economic estimation. *Environmental Health* 16.1. 2017; Landrigan PJ. et al. The Lancet Commission on pollution and health. *The Lancet*. 2017; Rachel Carson quote: Carson R. *Silent Spring*. NY: Fawcett Crest 5th edition, 1967, original 1962. p. 244; Sylvia Earle quote: Earle S. Natural History Museum Annual Lecture. Channel 4 News. UK Dec 3, 2017. www.channel4.com/news/; USA NIEHS/EPA. Children's Environmental Health and Disease Prevention Research Centers. *Impact Report*. 2017.

119 Deadly dust • Indoor toxic chemicals

Gore, AC et al. EDC-2: The Endocrine Society's second scientific statement on endocrine-disrupting chemicals. *Endocrine Reviews* 36, no. 6 (2015): E1-E150; Knower KC et al. Endocrine disruption of the epigenome: a breast cancer link. *Endocrine-related cancer* 21, no. 2 (2014): T33-T55; Mitro SD. et al. Consumer product chemicals in indoor dust: a quantitative meta-analysis of US studies. E*nvironmental Science and Technology*. Oct 4, 2016. US EPA. Indoor Air Quality. Pesticides' Impact on Indoor Air Quality. www.epa.gov

120 Deadly air

Prüss-Ustün A. et al. *Preventing Disease through Healthy Environments: A Global Assessment of the Burden of Disease from Environmental Risks.* WHO. Geneva. 2012; Smith KR. et al. Millions dead: how do we know and what does it mean? Methods used in the comparative risk assessment of household air pollution. *Annual Review of Public Health* 35 (2014): 185–206; WHO. *Burden of disease from household air pollution for 2012.* Summary of results; WHO. *Guidelines for Indoor Air Quality: Household Fuel Combustion.* 2014; WHO. *Ambient Air Pollution: A global assessment of exposure and burden of disease.* 2012; WHO. Global Health Observatory Data: Household Air Pollution. www.who.int/gho/phe/indoor air pollution/en/

121 Don't eat the fish

Fontaine J. et al. Re-Evaluation of Blood Mercury, Lead and Cadmium Concentrations in the Inuit Population of Nunavik (Québec): A Cross-Sectional Study. *Environmental Health* 7 (2008): 25. *PMC.* Web. Dec. 6 2017; Mortensen ME. et al. Total and methyl mercury in whole blood measured for the first time in the US population: NHANES 2011 2012. *Environmental Research* 134 (2014): 257-264; UN Environment, BRI, IPEN. *Mercury Monitoring in Women of Child-Bearing Age in the Asia and the Pacific Region.* April 2017.

Part Six WORK

123 Segregated work

American Dental Association. Women in Dentistry. www.ada.org; Catalyst. Women in Male-Dominated Industries and Occupations. May 30, 2017. www.catalyst.org; Chalabi M. Dear Mona, How many flight attendants are men? Oct 3, 2014. fivethirtyeight.com; Gender Gap Grader. How many women in "the Airman Database"? www.gendergapgrader.com/studies/airline-pilots/; Joshi S. Meet India's courageous women cab drivers. Dec 14, 2015. www.mashable.com; Kelly G. Veterinary medicine is a woman's world. May 07, 2017. www.vmdtoday.com; Medical Council of New Zealand. Workforce statistics: The New Zealand Medical Workforce. *www.mcnz.org.nz;* UN. *The World's Women 2015: Trends and Statistics;* UNESCO. Percentage of female teachers by level of education. www.data.uis.unesco.org; Women in Informal Employment: Globalizing and Organizing. Women in India's Construction Industry. www.wiego.

org; World Bank. World Development Report. Chapter 5. *Gender* Equality and Development. 2012; WHO. Global Health Observatory Data. apps.who.int/gho/data/view.main.92400

124–125 Women in the workforce

ILO. Labour Force Participation by Age and Sex. www.ilo.org/ilostat; OECD. Labour force participation rate (indicator). 2017. www.stats.oecd.org

124 Show me the money

USAID. The DHS Program. Demographic and Health surveys. www.dhsprogram.com/data/available-datasets.cfm

126–127 The earnings gap

AAUW. *The Simple Truth about the Gender Pay Gap.* 2017; BBC's 9% gender pay gap revealed. October 4, 2017. www.bbc.com/news/entertainment-arts-41497265; Business and Human Rights Resource Center. Walmart Lawsuit. www.business-humanrights.org/en/walmart-lawsuit-re-gender-discrimination-in-usa; Drogan R. *Statistical Analysis of Gender Patterns in Wal-Mart Workforce.* 2003. www.walmartclass.com/staticdata/reports/r2.pdf; Eurostat. Labour Market Tables, Earnings. www.ec.europa.eu/eurostat/web/labour-market/earnings/main-tables; ILO. *Global Wage Report 2016/17: Wage inequality in the workplace*; Kottasova I. Iceland makes it illegal to pay women less than men. CNN Money. January 3, 2018. http://money.cnn.com

128–129 Women's work

ILO. Informal employment. www.ilo.org/ilostat/

128–129 The global assembly line • Export processing zones

Beneria L. "Globalization and Gender: Employment Effects", workshop. Cairo. 2005; Boyenge J. ILO database on export processing zones (revised). ILO. 2007; Enloe C. *Bananas, Beaches and Buses.* Berkeley: University of California Press. 2014; Hoskins T. Reliving the Rana Plaza factory collapse: A history of cities in 50 buildings, day 22. www.theguardian.com; Sukthankar A. and Gopalakrishnan R. Freedom of association for women workers in EPZs: a manual. ILO. 2012.

130 It's lonely at the top

For EU countries, Iceland, Norway, and Turkey, data refers to the proportion of seats held by women on boards for the largest 50 members of the primary blue-chip index in the country concerned (including only those companies that are registered in the given country). "Board members" refers to all members of the highest decision-making body in the given company, such as the board

of directors for a company in a unitary system, or the supervisory board in the case of a company in a two-tier system. For countries with data based on MSCI (2015), data refer to the proportion of seats held by women on boards for companies covered by the MSCI's "global director reference universe", a sample of 4,218 global companies covering all companies of the MSCI ACWI, World, EAFE, and Emerging Markets indexes, plus an additional 1,700 large and mid-cap developed market companies, 900 of which are either incorporated or primarily traded in the United States.

The Netherlands, France, Germany, Belgium, and Italy have enacted board quota laws since 2011. In India, a gender quota law requires that every board have at least one female director.

Guynn J. Women can't crack the glass ceiling when it comes to tech boards. Aug 25, 2017. www.usatoday.com; Harvard Law School Forum. Gender Parity on Boards around the World. Jan 5, 2017. www.corpgov.law.harvard.edu/2017/01/05/gender-parity-on-boards-around-the-world/; Jones S. White Men Account for 72% of Corporate Leaderships of the Fortune 500 Companies. June 9, 2017. www.fortune.com; OECD. Female share of seats on boards of the largest publicly listed companies. www.stats.oecd.org/index.aspx?queryid=54753; Tam P. Dec 30, 2016. Join Our Board: Companies Hotly Pursue New Wave of Women in Tech. www.nytimes.com; The Economist. The glass ceiling index 2017. www.infographics.economist.com/2017/glass-ceiling/

131 Maternity and paternity leave

ILO. *Maternity and paternity at work: law and practice across the world.* 2014.

132 Unemployment

ILO. Key Indicators of the Labour Market. ILO Stats. 2017.

132 Race and gender: intersectionality at work

Department of Women, South Africa. *The Status of Women in the South African Economy.* 2015; US Department of Labor, Bureau of Labor Statistics. www.bls.gov/web/empsit/cpsee_e16.htm

133 Part-time work

ILO. Key Indicators of the Labour Market, Time-Related Unemployment; ILO. INWORK *Policy Brief 7, The Diversity of "Marginal" Part-Time Employment.*

134 Domestic and care work

UN Statistics Division. Unpaid work. Minimum Set of Gender Indicators. www.genderstats.un.org/#/indicators; Fletcher R. Women spend 50% more time in unpaid housework. June 01, 2017. www.cbc.ca; OECD Stats. Employment: Time spent in paid and unpaid work by sex. www.stats. oecd.org; Bureau of Labor Statistics. American Time Use Survey. Charts by topic: Household activities. www. bls.gov

135 Who does the laundry?

Singh A. 36 household chores men don't bother to do. Oct 6, 2014. www. telegraph.co.uk

136 Household decision-makers

USAID. The DHS Program. Demographic and Health Surveys, Country Reports. www.dhsprogram.com

137 Child labor

ILO. Global estimates of child labour: Results and trends, 2012–2016. 2017; UNICEF. Child Labor Database. www. data.unicef.org/topic/child-protection/child-labour/

138 Walking for water • Who is collecting water?

Office of the UN High Commissioner for Human Rights. *The Right to Water. Human Rights Fact Sheet #35.* 2010; UN Women. SDG 6: Ensure availability and sustainable management of water and sanitation for all. 2016; UN Women. *Progress of the World's Women, 2015–16: Transforming Economies, Realizing Rights*; UNEP. *Global Gender and Environment Outlook.* 2016; UN Department of Economic and Social Affairs, Statistics Division. *The World's Women 2015: Trends and Statistics.*

139–141 Agricultural work • Women employed in agricultural research • Farmer's access to extension workers

Action Aid. Policy Brief 2015: Delivering Women Farmers' Rights; Archambault CS. and Zoomers A. eds. *Global Trends in Land Tenure Reform: Gender Impacts.* London: Routledge, 2015; Beintema N. An assessment of the gender gap in African agricultural research capacities *Journal of Gender, Agriculture and Food Security* Vol 2, Issue 1. 2017; Doss C. et al. Women in agriculture: Four myths. *Global Food Security.* Nov 6, 2017; Global Forum for Rural Advisory Services. Fact Sheet on Extension Services. June 2012; World Bank. Employment in Agriculture, Female (% of female employment). www.data. worldbank.org

142 Primary responsibility for farm tasks • Gendered pathways of pesticide exposure

Catholic Relief Services. Women's work in Coffee. www.coffeelands.crs.org; FAO/ EU/ Pesticide Action Network. Protecting farmers and vulnerable groups from pesticide poisoning. May 2014–2015; Lusiba GS. et al. Intra-household gender division of labour and decision-making on rice postharvest handling practices: A case of Eastern Uganda. *Cogent Social Sciences* 3.1. 2017; UNEP. *Global Gender and Environment Outlook.* 2016.

143 Capture fishing • Fish processing • Fish farming

Asian Fisheries Society. Gender in Aquaculture and Fisheries: Engendering Security in Aquaculture and Fisheries. Vol 30S. 2017; Brugere C. and Williams M. Women in aquaculture profile. 2017. www. genderaquafish.org/portfolio/women-in-aquaculture/; FAO National Aquaculture Sector Overview (NASO) Fact Sheets; FAO. *The State of World Fisheries and Aquaculture 2016. Contributing to food security and nutrition for all*; UNEP. Global Gender and Environment Outlook. 2016; World Bank. *Hidden harvest: The global contribution of capture fisheries.* 2012; World Bank/FAO. Gender in agriculture sourcebook. 2018.

144–145 Migrating for work • Domestic work

Altorjai S. and Batalova J. Immigrant Health-Care Workers in the United States. Migration Information Source. June 28, 2017; Cortés P. and Pan J. Foreign Nurse Importation to the United States and the Supply of Native Registered Nurses. *Federal Reserve Bank of Boston Working Papers.* July 31, 2014; ILO. Global estimates of migrant workers and migrant domestic workers: results and methodology. 2015; ILO. *Domestic workers across the world: global and regional statistics and the extent of legal protection.* 2013; International Migration Organization. www.gmdac. iom.int/gmdac-migfacts-international-migration; House of Commons Briefing Paper. # 7783. *NHS Staff from Overseas.* Oct 16, 2017; Li, H. The benefits and caveats of international nurse migration, *International Journal of Nursing Sciences* Volume 1, Issue 3, September 2014: 314–317; McCabe K. Foreign-Born Health Care Workers in the United States. June 27, 2012. www.migrationpolicy.org; Philippine Government. Overseas workers. www.poea.gov.ph/ofwstat/compendium/2015.pdf; www.poea. gov.ph/ofwstat/deppercountry/2010. pdf; WHO. Migration of health workers: the WHO code of practice and the global economic crisis. 2014.

Part 7 EDUCATION AND CONNECTIVITY

147 Average years of schooling

UN. The *World's Women 2015: Trends and Statistics*; UNWomen. *Progress of the World's Women 2015–2016: Transforming Economies, Realizing Rights.*

148–149 Not making the grade • Gender gaps in primary school completion • Income and school completion

UNICEF. Primary Education. www.data. unicef.org/topic/education/primary-education/; World Bank. World Development Indicators. *Education Completion and Outcomes.* wdi. worldbank.org/table/2.10#

150–151 Beyond secondary

UNESCO. Gross enrolment ratio by level of education. www.data.uis.unesco. org/?queryid=142

150 Race, ethnicity, and gender, USA

National Center for Education Statistics. Digest of Education Statistics.

152–153 Progress by degrees • Higher education

D'ujanga FM. et al. Female physicists in Ugandan universities. AIP conference proceedings, 1697. 2016; Reid DM. *Cairo University and the Making of Modern Egypt.* Cambridge: CUP, 1990; The University of Tokyo. History of Todai Women. www.kyodo-sankaku.u-tokyo.ac.jp; Women's access to higher education: an overview (1860–1948). July 21, 2012. www.herstoria.com

154 520 million women can't read this

World Bank. DataBank. Literacy rate, adult female. www.data. worldbank.org/indicator/SE.ADT.LITR. FE.ZS?end=2015&start=2015

155–156 Looking good • Big leaps forward

UN. The *World's Women 2015: Trends and Statistics*; World Bank. DataBank. Literacy rate, adult female. www.data. worldbank.org/indicator/SE.ADT.LITR. FE.ZS?end=2015&start=2015

157 Functional illiteracy

ETS Research. Understanding the Basic Reading Skills of US Adults: Reading Components in the PIAAC Literacy Survey. www.ets.org; OECD. *Time for the U.S. to Reskill?: What the Survey of Adult Skills Says.* 2013; Rampey, BD. et al. Highlights from the US PIAAC Survey of Incarcerated Adults: Their Skills, Work Experience, Education, and Training. Program for the International Assessment of Adult Competencies, 2014 (NCES 2016-040). 2016; US Department of Education, National Center for Education Statistics, Program for the International Assessment of Adult Competencies (PIAAC), 2012 and 2014.

158–159 When computers were women • Boys' own world

Blitz M. The true story of "Hidden Figures". *Popular Mechanics*. Feb 3, 2017; Engel K. Admiral "Amazing Grace" Hopper, pioneering computer programmer. Oct 21, 2013. www.amazingwomeninhistory.com; Fessenden M. What happened to all the women in computer science? Oct 22, 2014. www.smithsonianmag.com; Galvin G. Study: Middle school is key to girls' coding interest. Oct 20, 2016. www.usnews.com; Garber M. Computing power used to be measured in kilo-girls. *The Atlantic*. Oct 16, 2013; Henn, S. When women stopped coding. Oct 21, 2014. www.npr.org; National Center for Education Statistics. www.nces.ed.gov/; NPR. "Most Beautiful Woman" by Day, Inventor by Night. Nov 22, 2011. www.npr.org; The ENIAC programmers project. www.eniacprogrammers.org/; Varma R. and Kapur D. Decoding Femininity in Computer Science in India. *Communications of the ACM*, Vol. 58 No. 5: 56–62. www.cacm.acm.org; Wenner M. Hedy Lamarr, Not Just a Petty Face. *Scientific American*. June 3, 2008.

160 Percentage of households with a computer • Percentage of American households...

Anderson M. and Perrin A. Disabled Americans are less likely to use technology. www.pewresearch.org; Camille R. and Lewis JM. Computer and Internet Use in the United States: 2015; Internet use by gender. Jan 11, 2017. www.pewresearch.org; ITU. Key ICT indicators. www.itu.int; Perrin A. Digital gap between rural and non-rural America persists. www.pewresearch.org; US Census Bureau. Computer and Internet Use in the United States: 2015. Report number: ACS-37. 2107.

161 Gender divide by country

ITU. Gender Internet stats 2017. www.itu.int

162 Digital divide • Gender divide by region

ITU. ICT Facts and Figures 2016; ITU. ICT Facts and Figures 2017; ITU. Measuring the Information Society. 2016; World Bank. Individuals using the internet, percentage of population. www.data.worldbank.org/indicator/IT.NET.USER.ZS

163 Keeping up with the news • Keeping up with health

ITU. Measuring the Information Society. 2016; Pew Research. Internet seen as positive influence on education, negative on morality in emerging and developing nations. 2015.

165 #Online harassment

Duggan M. Online Harassment 2017. July 11, 2017. www.pewinternet.org; Facebook Newsroom. Facebook Diversity Update: Positive Hiring Trends Show Progress. July 14, 2016. newsroom.fb.com; Ghosh, S. Google is making slow progress on hiring people who aren't white men. June 30, 2017. www.businessinsider.com/; Siminoff J. Building a more inclusive Twitter. Jan 19, 2017. blog.twitter.com; Wagner K. Twitter says it "met many" of its goals around diversity last year, so it's setting new goals for 2017. Jan 19, 2017. www.recode.net

166–168 The myth of the connected world • For some women, the gap is bigger still • Closing the gap • Can't afford it...

Dellman L. and Malhotra A. Why the vast majority of women in India will never own a smartphone. Oct 13, 2016. www.wsj.com; Connected Women. Bridging the Gender Gap: Mobile access and usage in low- and middle-income countries. 2015. www.gsma.com; UNCTAD. Measuring ICT and gender: An assessment. 2014; World Economic Forum. Global Gender Gap Report. 2016.

Part Eight PROPERTY AND POVERTY

170–171 Property: Women's rights to own, use, and control land • Ownership of "household owned" land in Africa • Women as a proportion of agricultural land-holders

Note: The "agricultural holder" has technical and economic responsibility for the agricultural unit of production.

Doss C. et al. *IFPRI Discussion Paper* 01308. Gender Inequalities in Ownership and Control of Land in Africa: Myths versus Reality. Dec 2013; FAO. Gender and Land Rights Database. www.fao.org; Landesa. Rural Development Institute. www.landesa.org; Massay G. Africa's women are still waiting for equal inheritance rights. June 21, 2017. www.womendeliver.org; OECD. *Social Instructions and Gender index 2014 Synthesis Report*; UN. The *World's Women 2015: Trends and Statistics*; UNEP. *Global Gender and Environment Outlook*. 2016; Women's land: Closing the gender gap in Sub-Saharan Africa. www.womendeliver.org

171 Home ownership in the USA

Rickert L. US Census Bureau: Native American Statistics. Nov 24, 2016. www.nativenewsonline.net; US Census. Table 15. Annual estimates of the housing inventory by age and family status and Table 16: Homeownership rates by race and ethnicity. www.census.gov

172 Inheritance

Iqbal, S. *Women, Business and the Law 2016: Getting to Equal*. World Bank Group. 2015; Dray K. "This is some Jane Austen-level BS": why it's time to stamp out Britain's sexist inheritance rules. *Stylist*. 2016; Lyall S. Son and heir? June 22, 2013. www.nytimes.com; Women could inherit if they change gender, says Earl. Nov 30, 2017. www.bbc.com; World Economic Forum. The *Global Gender Gap Report 2017*.

173 No reserves

Demirguc-Kunt A. et al. The Global Findex Database 2014: Measuring Financial Inclusion around the World. *Policy Research Working Paper* 7255. World Bank. Washington DC. 2015; World Bank. Global Findex Database 2014: Measuring Financial Inclusion Around the World.

174 Living on the edge

UNDP. Human Development Reports. Multidimensional Poverty. www.hdr.undp.org

175 Extreme poverty

UNDP Human Development Reports. Population living below income poverty line. www.hdr.undp.org

176 At risk of poverty in Europe

Eurostat. At-risk-of-poverty rate by sex. www.ec.europa.eu

177 Penniless in Latin America

Economic Commission for Latin America and the Caribbean (ECLAC). *Social Panorama of Latin America, 2015*. Santiago, 2016.

178–179 Profile of poverty, USA • Profile of wealth, USA

Economic Policy Institute. Racial gaps in wages, wealth, and more: a quick recap. Jan 26 2017. www.epi.org; Economic Policy Institute. 2016 ACS shows stubbornly high Native American poverty and different degrees of economic well-being for Asian ethnic groups. Sept 15, 2017. www.epi.org; Heller School for Social Policy and Management. We need to talk about the Gender Wealth Gap. Sept 27, 2016. www.huffingtonpost.com; Semega J. et al. US Census

Bureau, Current Population Reports, P60-259, Income and Poverty in the United States: 2016, US Government Printing Office, Washington, DC, 2017; US Census Bureau. Facts for Features: American Indian and Alaska Native Heritage Month: November 2015; US Census Bureau. Wealth, Asset Ownership, and Debt of Households Detailed Tables: 2013.

180–181 Rich world / poor world

Ratio of CEO pay to the average person's income, technical note: CEO pay is in companies that are members of each country's primary equity index.

Allen K. UK bosses will earn more in two and a half days than workers earn all year. Jan 4, 2017. www.theguardian.com; Bloomberg News. Bloomberg Pay Index. Best Paid Executives 2016. www.bloomberg.com/graphics/2017-highest-paid-ceos/; Bloomberg News. The best and worst countries to be a rich CEO. November 2016; Credit Suisse. Global Wealth Report 2017; High Pay Centre. 10% pay rise? That'll do nicely. www.highpaycentre.org; OXFAM. 5 Shocking Facts About Extreme Global Inequality; OXFAM. Reward work, not wealth: To end the inequality crisis, we must build an economy for ordinary working people, not the rich and powerful. *Briefing Paper* January 22, 2018; Mayah E. et al. *Inequality in Nigeria: Exploring the drivers.* OXFAM. 2017; World Economic Forum. *The Global Risks Report 2017;* World Economic Forum. *The Inclusive Development Index 2018.*

182 Banking on it

Demirguc-Kunt A. et al. The Global Findex Database 2014: Measuring Financial Inclusion around the World. *Policy Research Working Paper* 7255, World Bank, Washington, DC. 2015; Tavneet S. and Jack W. The long-run poverty and gender impacts of mobile money. *Science* 354.6317 (2016): 1288-1292; UN. *The World's Women 2015: Trends and Statistics;* World Bank. Global Findex Database 2014: Financial Inclusion.

Part Nine POWER

184–187 Votes for women

Daley C. and Nolan M. *Suffrage and Beyond: International Feminist Perspectives.* NY: NYU. 1994; Inter-Parliamentary Union. www.ipu.org; UNDP. *Arab Human Development Report*, 2005.

188–189 Militaries

Enloe C. *Globalization and Militarism: Feminists Make the Link.* Rowman & Littlefield. 2016; NATO. Summary of the National Reports of NATO Member and Partner Nations to the NATO Committee on Gender Perspectives. 2016; Mohan M. Rape and no periods in North Korea's army. Nov 21, 2017. www.bbc.co.uk; South African Army. Republic of South Africa; Celebrating Women's Month: Rise of Women in the SA Army. Aug 17, 2017; Stockholm International Peace Research Institute (SIPRI). Military versus social expenditure: the opportunity cost of world military spending. April 5, 2016; Telsur News. Feb 27, 2018. Saudi Arabia government to allow women to join army. www.telesurtv.net; UN Women. www.unwomen.org/en/what-we-do/peace-and-security/facts-and-figures; US DoD. Annual Report on Sexual Assault in the Military; Fiscal Year 2016; Women in the military in Africa. Jan 27, 2017. www.joburgpost.co.za

190–191 Women in national government

Inter-Parliamentary Union. Women in National Parliaments Database. www.ipu.org/wmn-e/classif.htm

192 Women in ministerial positions

World Bank. Gender Statistics. www.databank.worldbank.org/data/reports.aspx?Code=SG.GEN.MNST.ZS&id=2ddc971b&report_name=Gender_Indicators_Report&populartype=series#

193 European Parliament

European Parliamentary Research Service. *Women in Parliaments.* www.europarl.europa.eu/RegData/etudes/ATAG/2017/599314/EPRS_ATA(2017)599314_EN.pdf

194 Quotas for national government

United Nations, 2015. The *World's Women 2015: Trends and Statistics;* International Institute for Democracy and Electoral Assistance. Gender Quota Database. www.idea.int/data-tools/data/gender-quotas/database

195 Women at the United Nations

Bryant N. At the UN women play increasingly powerful roles. 17 Nov 2014. www.bbc.com; Data on the status of women in the UN. www.unwomen.org/en/how-we-work/un-system-coordination/women-in-the-united-nations/current-status-of-women

196–197 Feminisms

The pink pussyhat™ was originally designed as a symbol of defiance against US presidential candidate Trump's boasts about sexually abusing women; it became the symbol of the 2017 Women's March and endures as a signifier of broader resistance against patriarchal privilege.

Pressman J. and Chenoweth E. Women's Marches. Crowd Estimates. docs.google.com/spreadsheets/d/1xa0iLqYKz8x9Yc_rfhtmSOJQ2EGgeUVjvV4A8LslaxY/htmlview?sle=true#gid=0; Women's March. www.womensmarch.com/sisters

Picture credits

Page 49: Marry-your-rapist laws: advertisement for ABAAD, www.abaadmena.org.

Page 94: A campaign against female genital mutilation – road sign near Kapchorwa, Uganda. Photographer: Amnon Shavit, Wikimedia Commons.

Page 117: Right to pee: photograph courtesy of DNA Syndication.

Page 135: "Mercy, it's the revolution" cartoon: reprinted with permission of the author, Nicole Hollander.

Index